CALIFORNIA GOVERNMENT AND POLITICS ANNUAL 1992-93

EDITED BY THOMAS R. HOEBER & CHARLES M. PRICE

CALIFORNIA JOURNAL PRESS

ISBN: 0-930302-83-4
ISSN: 0084-8271

INTRODUCTION

The California Phenomenon

The California system of government is the same in bold outline as the government of the United States, with three theoretically equal branches of government operating under the supreme law of the land, the Constitution. Nevertheless, there are some significant differences:

• The California Constitution is far more detailed than the United States Constitution and, thus, the Governor and the Legislature have far less power and freedom than the President and Congress. Matters that are left to the statute-writers in Washington are covered in detail in the California Constitution, taking these issues out of the hands of the Governor and Legislature. The judiciary, on the other hand, may be even more powerful because this branch is in charge of interpreting the constitution.

• Normally, the speaker of the Assembly has far more power in Sacramento than any single member of Congress in Washington because this official controls virtually all committee appointments. Few bills pass over the speaker's objection. However the power of particular speakers ebbs and flows depending on factors such as their personalities, the size of their party's majority and the loyalty of their parties caucus.

• The people at large have much more control over California government than over national government because they have the powers of initiative, referendum and recall, giving them the ultimate voice in all matters that are not in conflict with the United States Constitution. Most major fiscal decisions, such as the enactment of general-obligation bond issues and the raising of local taxes, also cannot be made without voter approval.

Other factors make California unique as well. It has been the land of superb climate, rapid growth, a seemingly easy pot of gold, and the glamor of movie stars. Its government and politics reflect the excitement of a land of opportunity and colorful characters, and the news media look to California for the bizarre and offbeat. These unique characteristics may be fading, however. No longer is California the promised land; smog has dulled the climate; unemployment runs about the same as elsewhere and sometimes higher; and the movie industry is far from what it used to be. California is experiencing the ills of a mature society: slowed financial growth, reduced national defense spending with the end of the Cold War, declining infrastructure, burgeoning population, especially among new immigrants from foreign lands, and the need for urban renewal. California, in short, is no longer the land of milk and honey, although there are many who still view it as a preview of what will follow in the other 49 states.

Constitution

Every few years the California Legislature prints a paperback book with up-to-date versions of the United States and California Constitutions. The document that is the basic law of the entire nation takes up 27 pages; but the California Constitution takes up three times as much space (and twice as much just for the index).

The state constitution contains 21 articles describing, in great detail the bill of rights, the powers of various branches of government and basic state law in such fields as education, local government, corporations, taxation, water, harbor frontages, state debt, homesteading, motor vehicles, civil service, open space, public housing, and even the minimum drinking age.

The California Constitution wasn't always such a long-winded document. The first constitution, adopted in 1849 (one year before California was admitted into the Union), was a basic statement of the rights of the people and the responsibility of the three branches of government. Peter H. Burnett was elected California's first governor in November 1849, and the first Legislature convened shortly thereafter to levy taxes, establish cities and counties, put the courts into operation, and borrow enough money to grease the wheels of state government. Over the next 30 years, only three major changes were made to this constitution. This stands in sharp contrast to the current practice of adopting amendments every election year.

Massive unrest produced a greatly expanded new constitution in 1879. There was tremendous distrust of the state government, especially the Legislature, and demands were made for greater public control over taxation. The state's population had increased 17-fold in its first three decades. A drought and unfavorable economic conditions had produced mass unemployment. The railroad bloc practically ran the state and was an obvious target. Farmers were in revolt against the railroads and other businessmen. Unemployed whites joined the Workingman's Party to seek a ban against imported Chinese labor. Constitutional reform was seen as a solution, and a convention was called in 1878. The result was an extremely detailed document, which was adopted the next year by a comfortable but not overwhelming margin. The document remains the basic law of California, although it has been amended hundreds of times.

But despite the goals of those who demanded the convention, the second constitution did not provide major reform. That was to come later with Hiram Johnson and the Progressives, who instituted the initiative, referendum and recall.

Amending the Constitution

There are three ways amendments to the California Constitution may be placed on the ballot for approval by a majority of the voters: by initiative petition now requiring over 600,000 signatures of registered voters, by legislative proposal, and by constitutional convention.

• *The initiative*. Almost every election California voters decide the fate of one or more measures placed on the ballot through the initiative process. The initiative was designed as a method of exerting public control over the Legislature, so that bills ignored by the lawmakers could be put into effect. In recent years, elected officials themselves have sponsored initiatives when they are unable to get their way in the Legislature. Beginning in the late 1970's the initiative has been used more and more frequently by special interest groups, the very element the initiative was created to counter. The initiative can also be used to enact statutes, and fewer signatures are required to qualify these measure for the ballot.

• *Legislative proposal*. Every year, legislators introduce dozens of proposed constitutional amendments. A small percentage receive the necessary two-thirds vote of each house to qualify for the ballot. A 1983 law requires that ballot measures be numbered consecutively from election to election, starting with November 1982, to avoid confusion. Thus, for example, the November 1990 ballot measures were numbered 124 to 151.

• *Convention*. The constitution provides that the Legislature may call a constitutional convention by a two-thirds vote of both houses. However, it has not done so since 1878. Instead the Legislature has chosen to form a revision commission because it can control the commission and its recommendations. Such a commission existed from 1963 to 1970. The commission had some successes during those years and managed to reduce the size of the constitution considerably. From time to time sentiment is expressed for re-establishing the commission to continue the work of streamlining the state's supreme legal document. 🏛

WITH AN INTRODUCTION BY LARRY BERG

Reprinted from *California Journal*, January 1992

California had scarcely two million citizens in 1909 when Lord James Bryce, British ambassador to the United States, visited the state and asked a prophetic question: "What will happen when California is filled by 50 millions of people and its valuation is five times what it is now? There will be more people — as many as the country can support — and the real question will be not about making more wealth or having more people, but whether the people will then be happier

Dan Walters is a political columnist for The Sacramento Bee *and author of "The New California." This article is a shortened version of Chapter 1 of the second edition of "The New California," due for publication in February.*

or better than they have been hitherto or are at this moment."

Eighty-plus years later, California is more than halfway toward that 50-million mark and has become America's most diverse, most populous and most economically, culturally and politically potent state. But without knowing it, Californians are still seeking answers to Lord Bryce's question as they career toward the 21st Century.

From San Ysidro to Susanville, from Ventura to Volcano, from Moreno Valley to Moraga, no region of the state is being left untouched as California fashions a 21st Century civilization like nothing ever seen on the North American continent: ethnically complex, with distinct socio-economic classes; competitive; technologically sophisticated; older and more harried; and, unless a cadre of new civic and political leader-

ship emerges, a society that loses its communal identity and evolves into a collection of mutually hostile tribes.

California's once-powerful industrial economy, created during the emergency of World War II and later expanded to serve both Cold War and civilian demands, has given way to a post-industrial hybrid economy that rests on multiple bases and resembles that of a major nation more than that of a typical American state.

In a single generation, hundreds of lumber mills, auto and tire factories, steel plants, canneries, railroad yards, shipyards and other basic industries have closed. Of those that survive, many have downgraded their wage structures to meet foreign competition. Deregulation of trucking, telephone service and airlines has made them more competitive but also has forced

1992-1993

5

Ethnicity

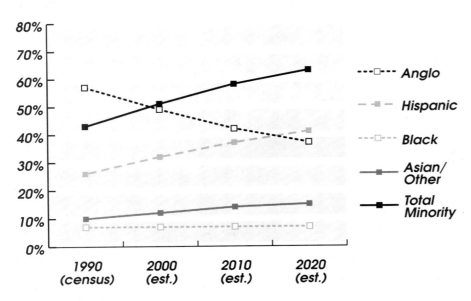

Legend:
- ---□--- Anglo
- ----■---- Hispanic
- ---□--- Black
- ---■--- Asian/Other
- ──■── Total Minority

X-axis: 1990 (census), 2000 (est.), 2010 (est.), 2020 (est.)

Y-axis: 0% to 80%

their employees to accept lower wages. And the new industrial jobs that have been created, especially those in high-tech and services, are overwhelmingly non-union, with non-professional wage scales in the sub-$12 per hour range.

At the same time, whole new industries have emerged, based on trade with burgeoning Pacific Rim nations, on highly sophisticated technology and on information; new industries that created three million jobs during the 1980s and allowed California to absorb a record increase in population while lowering its unemployment rate before a severe recession took told in 1990.

Between traditional industry's contraction and new industry's expansion lie the seeds of socio-economic stratification. Opportunities for the children of the postwar industrial middle class have been reduced, or at least become more contrasting. They and the young immigrants who continue to pour into California must either prepare themselves for expanding opportunities in technical, managerial, creative and professional fields or be content with relatively low-paying service industry jobs.

California's work force, therefore, is being squeezed like a tube of toothpaste: an expanding overclass at the top, earning the $40,000-plus salaries, buying the homes, living the California good life; and an exploding underclass at the bottom, ill-educated, ill-served by overburdened social services, struggling to find affordable housing, forgoing medical care and seeing the doors of opportunity become more difficult to open; and an economic and social middle that stagnates or even declines. And it is a change that is punctuated by the state's rapidly evolving ethnic structure, one in which today's minorities will soon become the collective majority. The economic and social differences are likely to become more distinct as California continues to move away from the egalitarian ideal.

Economists Leon Bouvier and Philip Martin, in a mid-1980s peek into California's future for the Washington-based Population Reference Bureau, described that scenario as "the possible emerging of a two-tier economy with Asians and non-Hispanic whites competing for high-status positions while Hispanics and Blacks struggle to get the low-paying service jobs." They noted that since 1970, "employment growth has shifted from high-wage manufacturing and government sectors to the lower-wage trade and service firms that are most likely to hire unskilled immigrants..."

End-of-decade economic data verified their prediction. Between 1982 and 1990, California's manufacturers added about a quarter-million jobs, but the service and trade sectors created nearly two million. Between 1972 and 1989, manufacturing dropped from nearly 21 percent of the state's jobs to about 17 percent. Jobs at the lower end of the scale ($5000 to $15,000 per year) and those at the upper end ($40,000 to $50,000 per year) grew two to three times faster than middle-income jobs ($25,000 to $30,000 per year). Increasingly, California families have achieved or clung to middle-class status only by merging paychecks of two or more workers.

There are strong indications that these trends will continue in the 1990s. The state Employment Development Department estimates that total California employment will increase by nearly one-third between 1987 and 2000, from 11.7 million to 15.4 million jobs, with above-average increases in trade, finance and services, and sub-par growth in manufacturing, transportation, communication, mining and government categories. The Center for the Continuing Study of the California Economy is even more optimistic, seeing employment in the state approach 17.5 million by 2000 with job and personal-income growth rates in the 1990s that are far above those of the nation as a whole and outstripping even population growth.

"This is probably California's last great growth surge," said economist Stephen Levy of the Palo Alto-based economic study center. "It is entirely possible that the state's population, which will go from 30 million to 40 million in 20 years, may never each the 50-million mark." Levy said that lower birth rates should slow California's population growth after 2010.

There is, however, dissent from some economists who believe that California peaked out in the 1980s and now faces a bleak economic future because of its deteriorating infrastructure and a competitive posture vis-a-vis other states and nations. They have noted a seemingly accelerated abandonment of California by major employers, especially manufacturers, who shift or expand plants in other states and nations because of California's above-average operational costs.

George Salem, a banking analyst for Prudential Securities, created a stir in California economic circles in 1991 when he circulated a report suggesting that the state "shows new evidence of structural weakness" and could face the kind of severe economic dislocation that struck Massachusetts and Texas during the 1980s.

At the time that Salem delivered his startling verdict, the state was experiencing a severe recession, with unemployment having jumped more than 2 percent since the go-go days of the 1980s. During the first year of the recession, from mid-1990 to mid-1991, the state lost an astonishing 380,000 jobs — roughly a year's employment growth during the expansive years of the 1980s. And despite the recession, which economists said was exacerbated by such localized factors as a record freeze and cutbacks in military procurement spending, California continued to experience huge levels of migration and child birth that drove its population upward by some 800,000 persons a year, thus raising doubts whether the state could continue to absorb newcomers or would face a future of continued economic uncertainty.

At the very least, the recession accelerated the evolution from an industrial to a post-industrial economy and thus the stratification of California society.

And if stratification happens, it may set the stage for a 21st Century political climate that pits haves against have-nots, with the political middle declining along with the economic middle and both major parties being compelled to realign themselves to the new socio-economic reality. Lewis Butler and Bruce Kelley of California Tomorrow, an organization devoted to worrying about California's future, use a harsh term to describe what is happening: segregation. This can be avoided, they wrote in 1989, only if people of different classes, colors and cultures live, work and go to school together.

The data of change, gleaned from a variety of public and private sources, is staggering:

• California's population, less than 16 million in 1960, grew by nearly 50 percent to 23.8 million by 1980, hit 30 million by 1990 and is expected to top 36 million by 2000 and climb to more than 40 million by 2010.

• The Anglo population (what demographers call "non-Hispanic white") is virtually stagnant. In fact, the Anglo population may begin to decline before the turn of the century, and a low Anglo birthrate means that its portion of the population is growing older faster than others, with median age already at least 15 years higher than the non-Anglo population.

• Some three-quarters of the near-term population growth and nearly all long-term growth is among Hispanics and Asians. California already is home to more than a third of the Asians who live in the United States, and the proportion of Californians who have Asian ancestry swelled from 4 percent to 10 percent in just a decade, replacing blacks as the state's third-largest major ethnic group.

• The Hispanic population, meanwhile, is being expanded by a high level of legal and illegal immigration from Latin America, mostly Mexico, and by a birthrate that is nearly twice that of Anglos. Demographers expect the continued political unrest and economic chaos in Latin America to push millions of Latino immigrants across a porous border into California, and even economic reform in Mexico will not have a major impact on that trend for years.

• The Black population is relatively stagnant, fixed at under 8 percent of the total; it's not shrinking but grows only at the rate of the overall population.

• Sometime before 2000, perhaps as early as 1996, Anglos will be a minority for the first time — a decade earlier than demographers had expected in the mid-1980s. A generation later, Hispanics and Anglos will be about equal in population, approximately 38 percent each.

• Despite an evening-out of population among the state's large ethnic groups, there are growing disparties in education and economic attainment. Hispanics and Blacks are far more likely to drop out of high school and less likely to obtain college educations than either Anglos or Asians, thereby becoming less able to compete for the well-paying professional and technical jobs that California is continuing to produce.

• With high birthrates among recent immigrants, the overall status of California's children has deteriorated markedly in recent years. A quarter of California's mothers are unwed and disproportionately high numbers of newborn babies suffer from low birth weights, drug addictions and other maladies. And as vaccination rates for children decline, once-conquered childhood diseases such as measles are staging alarming comebacks.

• Some 20 percent of California's 30 million residents lack any kind of health insurance, either private or public. This accounts for 20 percent of the nation's uninsured, even though the state contains just over 12 percent of the American population.

But the signs of change are to be found in more than numbers. They are to be found in the changing California landscape. They are found in such places as Moreno Valley, a small community in the semi-desert of Riverside County, which was the state's fastest-growing county in the 1980s. Moreno Valley just became a city in the mid-1980s and within a few months had a population of more than 100,000, mostly young families. It was graphic evidence of one of the most important social trends of the 1980s: dispersal of the economy and population from coastal enclaves to interior valleys and hills.

That phenomenon was fueled, in part, by the changes in the economy, especially the advent of portable jobs in burgeoning technical and service fields — jobs that do not depend on proximity to raw materials or even to transportation centers and that can be moved out of traditional urban employment centers and into the suburbs, thus allowing workers to move even further into the countryside for more pleasant surroundings and less-expensive housing. The move to the interior is evident from Escondido in northern San Diego through San Bernardino and Riverside counties to the Central Valley as far north as Redding.

It is largely, however, a movement of Anglos. And it contributes, as do continued high rates of immigration, to radical social surgery on the face of California's cities. As whites flee the cities, their places are taken by foreign immigrants who pack themselves ever more densely into stocks of housing that are not expanding.

Los Angeles, the new American melting pot, lost 500,000 Anglos between 1970 and 1980 and is headed for a 60 percent Hispanic population by the turn of the century. There are more than 100 separate languages spoken at Los Angeles area schools, 75 of them at Hollywood High School alone. Conversely, San Francisco, once a polyglot, is becoming a Beverly Hills-like enclave of the Anglo-Asian affluent, driving its middle classes to the suburbs and its Blacks across the bay to Oakland by development policies that favor high-income professionals. One-time farm towns of the Central Valley are diversifying their economies and flirting with metropolitan status.

In addition, whole regions of the

state, especially those north of the San Francisco-Sacramento axis, have seen their basic industries of timber and agriculture decline and nothing emerge to replace them. The result: economic and social stagnation that forces the young to seek jobs in growth areas.

The growth in and changing composition of California's population during the next 30 to 40 years will put an incredible strain on transportation systems, water supplies, sewage treatment, housing supply, educational facilities — what those in the public policy trade call "infrastructure." The California Economic Development Corporation has warned that without a massive overhaul of transportation policies, traffic congestion will increase by 15 percent a year.

Local officials throughout the state, especially in high-growth areas, already feel the strain and are compelled to take extraordinary steps to deal with it. But as they and state officials seek the billions of dollars needed to build and staff public facilities, they collide with another phenomenon that evolved in 1980s California: resistance to new taxes among voters who are not representative of the diverse new California but carry-overs from an earlier era. At the precise moment that California's political leaders confront a society that grows more complex as it grows numerically, California's voters are numerically stagnant, overwhelmingly white, middle-aged and middle-class, with conservative atttitudes toward taxes first felt with the passage of Proposition 13 in 1978 but still being expressed in the 1990s. The effect of these twin, contradictory pressures is to contribute to the political confusion and deadlock that marked the 1980s.

Politicians fear voter backlash if they propose new government programs, or expand old programs due to the pressures from expanded caseloads. And both the state and local governments have direct restraints on spending imposed by a Proposition 13 aftermath (Proposition 4), approved by voters in 1979 and modified only slightly in 1990.

The Legislature, moreover, has become preoccupied with internal power struggles and a series of image-bending scandals. Both it and the governor of the 1980s, Republican George Deukmejian, seemed disinterested in dealing with the far-reaching public policy issues that dynamic socio-economic change creates. Instead, they played games of political one-upsmanship that led to an explosion of initiative ballot measures that also contributed to the state's political paralysis. As the 1990s dawned, many were openly saying that California may have become ungovernable in traditional terms.

That was what Stu Spencer, a veteran Republican political strategist, told U.S. Senator Pete Wilson when Wilson, fresh off a Senate re-election victory in 1988, began thinking about running for governor in 1990. But Wilson, pressured by state and national Republican leaders to run and keep the Capitol in GOP hands for the all-critical reapportionment that was to follow the 1990 census, decided to run anyway. Wilson defeated Democrat Dianne Feinstein, the former mayor of San Francisco, in the November 1990 election. But the fact that both candidates came from the political middle indicated that voters yearned for new leadership.

Wilson came into office in 1991 determined to make California's government work again by shifting emphasis from remedial to preventive in education and social services and by proposing a first-ever statewide growth-management program aimed at bringing some order to the state's chaotic development patterns. But Wilson faced a monstrous state budget crisis born of recession and of a decade of ignoring the conflict between anti-tax fever and huge levels of population growth. He faced, too, a Legislature that was beset by scandal and torn apart by factional and partisan infighting.

As the traditional forms of governance lock up, what may be emerging is a new form of quasi-public, quasi-private governance in which local economic and civic interests, working in concert with local governments, create new vehicles for the improvement of infrastructure. In Santa Clara County, for example, the high-tech industry supported a successful drive to persuade local voters to raise sales taxes to finance better highways after it became apparent that more aid would not be forthcoming from Sacramento. Dozens of other counties followed suit and, in a rare major policy action in the Capitol, Deukmejian and legislators agreed on a comprehensive transportation-financing plan eventually enacted by voters in 1990.

Bond issues, lease-purchase contracts and other forms of creative financing have been used by local officials to finance infrastructure improvements.

But as with other aspects of California culture, it is widening the gap between the haves and the have-nots and weakening the bonds of a broader community. Affluent, growing areas can afford to make such improvements while poor areas with stagnant economies cannot. In 21st Century California, what kind of highways serve motorists, how crowded the schools, how dependable the water supply may depend on where one lives.

The demands of affluent parents for better elementary and high school education got results in Sacramento. But California has continued to lag behind in its overall educational performance, especially in services to the non-affluent, non-Anglo and non-English speakers, as it struggled to cope with record growth in school enrollment. By 1990, the average Latino adult in California had three fewer years of education than Anglo, Asian or Black adults.

Dropout rates among minorities showed little improvement in the 1980s. The community college system, once California's traditional educational ladder for the economically disadvantaged, drifted in the 1980s, a victim of post-Proposition 13 budget restraints and a seeming lack of purpose. Finally, in the late 1980s, there was an effort to revive the system and redirect it back to its original purpose, but no one was certain the reforms would work.

Although California's minority population is growing faster than the Anglo population, the state's public and private universities and colleges remain bastions of Anglo and Asian aspirations. Hispanics, now more than 25 percent of the population, represented less than 10 percent of the undergraduate enrollment at the University of California in 1988, while Blacks were less than 5 percent. Asians were nearly 30 percent of UC's undergraduate enrollment — three times their proportion of the overall population.

California's public schools, anticipating the change that will occur in the larger population a decade years later, acquired a non-Anglo student population in the late 1980s even as they absorbed growth rates that approached 200,000 a year.

But the public school system is producing widely disparate results.

According to the California Postsecondary Education System, only 3.6 percent of 1985's Black high school graduates and 4.9 percent of Hispanic high school graduates were eligible for University of California admission; 13 percent of Anglo graduates and 26 percent of Asians were qualified. Asians, even those who only recently migrated from Southeast Asia, are doing very well in the state's schools — a by-product, sociologists believe, of the Asian cultural impetus to excel that may be missing from other minorities.

The high level of Asian education and economic achievement, markedly above those of the population as a whole, has led many demographers to see them as part of an Anglo-Asian overclass that will dominate California's two-tier society of the 21st Century.

And if the elementary and high schools become dominated by Hispanic and Black students while an aging and stagnant Anglo population produces relatively few school-age children — and sends many of them to private schools — it is questionable whether the overclass will be willing to invest the money in public education. One poll taken for the California Teachers Association indicates that older, white voters are less supportive of public education that other groups; by one estimate, fewer than 20 percent of California voters are parents of public school students and the percentage is declining.

Some Hispanic and Black leaders fear that public education, and especially programs geared to the needs of their children, will be neglected in the 21st Century by a dominant class that has little direct interest in it. Indeed, some see Proposition 13 and its anti-government, anti-tax aftershocks as the first indications of growing disinterest.

Because of myriad pressures, California's political structure in the 1980s seemed incapable of dealing with the change. With professionalization of the Legislature and rising partisanship, the Capitol in the 1980s evolved into a place where the petty concerns of internal politics came to dominate the more pressing needs of the real world. In the largest context, political leaders could not simultaneously meet the needs of the state's large and diverse population and obey the mandates of its politically active and somewhat conservative middle and upper-middle classes.

That tension, which increased steadily during the decade, resulted in an explosion of ballot measures whose fate, both positive and negative, did little to clarify the situation.

If California is evolving into a two-tier society as present trends indicate, it will have vast political consequences. There seems to be an overall swing toward conservatism and the Republican Party in California already. As the state was voting overwhelmingly for President Ronald Reagan's re-election in 1984, for example, it also was giving a plurality of its votes to Republican congressional candidates — despite the fact that a partisan congressional redistricting plan enacted in 1982 handed firm control of the congressional delegation to Democrats.

Pollster Mervin Field reported in 1985 that his survey of voter identification shows the GOP having drawn even with the Democrats for the first time in recent history, a trend that held firm as the 1980s evolved into the 1990s. Democratic voter registration, which approached 60 percent in the mid-1970s, slipped below 50 percent for the first time in more than 50 years.

It seems that Anglo voters and middle- to upper-income Asians and Hispanics are identifying more strongly with the Republican Party. And while they may be outnumbered in the overall population, they are most likely to register and to vote.

Lower-income Hispanics and Asians are not participating in California's political process. Asians have the overall lowest levels of political activity of any ethnic group; by 1990, they were 10 percent of the state's population but scarcely 2 percent to 3 percent of the dependable voters. Blacks are more politically active — and overwhelmingly Democratic — but are a stagnant or even declining portion of the state's population. The industrial middle class, the traditional backbone of the Democratic Party, is shrinking because of economic changes.

These trends create a huge dilemma for the Democratic Party. To appeal to the overclass, it must move its ideological identity to the right, putting less stress on providing government programs to the poor. In doing so, it turns its back on some of its most active constituencies and on the liberal ideological bent of its current leaders. But to organize the unorganized runs the risk of further alienating Anglo, middle-income voters and faces enormous barriers of language, non-citizenship and a lack of political tradition among newly arrived immigrants.

The most liklely political scenario for California in the 1990s, and at least the early years of the 21st century, is for dominance by an affluent, politically active overclass using its position to protect its privileges against the larger but weaker underclass. It's a social situation that benefits the Republican Party, which has undergone a quiet evolution into a decidedly more moderate institution as it has expanded its reach. That shift is personified by Governor Wilson, a one-time party pariah for his centrist views. If the Wilsonite philosophy — tough on crime, conservative on taxes and spending; liberal on abortion and environmental issues — becomes the dominant image of the Republican Party, Democrats may be doomed to minority party status in the nation's largest state.

Evolving political power, however, is just one aspect, and probably not the most important one, of a unique culture that continually redefines itself as it expands and diversifies. Clearly, some of California's golden sheen has been tarnished by its social and economic complexities: tangled freeways, high housing prices, rising fear of crime and congested public facilities. A 1989 Field Institute poll revealed a sharp drop in Californians' sense of pride about living in the state. In previous polls, about 75 percent of those responding had rated California "one of the best places to live." But the 1989 poll saw that drop to under 60 percent.

There is some evidence that California's crushing social and economic problems are sinking in on both the state's civic leadership and the larger population. Cadres of civic leaders have been formed, both statewide and at regional and local levels, to explore workable approaches to such pithy issues as regional government, education, water, growth and, most of all, rising levels of social friction.

"California is just entering what may be its most crucial decades since the Mexican War ended in the 1840s," Bouvier and Martin conclude in their study of the state. "The state will never be the same; yet, as with the nation, it remains unfinished. ... The important question is: How will the state adjust to these demographic changes and all their repercussions?"

It's a question whose answer, if anything, is becoming more elusive. 🏛

Pete to immigrants: "Don't huddle here."

GOVERNOR SAYS BREATHING HERE AIN'T FREE

By Danielle Starkey

Reprinted from *California Journal*, March 1992

Late last year, when Governor Pete Wilson blamed a significant share of the state's budget woes on "shifting demographics," he focused the state's attention on two groups — immigrants and the poor — which have often been blamed during times of economic ill.

Apparently counting on voters' hostility — or at least indifference — to these groups, Wilson said that immigrants and welfare mothers are multiplying more rapidly than taxpayers, a trend that would contribute to a state budget shortfall that might reach $20 billion by the year 2000 if the situation is not corrected. The message was clear: If the costs of tending to the poor and the newly-arrived aren't brought down, the rest of us are going to suffer.

Using the tough language of an election-year reformer, the governor said he would remove some of the incentive for newcomers to migrate by proposing a constitutional amendment that would reduce California's attraction as a "welfare magnet," as well as wean welfare recipients from their welfare dependency. Among his proposals were to cut welfare benefits, now $663 for a family of three (fourth highest in the nation, and $86 per month more than what New York pays) by up to 25 percent and to impose a "pay freeze" on newcomers so that for one year, their welfare payments could not exceed the amount they would have received had they not moved to California.

Wilson maintains that the financial consequences of the population changes are real, and that we should not shy away from dealing with them even though it may mean hardship for some of the most defenseless in our society. The welfare of the hard-working middle class is also at stake.

In his state-of-the-state address, Wilson asserted that "spending reform and welfare reform are one and the same."

"Runaway spending is unfair to California taxpayers. And it's not fair to job-seekers, or to the working men and women of California — the breadwinners," Wilson said.

That it also happens to make good election-year politics for a governor frantically trying to backfill a budget deficit that might exceed $5 billion this year even after raising taxes some $8 billion last year — well, that's merely a nice coincidence.

"There are some real changes in the state's demography, and there isn't enough money to be as generous as we have been in the past, specifically in our welfare payments," insists Wilson Press Secretary Bill Livingstone.

Wilson's critics roared their disapproval, accusing him of looking for scapegoats for California's recession-mired economy. By raising a divisive and racially charged issue, they said, the governor was camouflaging his true aim of gaining greater budgetary powers for himself, since those measures are incongruously included in his welfare reform package that he is trying to qualify for the November ballot.

In any case, they said, it is not the immigrants nor the poor that are the enemy of a balanced budget but rather the policies of successive Republican administrations and initiative measures that have eroded the state's tax sources.

There is substantial evidence for this. For all Wilson's rhetoric, the Aid to Families with Dependent Children program (AFDC), the state's basic welfare effort, is expected to cost the state's general fund only $2.8 billion this year — 6.4 percent of a $43.7 billion budget. The rising costs of welfare are small compared to the rising costs of education, health care or operating the state's prisons. Indeed, if Wilson wins passage of his welfare cuts, during the next fiscal year Californians will spend more on prisons than they do on welfare. Still, Wilson's pitch has struck a resounding chord at a time when people are worried about getting their share of what is often perceived as a shrinking pie.

What are the economic impacts of having hundreds of thousands of immigrants move to California each year?

In a November report, "California's Growing Taxpayer Squeeze," the state Department of Finance pointed to recent census figures which project that California, with a population of 29.7 million, will become home to an additional 6.3 million in the next 10 years, 44 percent of them foreign immigrants. In addition, the report said, about 75 percent of California's migrants in the 1980s were foreign born.

"For the vast majority of these new residents, English is a second language. Lack of English language skills places extra demands on the school systems and also limits employment opportunities for adult immigrants," the report said.

The report also said that in 1980, there were 6.9 taxpayers for every welfare recipient, a number projected to drop to 2.94 taxpayers per welfare recipient by the year 2000.

Are the finance report and the governor's gloomy forecasts about the burgeoning welfare caseload more than an election-year gimmick? Are recent foreign immigrants, who have been moving to California at a rate of about 285,000 per year, chomping their way through public-assistance programs? Or are immigrants an economic and cultural asset to California, that keeps U.S. businesses competitive and contribute more in taxes than they use in public services (like welfare) that they are too frightened, ignorant, unwilling or ineligible to use?

This cost-benefit computation is fraught with difficulties. For one thing, it depends foremost on a reasonably accurate count of immigrants, many of whom believe their lives depend on eluding notice. It also tosses into a heap a wildly diverse group, including refugees from Poland, Mexican agricultural workers intending to stay for one season and Korean professionals holding advanced degrees, and calculates how they will act as a group — such as whether they will sign up for welfare, if eligible. It also must figure in how much in taxes the immigrants as a group pay, including payroll, social security and sales taxes, then contrast that with the types and amount of public services they use.

If immigrants keep prices down by accepting low-paying jobs, what effect does this have on the rest of the labor market? How much leverage do these low-paid workers give to U.S. companies to be competitive abroad, and to expand their domestic operations? How much foreign investment do immigrants attract, which in turn supports local business activities that translates into jobs?

Will California see the number of welfare cases jump in June of this year when immigrants recently legalized under the Immigration Reform and Control Act of 1986 (IRCA) are finally allowed to sign up for these programs without fear of being deported?

Beginning to sound like a daunting task? Some studies dispute the premise that immigrants are an economic burden; others say that it's impossible to calculate. But what economists, sociologists and others looking at the issue are finding runs counter to some persistent myths:

• Although communities with a high concentration of immigrants pay a disproportionate share of costs to educate and provide medical care for them, immigrants' overall tax payments — about two-thirds of which go to the federal government — far exceed the cost of what they use in public services.

• While not all foreign immigrants arrive in California without job skills, a significant portion take low-paying jobs that have helped keep U.S. businesses competitive; others have started their own businesses, some of which are successfully competing with international firms.

• Immigrants traditionally have not displaced domestic workers, and instead have competed for jobs with other, newer immigrants. But as the nation's labor market shifts from a manufacturing base to high-technology and service industries, that situation could change.

"Contrary to conventional wisdom, immigrants don't tend to be users of public services any more than the native population. In fact, immigrants tend to pay more in taxes than they use in social and public services," said Stephen Moore, an economist at the Washington, D.C.-based CATO Institute, a Libertarian think tank.

But about 65 percent of that money goes to the federal government, which has not been returning it to states with large immigrant populations at the rate promised under the 1986 Immigration Reform and Control Act, Moore said. Consequently, state and local governments absorb more than their share of costs.

"One perfect example is education," Moore said. "Immigrants, many of whom come here in their peak child-bearing years, put their children in the school system. Clearly, in many California towns, that gets to be very difficult." (In the past decade, the number of California schoolchildren with limited English has more than doubled to 986,000, or one in every five children.)

On the other hand, Moore noted, most of the people who move here came to work, and when they work, the majority pay social security and unemployment insurance, for example, usually without getting the benefits of these when they retire or get laid off. In effect, they are subsidizing the country's aging population, which is relying on a dwindling number of domestic workers to keep the social security system from going bankrupt.

"And the illegals, they're a great windfall because they use almost no public services," said Moore. "The last thing they want to do is go to the government and ask for services. They're too afraid of getting caught. They never collect a dime of social security, and you don't find too many collecting unemployment benefits, but those taxes are deducted from their paychecks." (By law, illegals are barred from receiving federal welfare, food stamps and unemployment.)

Before going further, it's important to note that "immigrants" generally are divided into four categories, and while all are eligible to receive emergency medical care and pregnancy services, not all can get financial assistance:

• Refugees. The majority of these are fleeing political persecution in their native country, and Congress and the president decide how many of them will be admitted to the United States each year. These individuals are eligible to receive all benefits.

• Legalized aliens. These are people who entered the United States illegally but have applied for temporary residence under the federal immigration-reform law. These individuals are prohibited from applying for financial assistance for five years. The penalty for doing so is deportation. However, if these legalized aliens have children while living in this country, their children are eligible for benefits. Approximately three million people applied for lawful resident status under IRCA, and about half of them have settled in California. Most are from Mexico, (74.7 percent); followed by Central America (9.4 percent) and the Caribbean (4.1 percent).

• Undocumented aliens. These are people who are living here illegally. No one knows how many there are, but the state estimates that 100,000 illegal immigrants move to California each year.

• Documented aliens. These are people who are admitted to the country under existing immigration laws and includes mostly individuals who are joining family members who are already citizens, who have special desired job skills, or significant amounts of money to invest here.

O f the nine million or so people in all four categories who have immigrated to the United States in the 1980s, about 2.3 million of them settled in Los Angeles County. While undocumented aliens represent only a part of the immigrant population, they have been the subject of a great deal of study by L.A. county officials.

An April 1991 report to L.A. supervisors by chief administrative officer Richard Dixon said, "At the local level, the costs of services provided to undocumented aliens (and their citizen children) continue to escalate and are not fully offset by local revenues received from them." (Estimated revenues from undocumented aliens in 1990-91 to county coffers was $137.6 million. At the same time, the county's estimated cost for that population was $413.8 million, a shortfall of $276.2 million.)

However, the report found, "Total revenues received by all levels of government from undocumented aliens greatly exceed their total cost to the county, but most revenues are received by the federal and state governments." (The county has estimated that 770,000 undocumented aliens were living in Los Angeles in 1990-91, and that they paid $2.96 billion in revenues.)

The report said that the cost of providing welfare aid to citizen children and, eventually, their families, "could easily reach $1 billion a year by the end of the decade, even if illegal immigration levels off... due to the high birth rate of the undocumented alien population who are disproportionately

of child-bearing age" and because residents legalized under IRCA will be eligible for aid beginning in May, and they may be waiting in the wings to apply for it.

Tom Lee, a supervisor with the state Department of Social Services, says that these assumptions are "unfair" to the newly legalized population. "We're talking about people who have been underground for many years, working, and not taking advantage of services," he said.

Indeed, studies show that most of the newly legalized are working. For example, a 1989 survey prepared for the state Health and Welfare Agency by the Comprehensive Adult Student Assessment System found that three-quarters of the legalized aliens interviewed had been working full-time in the month before the interview, and an additional 10 percent said they had been working part-time.

Nevertheless, says the Wilson administration, the 1990 census and "current demographic trends," point to a 141 percent increase in the number of welfare cases in the 1990s. "To the extent the state is required to fund entitlement programs like welfare, it will crowd out spending on education, public safety and preventive programs," said Livingstone.

Others say the recession is to blame for a jump in welfare cases, and once it eases, the number will drop down.

"What [the Wilson administration] seems to be saying is that the AFDC caseload would grow as much as 9 percent a year over the next 10 years, when in fact, before the recession hit, AFDC was growing at about 2 percent to 4 percent a year," said Edward Lazere, a research analyst at the Washington, D.C.-based Center on Budget and Policy Priorities. "The main gripe we have is their claim that the recession has no effect on the welfare caseload. That's completely counterintuitive."

In January, Russell Gould, secretary of the state Health and Welfare Agency, said that welfare advocates who "claim that the recession alone is to blame for the dramatic caseload increase in the past four years are not facing reality." As proof, he said, "From 1981-83, in the midst of a severe recession, the number of single-parent families on aid grew by only 2 percent. Conversely, the current trend of rapid increases in caseload began in 1988, and were well underway by 1989-90."

His analysis invites closer inspection.

Single-parent families are least likely to be affected by a recession because they probably weren't working in the first place because it's unlikely they could afford child care.

However, rises and falls in the AFDC "employed parent" category (two parents, both unemployed) would more likely reflect whether the recession has had an impact. And that is the category that grew faster than any other from 1989-90 to 1990-91, according to figures from Gould's own Department of Social Services.

In 1989-90 there were 75,579 cases in AFDC's two-parent category, a number that has been roughly constant (in the 70,000s) since 1983-84, at the tail end of the last recession, when the number was up to 83,055. In 1990-91 the AFDC category covering two-parent families jumped to 93,379, an increase of 24 percent, while the single-parent group went from 560,676 to 613,131, an increase of less than 10 percent.

To test the supposition that immigrants (through their U.S-born children) are responsible for much of the upswing in welfare cases, it might be useful to compare the rate of increase of child-only cases (which includes, but is not limited to, children of immigrants) with adult cases. Here too, however, caseloads grew roughly at the same rate until last year, the first year of the recession, when both shot up. For example, from 1986-89, the number of child-only cases actually dropped, from 92,170 to 89,367, while the number of adult-headed cases grew from 581,253 to 598,780. But both jumped when the recession began. The number of child-only cases went from 107,070 to 141,848 and adult cases went from 636,255 to 706,510.

Lee, with the state Department of Social Services, said it may be easier to evaluate potential costs of immigrants by looking at their use of health services, "because there's more of a life-or-death need for a doctor's treatment. "They would think, 'I can do with less food for a while, but if I don't get to a doctor, I might lose an arm or die.'"

In November, a state Department of Finance report did say that, "While immigrants and refugees accounted for only 1.3 percent of the Medi-Cal caseload in 1980, those groups accounted for over 4.5 percent of the program's beneficiaries in 1990."

When interviewed, however, the state demographer who helped prepare the report acknowledged that the percentage used in 1980 referred only to refugees, not to all immigrants. Adding other immigrants into the 1990 figure artificially inflates the rate of increase.

"Any medical care associated with that population would have been picked up by the county, at county hospitals," said Kathryn Perry, associate secretary for public affairs at the state Health and Welfare Agency. "County hospitals have always provided a safety net for the poor [and] there's not a word [in the law] that says you have to be a legal resident to get treatment."

Apart from the question of what immigrants take is the question of what they give back, culturally and economically.

"What we proudly call 'American' today is not the Puritan of the 18th Century," said Paula Fass, a history professor at UC Berkeley. "The need to confront heterogeneity on a daily basis is one of the glories of American culture."

That diversity is a plus in a world that's quickly heading toward global markets and global communities, she said.

And while the children of immigrants will be heavy users of education systems, they also should be considered an investment in the nation's future, said Paul Ong, a labor economist and UCLA professor in urban planning.

"This country has been having a hard time convincing our own students to go into very specialized fields, particularly fields that emphasize research. Clearly, to remain on the cutting edge of technology, we need people with those skills, and a good number of the people filling that demand are Asian immigrants," Ong said.

In addition, he said, Asian-owned businesses are the most dynamic sector of the state's economy. He said there was a 255 percent increase in the number of new Asian companies from 1977-87, compared with a 35 percent growth in firms for the state as a whole.

"These businesses create jobs," he said.

Do immigrants working for lower wages take jobs from natives? Not according to Robert Valdez, a UCLA professor of health policy and management and an analyst with the Rand Corporation who co-wrote in 1986 with Kevin McCarthy, "The Current and Future Effects of Mexican Immigration to California."

"Immigrants and the native-born population function in different labor markets," he said. "The groups most impacted by immigrants are other immigrants who have been here for some time, who are in low-paying, low-mobility jobs."

The availability of a large pool of low-wage, Mexican-born workers statewide and especially in Los Angeles no doubt contributed to slower wage growth. But this has helped the state's manufacturing sector to maintain a better competitive position with foreign producers, according to Valdez.

According to his study, "For example, wages increased more slowly in Los Angeles (where the majority of immigrants are concentrated) than statewide, and the slower wage growth tends to be more pronounced in industries that rely heavily on Mexican workers (apparel and furniture) than in those that use Mexican workers sparingly (transportation and printing)."

But his study also found that, "Overall, wage levels of all workers (about 70 percent of whom are Anglos) and of black workers in California and Los Angeles are substantially higher than those of their counterparts nationwide.

"Thus, even if the presence of a large pool of Mexican workers has slowed wage increases, it has certainly not erased the earnings advantage enjoyed by California's Anglo and black workers. However, the picture among the state's Latino workers is more mixed. Although Latino workers in California and Los Angeles are at rough earnings parity with Latino workers nationwide, their wages have been growing more slowly (and) any displacement effects appear to be concentrated in the Latino population itself."

With so many studies either disproving the assertion that immigrants are a net drain on the state's economy, Democrats, welfare and immigrants rights' groups are focusing on Wilson's possible political objectives. Leo McElroy, a veteran, Sacramento-based manager of initiative campaigns, said the Republican governor's sagging popularity in an election year and before a possible 1996 run at the presidency is relevant.

"If you had a fan club meeting for the governor right now, I suspect you could hold it in a phone booth. To blunt this unpopularity, it looks to me as if he's selected a popular target for people's hostility," said McElroy.

"Immigrants are definably other than 'us;' they're people trying to join us and become us. But in an economy where it's perceived that there may not be enough of the pie to go around," immigrants can easily become the scapegoat, McElroy said.

And by calling the initiative "welfare reform" instead of "government reorganization," McElroy said Wilson is like "the magician who makes a dramatic gesture in the air with his left hand while slipping a rabbit into his hat with his right. "This could actually prove to be a mobilizing force for a lot of people who otherwise may not have voted, and who will be driven by anger at the governor to go to the polls. If he brings to the polls a lot of people injured by this who choose to fight it, he's not going to like the results."

One welfare-rights advocate already has proposed making voter registration a prerequisite to receiving welfare, McElroy added.

The Wilson administration has shrugged off their complaints and said hard times are forcing painful cuts everywhere, and that without welfare reform, budget reform is impossible.

"When people can't challenge the initiative on its merits, they begin name-calling," said Livingstone. "You must address the programs that are on auto-pilot spending that are causing the budget to be out of balance." 🏛

EXECUTIVE BRANCH & BUDGET

One might think from reading the state Constitution that California's chief executive has absolute authority. In reality, California's governor has, as does the President of the United States, power that is balanced by power of the other branches of government and the electorate. The governor reigns supreme in very few areas. One of them is appointments, but many of these are subject to confirmation by the state Senate. California's governor has remarkably few appointments compared to other states because the civil service system has long been established for all but the top policy posts. The governor also has prime responsibility for the fiscal affairs of state, but his budget is subject to alteration by the Legislature. The governor can reduce or eliminate items in the budget passed by the Legislature. This "line-item" veto is a very powerful tool for which President Bush has voiced envy. These vetoes, like any others, are subject to override by two-thirds vote of the Senate and Assembly, through this happens only rarely.

Governors are elected for four-year terms, with a new two-term limit established by Proposition 140 in November 1990. Historically, only Earl Warren was elected more than twice. The order of succession is the lieutenant governor, Senate president pro tempore, Assembly speaker, secretary of state, attorney general, treasurer and controller. The governor serves as the ceremonial chief of state, as president of the University of California Board of Regents and the State University and Colleges Board of Trustees, as unofficial leader of his party, and as the head of most administrative agencies through his subordinate appointees. The governor is deeply involved in the legislative process, through presentation of the budget, the office's veto power and the traditional presentation of a package of bills constituting a legislative program (and usually outlined in the annual "state-of-the-state" message).

Veto power

The veto is perhaps the governors most potent weapon, but it is essentially a negative power. Governors wield tremendous influence with members of their own party (because they often control the party structure, weak as it is, and because lawmakers like to stay on the good side of a governor so they can get projects for their districts and appointments for their friends). Consequently, vetoes are rarely overridden. When Governor Ronald Reagan had a

veto overridden during the 1973-74 session, it was the first over-ride since 1946. Jerry Brown was overridden during his first term on a death-penalty measure and overrides became almost commonplace in 1979, especially on fiscal issues. Neither George Deukmejian nor Pete Wilson have had a veto overridden.

Governors have the power to organize the administrative agencies of state government as they see fit, although the Legislature can veto major reorganization plans. Reagan organized his administration into four agencies headed by the secretaries of health and welfare, business and transportation, agriculture and services, and resources. The Department of Finance reported directly to the Governor. The cabinet met regularly and established policy for the administration. Once policy was set, every department had to follow it — whether or not it agreed.

The Jerry Brown administration employed the case-study method for solving problems and establishing policies. Cabinet sessions at the start were frequent, lengthy and argumentative — far less business-like than in the Reagan years. However Brown put agency executives on a loose leash once they learned what he expected from them. Jerry Brown created a fifth agency, the Youth and Adult Correctional Agency, and gave the departments of Food and Agriculture and Industrial Relations cabinet rank.

George Deukmejian, it was assumed, would be willing to bargain and compromise with the legislature on issues since, as a former legislator, he was used to a give and take process. His unyielding stance during his first year in office on issues like taxes and community college fees surprised many. Despite the fact that he was the sole Republican among the state's statewide officeholders and both houses of the Legislature were Democratic-controlled, Deukmejian wielded the powers of his office with considerable effect during his first two years. During his last six years, thanks largely to an eased fiscal condition, Deukmejian was more amenable to the wishes of the Democrats, but remained a hard-liner on fiscal issues. Neither George Deukemejian nor Pete Wilson has had a veto overridden.

Deukmejian's Republican successor, Governor Pete Wilson, selected a more moderate and pragmatic group of Cabinet secretaries. Wilson also has proposed establishing a new cabinet and agency: environmental protection, similar to one created administratively by Deukmejian.

Sharing executive power with the governor are a number of boards and commissions. The governor appoints most of their members and they in turn exercise independent authority. Among them:

University of California of Regents. Aside from the power of the purse, the Regents control the university system.

State University Trustees. This board has less power and prestige than the UC Regents but has been seeking increased independence.

Public Utilities Commission. The PUC sets rates for public utilities and also exercises allied responsibilities.

Franchise Tax Board. This board administers the state income tax and handles other revenue matters.

State Lands Commission. This commission exercises control over the state's oil-rich tidelands and other public properties.

Fair Political Practices Commission. This powerful agency was created by voters in June 1974 to police the state's Political Reform Act covering lobbyist activities, campaign contributions and conflicts of interest.

Energy Resources, Conservation and Development Commission. This commission also went into operation in 1975. It is charged with establishing overall state power policy and with the selection of sites for new power plants.

Agricultural Labor Relations Board. This agency supervises management-labor activities for the agricultural industry.

Lottery Commission. Created by the 1984 initiative to run what is, in effect, one of the nation's largest businesses.

Citizens Compensation Commission. This governmental unit was established by voters with the adoption of Prop. 112 of June 1990. This commission is charged with setting the salary level of all state elected officials except judges.

In a special category is the *State Board of Equalization,* composed of the state controller and four members elected by district. It collects the sales tax and other levies, and supervises county administration of the property tax. From time to time, governors propose elimination of the Board of Equalization and the Franchise Tax Board in favor of creating a Department of Revenue under the governor's control.

Statewide offices

In addition to the governor, the state Constitution requires the election of seven other statewide officials. All are limited to two four-year terms by Prop. 140. See box for a list of current incumbents, the individuals they defeated and their predecessors.

Here is a brief rundown of the duties of these other statewide officials:

• **Lieutenant Governor:** presides over the Senate, serves as a member of numerous state boards and commissions, and exercises the powers of chief executive when the governor leaves the state or is incapacitated.

• **Secretary of State**: the state's chief election officer; maintains all the state's official files and historical documents, including articles of incorporation; receives lobbyists' registrations and their monthly reports; receives campaign-contribution and conflict-of-interest disclosure forms.

• **Attorney General**: the state's chief law enforcement officer, legal advisor to state agencies.

• **Treasurer**: provides all banking services for the state, including sale of bonds and investment of securities.

• **Controller**: the principal accounting and disbursement officer for the state; administers inheritance and gift taxes and performs a variety of functions assigned by the Legislature, including publication of statistics on local government.

• **Superintendent of Public Instruction**: heads the state Department of Education, but most of the public schools are administered by local boards; state education policy is established by the state Board of Education, composed of gubernatorial appointees.

• **Insurance Commissioner**: This is a relatively new position created by the passage of Proposition 103 in 1988. The commissioner oversees the operations of the state Department of Insurance and has wide authority to approve or disapprove many types of insurance rates.

Constitutional Officers

	Incumbent (year first elected)	Defeated Nov. 1990	Predecessor
Governor	Pete Wilson (R) 1990	Dianne Feinstein (D)	George Deukmejian (R)
Lieutenant Governor	Leo T. McCarthy (D) 1982	Marian Bergeson (R)	Mike Curb (R)
Secretary of State	March Fong Eu (D) 1974	Joan Milke Flores (R)	Edmund G. Brown Jr. (D)
Attorney General	Dan Lungren (R) 1990	Arlo Smith (D)	John Van de Kamp (D)
Treasurer	Kathleen Brown (D) 1990	Tom Hayes (R)	Tom Hayes (R)
Insurance Commissioner	John Garamendi (D) 1990	Wes Bannister (R)	— none —
Controller	Gray Davis (D) 1986	Matt Fong (R)	Kenneth Cory (D)
Superintendent of Public Instruction	Louis (Bill) Honig 1982 (nonpartisan)	Won in Primary	Wilson Riles

Note: Minor-party candidates omitted.

California Executive Branch Organization

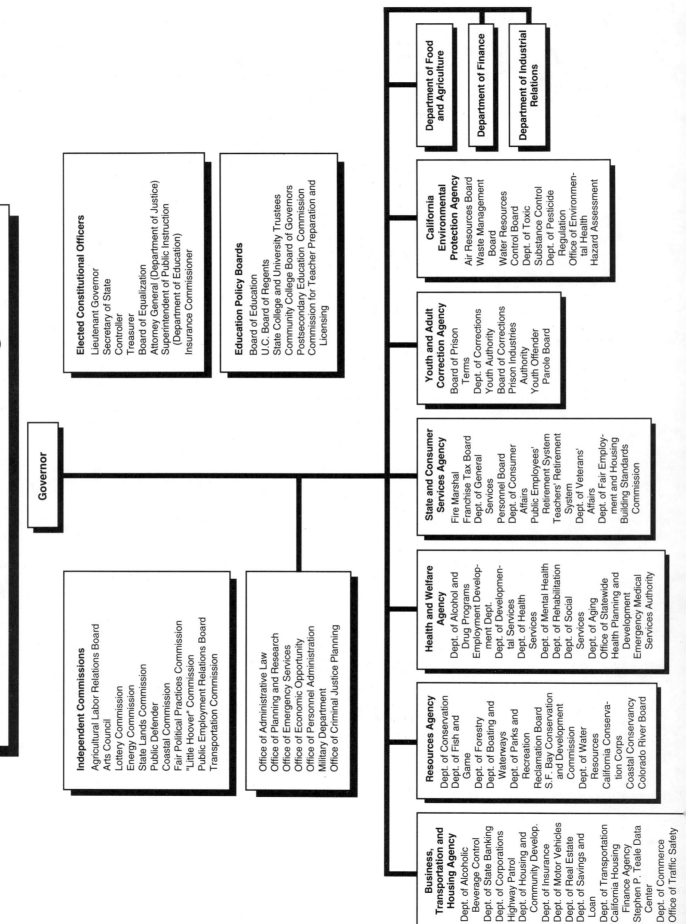

Governor

Elected Constitutional Officers
Lieutenant Governor
Secretary of State
Controller
Treasurer
Board of Equalization
Attorney General (Department of Justice)
Superintendent of Public Instruction
(Department of Education)
Insurance Commissioner

Education Policy Boards
Board of Education
U.C. Board of Regents
State College and University Trustees
Community College Board of Governors
Postsecondary Education Commission
Commission for Teacher Preparation and
Licensing

Independent Commissions
Agricultural Labor Relations Board
Arts Council
Lottery Commission
Energy Commission
State Lands Commission
Public Defender
Coastal Commission
Fair Political Practices Commission
"Little Hoover" Commission
Public Employment Relations Board
Transportation Commission

Office of Administrative Law
Office of Planning and Research
Office of Emergency Services
Office of Economic Opportunity
Office of Personnel Administration
Military Department
Office of Criminal Justice Planning

Department of Food and Agriculture

Department of Finance

Department of Industrial Relations

California Environmental Protection Agency
Air Resources Board
Waste Management Board
Water Resources Control Board
Dept. of Toxic Substance Control
Dept. of Pesticide Regulation
Office of Environmental Health Hazard Assessment

Youth and Adult Correction Agency
Board of Prison Terms
Dept. of Corrections
Youth Authority
Board of Corrections
Prison Industries Authority
Youth Offender Parole Board

State and Consumer Services Agency
Fire Marshal
Franchise Tax Board
Dept. of General Services
Personnel Board
Dept. of Consumer Affairs
Public Employees' Retirement System
Teachers' Retirement System
Dept. of Veterans' Affairs
Dept. of Fair Employment and Housing
Building Standards Commission

Health and Welfare Agency
Dept. of Alcohol and Drug Programs
Employment Development Dept.
Dept. of Developmental Services
Dept. of Health Services
Dept. of Mental Health
Dept. of Rehabilitation
Dept. of Social Services
Dept. of Aging
Office of Statewide Health Planning and Development
Emergency Medical Services Authority

Resources Agency
Dept. of Conservation
Dept. of Fish and Game
Dept. of Forestry
Dept. of Boating and Waterways
Dept. of Parks and Recreation
Reclamation Board
S.F. Bay Conservation and Development Commission
Dept. of Water Resources
California Conservation Corps
Coastal Conservancy
Colorado River Board

Business, Transportation and Housing Agency
Dept. of Alcoholic Beverage Control
Dept. of State Banking
Dept. of Corporations
Highway Patrol
Dept. of Housing and Community Develop.
Dept. of Insurance
Dept. of Motor Vehicles
Dept. of Real Estate
Dept. of Savings and Loan
Dept. of Transportation
California Housing Finance Agency
Stephen P. Teale Data Center
Dept. of Commerce
Office of Traffic Safety

State Finance

The governor is required by the state constitution to present a budget each January — an estimate of the state's expenditures and revenues for the fiscal year starting the following July 1st. In a state growing as fast as California, the budget increases dramatically no matter who is governor.

During the eight years Ronald Reagan was governor, the total budget doubled from $5 billion to $10 billion. Jerry Brown's first budget (1975-76) totaled $11.4 billion, and his final budget (1982-83) totaled $25.3 billion. George Deukmejian's first budget (1983-84) totaled $26.8 billion and his last budget (1990-91) was $54.4 billion. Governor Pete Wilson's first budget was $55.7 billion.

These figures can be misleading because they do not show how much the cost of state government has risen. Many of the increases were for the exclusive purpose of relieving-pressure on the property tax or on local government, especially after the passage of Proposition 13 in 1978. In fact, about two-thirds of each year's budget consists of allocations to schools and other elements of local government, and about half the state budget is for public education.

Budget process

The budget process in the Legislature involves detailed study of items that are questioned by the Legislature's fiscal specialist, the legislative analyst. For months, subcommittees of the Senate Budget and Fiscal Review Committee and the Assembly Ways and Means Committee pore over the budget and decide which items should be increased, reduced, added or eliminated. Eventually, the budget is packaged by the fiscal committees and sent to the floor of each house. As a practical matter, either the Senate or the Assembly bill becomes the vehicle for enactment of a budget. The first house to act sends its version of the bill to the other, which then puts its own figures into the legislation and sends it back to the house of origin. The changes are routinely rejected, and the budget is placed in the hands of a conference committee composed of members of both chambers. Even though the constitution requires that the budget be sent to the governor by June 15th, it is often much later before both houses are able to adopt a compromise because passage by a two-thirds majority is required.

Revenue

One major portion of the budget — estimated revenues — is not considered at all by the Legislature, except to verify that funds will be sufficient to meet anticipated expenditures. The difference between revenues and expenditures (with any carryover from the previous year taken into account) produces the projected surplus for the fiscal year.

About 85 percent of the revenue goes into the state general fund. The remaining 15 percent is collected from specific sources and placed in special funds (notably the motor vehicle fund) to be spent for specific purposes. Estimates in the governor's proposed budget for the 1992-93 fiscal year show anticipated revenue from all funds of $57 billion ($45.7 billion general fund; $11,326 special funds). Specific fund sources and their percent of total revenue are as follows:

Personal income tax, $19.5 billion (33.6%);
Sales tax, $18.6 billion (32.0%);
Bank & corporation taxes, $5.5 billion (9.4%);
Insurance, $1.2 billion (2.1%);
Motor vehicle (inc. gas tax), $7.1 billion (12.3%);
Tobacco, $685 million (1.2%);
Liquor, $313 million (0.5%);
Estate taxes, $540 million (0.9%);
Horse racing fees, $115 million (0.2%);
Other, $4.5 billion (7.8%).

Expenditures

Total proposed 1992-93 expenditures are $56.3 billion, not counting bond funds. Here are the major items of expenditure as proposed by the governor in January 1992:

Aid to schools K-12, $17.9 billion (31.8%);
Health and welfare, $15.9 billion (28.3%);
Higher education, $6.5 billion (11.6%);
Business, transportation and housing, $4.3 billion (7.7%);
Local government, $3.5 billion (5.5%);
Youth and adult corrections, $3.3 billion (5.9%);
Other, $4.8 billion (9.2%).

Clouding the fiscal picture in 1991-92, Governor Pete Wilson's first year as chief executive, was the unprecedented and massive deficit, which ultimately surpassed $14 billion. A deficit in the $6 billion range had to be dealt with for 1992-93.

While the Legislature can revise the budget in any way it sees fit, the governor has only two choices when he receives the bill act at the end of June: he can veto it in its entirety and thus force the Legislature to pass a new bill, or he can reduce and eliminate specific items (this is known as blue-penciling the budget through line-item veto). This latter is the practice traditionally used.

Until the budget is enacted, the Legislature cannot pass appropriations measures unless the governor provides a letter saying that the expenditure is needed on an emergency basis. Once the budget is passed, however, the Legislature can — and usually does — send the governor numerous bills containing appropriations. The governor can cut the entire appropriation or reduce the amount. (Each of these bills can contain only a single appropriation.) 🏛

Pete Wilson after one year

Natural disasters ... and other highlights from the governor's inaugural season

Reprinted from *California Journal*, December 1991

By Richard Zeiger

Pete Wilson's first year in office has been a year of disasters — some natural, some unnatural. The state had its fifth year of drought, a freeze, an urban fire and now white flies in the Imperial Valley.

It also faces a budget shortfall that at times appears bottomless, some $14.3 billion at the time the budget was passed in July and perhaps another $6 billion by budget-passing time next summer. Wilson arm-wrestled with the Legislature over the issue of reapportionment and he infuriated the state's gay community by vetoing its long-sought equal employment bill.

For a man who is used to being on top of the political agenda, whose campaign for governor seemed prepared for every possible contingency, actually holding the governorship must be something of a shock.

The unexpected and unrelenting crises have sidetracked Wilson from much of the ambitious agenda he hoped to tackle in his first year as governor. Instead he has done battle with unforseen events that have taken their toll on Wilson politically. His stock in the polls has plummeted; the California Poll indicated that the percentage of people who think he is doing a good or excellent job dropped from 36 percent in February to 29 percent in September. Perhaps more alarming, the percentage of those who say he is doing a poor or very poor job increased from 6 percent to 21 percent during those seven months.

Furthermore, the governor managed to alienate a substantial portion of his own political party, first by advocating more taxes than many of the more conservative Republicans could swallow and then by blocking a reapportionment plan advocated by some of the more conservative officeholders in his party who worried that a plan that drew more Republican districts would result in their own strongholds being weakened.

According to one Republican political observer, the bad-feelings could linger long enough to make Wilson a one-term governor.

Wilson himself doesn't totally dispute the notion, saying, "Hell, I could be a casualty. I could be a one-termer. But I don't think so because I think the recession will disappear."

Wilson notes he has "faced an unnatural series of natural disasters which has made a considerable claim on the time, treasury and energy that obviously we'd like to expend in other directions."

In the meantime, Wilson will have to travel down a very bumpy road.

The governor has already declared that he will approve no further tax increases, a notion supported by legislative leaders of both houses fearful of the election-year retribution that might be heaped on incumbents by voters who face tax boosts.

But foregoing taxes means Wilson and legislators must make even greater cuts in state services, cuts that Wilson last year called Draconian and this year look no more palatable.

"What is very clear is that we simply cannot impose additional taxes. The people can't afford to pay them and the businesses that have the option of doing so will locate elsewhere. As a result, we're going to have to do some terribly unpleasant things, things that I will hate doing and that the Legislature will hate doing," Wilson offered.

The last round of budget cuts, cuts which made up about half of the $14.3 billion deficit, were not popular with voters. Some 21 percent of California Poll respondents who were unhappy with Wilson cited cuts as the reason for their disapproval. But the taxes were even less popular, the reason for dislike by nearly a third of those who thought Wilson's performance poor.

Wilson's supporters, in fact, say that these contradictory results show that Wilson actually did a good job of sheparding his first budget through the Legislature — a contention largely confirmed by most of those interviewed for this story.

The budget gap was closed with a combination of tax increases, some temporary and some permanent, cuts in spending — including a reduction in payments to families on welfare — and the usual amount of fiscal gimmickry that drew the praises of all but the most hard-core anti-tax conservatives.

This group of intransigent Republicans, located almost exclusively in the Assembly, ironically might have pushed Wilson toward a more liberal position because of its failure to cooperate. These Republicans were so hard-core in their position that they took themselves out of the game, forcing Wilson to seek most of his votes from Democrats, Democrats who were inclined to favor taxes over spending cuts.

"I think that if there were more Republican votes, if there were more Republicans to begin with and we had gotten more of those votes to begin with, we could have gotten more in the way of spending cuts because we would have had to get fewer Democrats. To the extent they were unwilling to vote for certain spending cuts, they had no voice at all," Wilson said. The governor's anger at this group is all the greater because he believes they acted hypocritically in refusing any tax increase.

"The truth is, there wasn't anybody upstairs [in the Capitol] who was willing to vote for $14 billion in tax cuts," said the governor. "That's what I mean when I say that some of the ... critics were distinctly hypocritical, simply because the alterna-tive to those taxes that they couldn't bring themselves to vote for were spending cuts that they couldn't bring themselves to vote for either, or that they knew were utterly unrealistic because they knew there weren't enough votes. There were a few people who would be happy to vote for any spending cut, but not very many."

Things won't get much easier in this next round. These conservative Republicans remain angry. And Wilson this time cannot count on the assistance of Democrats.

For one thing, Democrats are very angry about Wilson's approach to reapportionment. They maintain Wilson never really intended to sign any reapportionment bill, except one that completely capitulated to Republican demands. They contend that his strategy all along was to send the matter to the state Supreme Court, dominated by Republicans appointed by Wilson and his predecessor, former Governor George Deukmejian.

"Pete Wilson is more anti-Legislature than any governor with whom I've served," said Assembly Speaker Willie Brown, who was a lawmaker when Ronald Reagan was governor. "He is without a Republican constituency in the Legislature, and he clearly has alienated the Democratic constituency. He has no prospects at all."

Brown also believes Wilson may become pinned down in the next year by a recall movement being supported by some public employee groups, retired government employee groups and perhaps tacitly by conservative Republicans. Brown believes there is a decent chance the recall will make it to the ballot, putting Wilson before the voters in 1992 along with George Bush's presidential reelection campaign.

If the economy stays bad, "He's in real trouble this year. For the first time, he'll be playing defense." Brown said.

Even if Wilson should survive the recall attempt, unless he gets a very big showing, Democrats will view him as vulnerable in 1994, Brown believes.

"If he goes in the mid-50s on the recall, I guarantee that Miss [Kathleen] Brown and Mr. [John] Garamendi will turn up the burners," said Brown.

Wilson will need Democratic help to get through this year's budget crises. If there were any easy cuts last time, they are gone now, and the governor readily admits he will have to go after big ticket — and popular — budget items to bring spending down. Among the most likely targets is education. Although grade schools and community colleges make up some 41 percent of the state budget, they were spared the worst cuts last time around.

Wilson says he doesn't mind spending on education, if the education system is effective. But these days he has taken to citing figures that show where the system fails, and he says for all the state's spending "we're not beginning to get what we're paying for."

The changes Wilson wants, including testing of students and teachers to determine which teachers are effective, is sure to be contested by powerful teacher unions and probably resisted by Democrats in the Legislature.

And Wilson needs to be aware of legislative sensibilities. Unlike Deukmejian, Wilson has an ambitious legislative program he wants to see enacted into law. He got some of it passed — particularly changes he advocated in the budget process and creation of an environmental protection agency — but lawmakers stopped him in other areas. They refused, for example, to approve his plan for a Department of Child

Development and Education, making it, in Wilson's words, "hostage to the reapportionment struggle. And I think that's inexcusable."

Wilson, though, had no compunctions about hostage-taking when he attempted to force the Legislature into approving some last-minute changes in the state's workers' compensation program, a proposal Wilson says he intends to revive this year.

Interpretations of Wilson's workers' compensation efforts vary. Wilson representatives say the governor had few expectations that the Legislature would comply but felt that he had to set the stage for further efforts this year. Critics of the effort say the governor was dragged into a squabble he was unlikely to win as a result of some bad advice from the business community, which has too much sway over the governor. Even with this bad advice, others offer, the governor was on the verge of winning that dispute when he blinked, backing off just as lawmakers were about to capitulate.

Wilson himself says that he had little choice but to take on the issue at budget time.

"When the hell would you ever have anything like the same leverage?" Wilson asked. "I could have avoided getting into trouble by not running for governor. I don't think ducking challenges is a particularly clever thing. I think the workers' comp situation is one where I think I was absolutely right. What they're saying is I should have ducked it."

In fact, the governor has found himself in several binds this year as a result of his inability to duck or deflect tricky questions. Most prominent was his veto of AB 101, the measure that would have barred employers from discriminating against individuals on the basis of sexual orientation.

Wilson insists he "never promised during the campaign" that he would sign the measure. But that impression was left with the gay community nonetheless, and it was outraged when Wilson finally vetoed the measure.

Some political observers have speculated that Wilson vetoed the proposal in order to shore up his deteriorating rapport with the most conservative wing of his own party and because he needed to protect the primary prospects of Republican John Seymour, Wilson's appointee as his successor in the U.S. Senate. Seymour faces a primary challenge from the right, and had the bill become law, there was the distinct possibility that a referendum would have been mounted to have it repealed — a proposal that might have been on the primary ballot along with Seymour. It would have become a magnet for right-wing voters who also may have voted against Seymour.

If Wilson wanted to placate the right, he failed. Included in his veto message was a sentence saying it was not intended to give solace to "bigots" and the narrow-minded, lines that the right took as a slap in the face.

Wilson dismisses these contentions, however, saying the bill was vetoed on legal grounds, that it was unnecessary because protections existed in current law — a position recently confirmed by an appellate court ruling — and because additional protections would place an undue burden on the business community. But the governor failed to get this message out to the gay community, which had other expectations. And with a public-opinion poll about to come out showing support for the measure, Wilson hurriedly vetoed it, setting off a wave of protests across the state.

The rash of bad timing has been attributed by the press,

in large measure, to the loss of Otto Bos, Wilson's longtime advisor whose tasks included handling the media. Bos, who died unexpectedly of a heart attack just before final deliberations on the budget, was the Wilson aide who worried about long-range political planning. He was widely respected among the press corps for his ability to put the most favorable "spin" on Wilson activities. Bos admirers believe he might have kept his boss out of some trouble, for example, by diffusing expectations of a Wilson signature on the gay-rights bill.

"Otto had that facility. He's one of only two people who can walk in and say, 'Governor, you're all f----- up.' [Chief of Staff] Bob White is the other, but he works primarily on internal matters. The governor desperately needs people who will tell him the truth, who have the ability to talk sense to him," offered one Republican observer.

Wilson Press Secretary Bill Livingstone admits that his office has been swamped by the crises siege of the past year, and he laments that there has been no time to look ahead. But he believes that, even had Bos been there, things would not have been much different.

Wilson agrees, saying in recent interviews that his decisions would have been the same, even had Bos been on hand to give advice.

In part, the pessimism about Wilson may be the result of higher expectations about the new administration. Wilson himself set an ambitious agenda for his governorship. But despite 16-hour days that have left the governor with a haggard look, Wilson has been unable to do all he wanted and to manage the crises at the same time.

Certainly the press, and probably the public, has become disenchanted with Wilson. After the lethargic Deukmejian years, expectations for Wilson were high, higher perhaps than any governor could meet, and the new administration in its early days did nothing to defuse these.

Now, there is a lot of talk among administration officials about how tough things have been because of the state's unending crises. Thus, these officials say, Wilson has done better than should have been expected.

Even if public perceptions are otherwise, predictions about Wilson's political demise are not universal and are probably premature. Observers note that Ronald Reagan managed to survive a first-year tax increase with his hard-line reputation intact.

If Wilson can somehow manage to cajole the Legislature into making more cuts and avoid further tax increases; if the economy improves and the state's financial coffers again fill; and perhaps if Mother Nature gives him — and the citizenry — a break, the governor still could end up in good shape when re-election time comes up in 1994.

In his state-of-the-state address last January, Wilson outlined "a new vision of government, a vision based on the old adage that an ounce of prevention is worth a pound of cure." But things have been so tough in California that the state has been hard put to purchase much of the medicine Wilson is advocating.

The country's recession is not of Wilson's making, but at least for the time being, he is one of its casualties.

Still, the governor maintains "my optimism continues."

"California is wonderfully positioned, both geographically and in terms of its being the most multicultural society in the world. We look both west across the Pacific and south to Mexico and Latin America for what I think are going to be very exciting economic times."

Wilson, lawmakers unleash

MONSTER

state budget

By Steven A. Capps

Reprinted from *California Journal*, September 1991

The process wasn't pretty and the end result far from perfect, but Governor Pete Wilson and the Legislature at least deserve credit for tackling the largest state budget deficit in the nation's history — and producing a new state budget only 16 days late.

When it was all over and the new budget signed into law 15 minutes before midnight on July 16th, state government emerged bruised and battered but still standing, operating under a patchwork $55.7 billion budget peppered with historic achievements or monumental blunders, depending on one's point of view.

The new budget included:

• the largest tax increase in state history, totaling more than $7 billion in income and sales tax hikes, increases in vehicle registration fees, the highest student fees ever and a hike in the liquor tax;

• elimination of a 56-year-old exemption from the sales tax for candy and snack foods, as well as for newspapers and magazines;

• a first-ever cut in monthly welfare grants for recipients of Aid to Families with Dependent Children, the state's largest welfare program;

• adoption of a "realignment" system to set counties on the road to financial independence from the state in running health and welfare programs;

• pay cuts, mandatory unpaid furloughs and, in some cases, layoffs of state workers — sticky issues yet to be

---

Steven A. Capps is a Capitol reporter for the San Francisco Examiner.

1991-92 Revenue Changes
($ In Millions)

Source: California State Budget
1991—1992

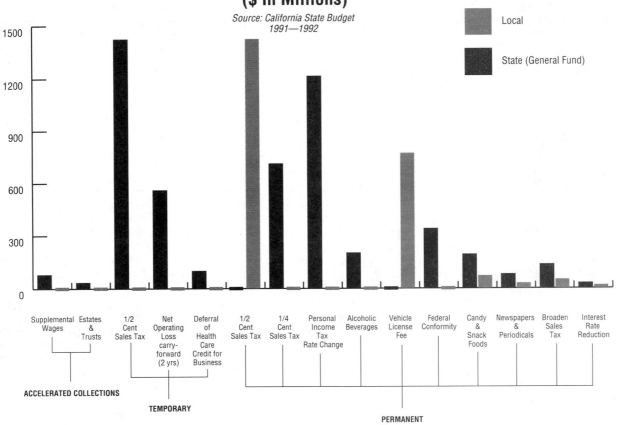

worked out at the collective bargaining table;

• a restructuring of the Public Employees Retirement System for state and local government workers, cutting surplus benefits and allowing the governor to appoint an outside actuary to monitor the performance of the system's governing board.

Adoption of the budget was not only of paramount interest to counties, cities, school districts and the tens of thousands of state employees that depend on the state for money, but also to Wall Street where the state markets its bonds. California's budget woes threatened its coveted triple-A bond rating by Wall Street firms, a rating that allows California to save millions in interest when selling its bonds. The bond-rating houses, after studying California's new budget, reaffirmed its triple-A credit rating, although the largest — Standard and Poor's — warned that it would be watching California's budget performance very closely in the coming years and might quickly downgrade the state if the budget were to fall out of balance again.

Many legislators, including those who helped fashion the new spending

plan, cautioned that it was precarious, based on economic growth not yet materializing. Even with a strong economic recovery late in the fiscal year, they warned, many of the budget's key components were merely quick fixes and California would be back in the fiscal soup in later years.

Senate Republican leader Ken Maddy of Fresno said expenditures would begin to outpace revenues within three years. And two key elements of the budget — the income tax hike and a freeze on automatic increases in welfare payments — both expire after five years.

Wilson, who carefully had avoided a "no-new-taxes" approach during his 1990 gubernatorial campaign, found himself facing a projected budget deficit immediately upon his election. Outgoing Governor George Deukmejian made a half-hearted attempt to ease the problem by calling the Legislature into special session shortly before leaving office, but Democrats would have none of it. Holding majorities in both houses of the Legislature, Democrats decided to wait and take their chances with the new Republican governor, decidedly more moderate than the two-term

Deukmejian.

When Wilson took office, his Department of Finance — headed by Tom Hayes, a popular but politically inexperienced former auditor general who had been appointed state treasurer by Deukmejian but then ran unsuccessfully for the job on the GOP ticket with Wilson — was estimating a projected deficit at a whopping $7.5 billion.

The budget gap stemmed from a combination of factors, including an economic recession that led to sagging tax revenues, plus increased caseloads for schools and social programs and built-in cost-of-living increases in state programs.

The $7.5 billion estimate was more than twice the gap faced by the state the year before, when adoption of the budget was a record month late as legislative Democrats battled with Deukmejian and conservative Republicans who were able to hold up the budget because of the two-thirds vote required for its passage.

In subsequent months, Wilson's estimate of a $7.5 billion gap proved overly optimistic.

Wilson unveiled his initial budget proposal in January 1991, and it included about $1.7 billion in new taxes and fees, including an increase in the tax on alcoholic beverages and application of the sales tax to candy, snack foods, newspapers and magazines. He called for a reduction in the renters' income tax credit, a 3 percent cut in monthly welfare benefits and permanent suspension of automatic cost-of-living increases in health and welfare programs.

And, in one of his more controversial moves, the governor asked for legislative approval for suspension of Proposition 98 — the voter-approved initiative guaranteeing schools at least 40 percent of all state revenue.

While his initial budget did not include a call for a statewide sales tax hike — that would come later as the economy worsened — he did propose a measure allowing counties and cities to raise their local sales taxes by a half-cent for anti-drug and anti-crime programs.

Members of his own party bemoaned these revenue boosts, saying more programs should be cut instead. But Wilson balked at further cutting, saying they would result in draconian elimination of needed state services.

The ink was barely dry on Wilson's January budget proposal when new estimates began to show the budget gap far worse than anyone had imagined. By the end of January, Legislative Analyst Elizabeth Hill was predicting the budget deficit at nearly $10 billion. In April, legislators returned from Easter recess to find that Wilson's own advisers were reporting a potential deficit of $12.6 billion.

To meet the growing shortfall, the governor came up with a new budget plan that disappointed many Republicans but delighted Democrats. While proposing new cuts loathsome to Democrats, he also acknowledged that half of the budget gap would have to be erased through tax increases. He proposed a one-and-one-quarter-cent increase in the statewide sales tax, and other tax increases for a total of about $6 billion in new revenue that caught Democrats by surprise. He also called for an 8.8 percent cut in welfare grants, an idea liberal Democrats vowed would never become law.

Somewhat arrogantly, the governor called his new budget package not a proposal but a "solution." His call for quick adoption would not be heeded.

Nor was the floodtide of bad news at an end. A few weeks later, as the economy continued its downward plunge, Department of Finance analysts began warning that the budget gap would be "larger than $13 billion." On May 20th, the department revised its official estimate of the deficit to $14.3 billion — the number that would be used through the remainder of the budget negotiations.

It was a staggering projection: California's deficit was larger than the entire general fund budgets of all but two states in the nation. The deficit was about 25 percent of the entire budget.

Wilson and legislative leaders plunged into closed-door negotiating sessions in his office. The first concrete agreement to emerge amounted to capitulation on the part of the governor: He agreed to drop his demand for suspension of Proposition 98, and the Legislature quickly passed a school finance bill that closed the books on nearly half of the budget.

The remaining issues, however, proved more difficult to resolve. Wilson and three of the Legislature's leaders — Assembly Speaker Willie Brown of San Francisco, Senate President pro Tem David Roberti of Los Angeles, and Senate GOP leader Maddy — saw eye-to-eye on a lot of matters. But the governor was having trouble with the Assembly Republican caucus.

Assembly GOP leader Ross Johnson of Fullerton said he could not speak for his divided caucus during the budget negotiations. Many of his conservative members were upset at the tax increases proposed by the new governor. Johnson merely acted as a go-between, carrying messages back to his colleagues, but could not guarantee votes.

A budget package was finally put together in late June, but among its elements was a 6 percent tax on cable television and telephone service sought by Wilson. The four leaders seemed in agreement, but then Democrats in the Assembly blocked the utility tax proposal and the package fell apart.

Rejection of the utilities bill set the stage for weeks of haggling over the final $2 billion needed to balance the budget. Various forms of a utility tax were discussed, but none seemed destined for approval.

Then the business community, led by the California Chamber of Commerce and the California Manufacturers Association, pulled the rug out from under Wilson. After figuring out that the utility tax would hit business hardest, the associations advised Wilson they would rather see some form of an income tax hike instead.

During his campaign and throughout the first months of his administration, Wilson had stood firm against an increase in the income tax, arguing that it would drive business out of Califor-

Where the General Fund comes from
1991-92 Fiscal Year

Where the General Fund goes
1991-92 Fiscal Year

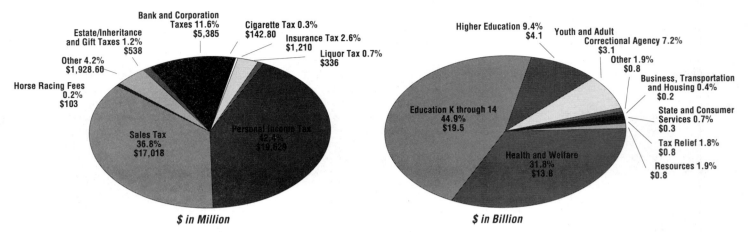

$ in Million

$ in Billion

Source: California State Budget 1991-92

nia. But business had spoken, and he listened.

The governor sent out word to the Legislature that he would agree to an income tax hike for the richest Californians, an idea being pushed by Democrats, but with a big catch: They would have to agree to legislation restricting claims under the state's workers' compensation program. At issue were claims filed for mental stress. Current law required employers to pay stress claims if the employee proves that at least 10 percent of the stress injury is caused by on-the-job condition.

Wilson and business wanted the standard raised to 50 percent but faced considerable opposition among Democrats and others with a vested interest in the workers' compensation system — trial lawyers, insurance companies, labor, manufacturers, ad infinitum. In choosing to fight over such a politically complex issue, Wilson bit off more than he could chew. Democrats finessed the issue by insisting that insurance company profits also be cut, thus converting those companies from supporters to opponents. In the end, Wilson got little more than a face-saving measure that left the 10 percent standard in place but prohibited workers from filing stress claims within the first six months of employment.

The governor also was forced to back off another controversial proposal — to reshape the 13-member Public Employees Retirement System board. Wilson wanted to replace it with a seven-member board, the majority of which he would appoint.

In the end, the board was left intact but the governor won approval for a change in PERS supplemental retirement benefits. Wilson also backed off his call for an 8.8 percent welfare cut, but did get a 4.4. percent cut — the first such cut in state history.

With the final issues resolved, only one task remained for Wilson. He still had to convince some members of his own party in the Assembly to vote for the budget. Without the support of the Assembly Republican leadership, Wilson had to peel off the votes one-by-one on each of the budget elements.

During the budget fight, Wilson at one time or another was able to pressure 16 different Assembly Republicans into voting for various elements of the budget, including the tax increases. Absent from these ranks was Minority Leader Johnson.

The number who finally voted for one piece of the budget or another was significant as it represented an exact majority of the 31-member caucus. And soon after the budget passed, 16 members of the Assembly Republican caucus voted to oust Johnson in favor of a new minority leader, Bill Jones of Fresno.

Jones made it clear on his first day as minority leader that he believed part of his job would be to help — not hinder — Republican Wilson as he went about pursuing his future policies in the Legislature.

"Part of the responsibility of the minority leader is to act as a floor leader for the governor and the positions of the administration," Jones said.

But Wilson still has his problems.

The most conservative members of the Assembly GOP caucus were openly critical of Wilson's budget solution. The most outspoken was Thousand Oaks Assemblyman Tom McClintock.

"God help us if he's ever across the table from the Russians in negotiations," McClintock said.

Wilson's assault on PERS and his call for pay cuts, mandatory furloughs and layoffs of state workers also created bitter enemies in the state workers' unions. Most of the $800 million in savings Wilson wanted in employee compensation was to be addressed in collective bargaining sessions, and those sessions were volatile. State workers unions refused to go along, and in some cases threatened strikes.

"We feel that the governor is trying to reshape government in his image to pave his way to the presidency," said Pat McConahay, spokeswoman for the largest state employee union, the California State Employees Association. "He isn't interested in cuts. He's interested in breaking the union."

Still, completion of such a difficult budget 16 days into the fiscal year was more than many in state government had hoped for. More pessimistic members of the Legislature had predicted no agreement until well into August.

"We have made the tough decisions now, thereby saving ourselves from a world of pain later on," Wilson said after signing the budget.

Only time will tell whether the first-term, moderate Republican governor really avoided that "world of pain" — or merely postponed it for a few years. 🏛

The economy: Gateway to the Pacific

Reprinted from *California Journal*, January 1990

By Tony Quinn

California: Wholly-owned subsidiary of Japan.
California: America's Third-World state

A description of California's future? Some people think so. The most salient difference between California in 1990 and the California of 1970 is a sense that we are losing our destiny, that we are being overrun by foreign money and foreign nationals.

It's a legitimate concern, but it's also the narrow focus of a much larger story. California's future is being shaped by personal decisions made hundreds of times a day somewhere across the globe.

A Soviet Jew, exit visa in hand, boards the plane in Moscow destined for Tel Aviv. In Frankfurt, putting aside pangs of conscience, he changes his ticket — for a flight to San Francisco.

The best and brightest of a Guatemalan village can take it no more. He starts his trek north, and doesn't stop until San Diego.

The Japanese banker, high in his tower above the glittering lights of Tokyo, spins a globe looking for the best place to invest his millions. His finger stops on Los Angeles.

In 1849 and a century later following World War II, the world rushed to California. Once again the world is rushing in, and California finds itself at the center of one of the greatest migrations of money and people in history. In 1986 and 1987 our population grew by 1.3 million people — the largest two-year gain in our history.

Half of these people, if demographers are to be believed, are immigrants from other nations, their emigration driven by events like the collapse of Latin American economies and uncertain political situations at home.

It isn't over. The Tienanmen massacre, El Salvador's civil war, worries about Hong Kong will all be reflected in California's population gains in the 1990s.

Why do they come here? Consider these facts: Since the end of the 1982 recession we have created 2.3 million new jobs, more than all of western Europe. Our gross state product has grown by 40 percent to more than $600 billion. That growth alone is equivalent to the entire economy of Australia or Spain.

The very dynamic of this state draws people. California is now a major manufacturing state. That wasn't true 20 years ago, even though we had more blue collar industries then. But American manufacturing is no longer driven by tradition-

The author is director of public affairs for Braun and Company, a business public relations company. He has written extensively on California demographics and politics.

al heavy industries, most of which cannot compete internationally.

California's growth industries in this decade, and for the foreseeable future, are those that compete in global markets. In recent years, the fastest manufacturing growth has come in high-technology industries such as electronics, California's bread-and-butter industry.

In the 1990s and into the next century, the information-age industries will be the fastest producers of economic wealth. Superconductors, lasers, gene manipulation, fiber optics and technologies with names we don't even know will continue to butter California's bread.

It is not so much a matter of absorbing new technologies. "We are trying to absorb multiple technologies at once," says Paul Saffo of Menlo Park's Institute for the Future.

California's strength has been a networking of these multiple technologies. We account for a third of the nation's high-technology companies. Our 5500 electronics and computer firms produced $63.5 billion in goods and services last year.

Electronic goods accounted for $3.6 billion of California's $27 billion export market, according to a study by the California Department of Commerce. Electrical components find a market overseas not open to other American products.

Because we succeed where much of the rest of America fails, we are less fearful of international commerce than other states. Protectionism is not welcome here; we pride ourselves in being more cosmopolitan. This includes our attitude toward Asian investment, particularly Japanese.

Accommodation of diverse cultures is a requirement for future economic success. The Asian presence here goes back decades, as does California's presence in Asia.

And, remarkably, it is just beginning. The twin phenomena of foreign investment and foreign immigration will do more to shape California's economy over the next two decades than anything else.

For one thing, they will help make Los Angeles America's most important city. It is already the nation's most culturally diverse. In the next decade Los Angeles County will lead the country in job growth, adding some 800,000 new jobs, many filled by new arrivals.

Guess which county will be number two? Orange County, with 620,000 new jobs. San Diego and Santa Clara Counties will be numbers six and seven. On the other hand, Cook County, Illinois, and Suffolk and Nassau Counties, New York, will be numbers 10, 16 and 30.

Around the turn of the century, Los Angeles County's population will exceed the five boroughs of New York. In the first decade of the 21st Century, assets of California financial institutions will exceed those of New York's banks.

But in this decade, that has changed. We now do more trade across the Pacific than the Atlantic. Japan is the new economic giant of the world, hotly pursued by the various Tigers of the Pacific: South Korea, Taiwan, Hong Kong, Singapore.

For the newly wealthy of the world, the sun rises in the west; America's day begins along its Pacific shore. And California is the beachhead from which, like it or not, Asians and Europeans are stamping an international character on the American economy.

Nothing will be more striking in the next 20 years than the impact of international commerce. Like almost everything else, the future happens here first, and the international stamp is already very visible here in California.

One of our two remaining automobile plants is a joint venture involving General Motors and Toyota. Both of our two remaining steel operations involve foreign companies. The state's only cotton mill is Japanese-owned.

Nevertheless, the role of foreign investment, and foreign immigration, will be dominant political and economic issues in California in the 1990s and beyond. Although foreign money accounts for less than 10 percent of investments in this state, it shows up in dramatic and sometimes painful ways. One might have thought our cultural birthright was up for grabs when Sony bought Columbia Pictures.

Yet the reality of the 1990s is that American industry cannot survive unless it can compete globally, and California, as the most international of America's continental states, cannot help but be a major player.

As long as America remains a debtor nation, we will draw foreign capital here, and more of it will land in California than anywhere else. But foreign capital, like domestic capital, does not operate in a vacuum. Most Japanese automobile companies placed their design centers in California because, in their view, California sets the style for the rest of the nation.

California is better integrated into the international economy, and thus should play the major role in reshaping a global market economy.

However, demographic trends may exert counter pressures. In 2010, according to the California Economic Development Corporation's "Vision 2010" study, California will have a population of almost 40 million, and almost all this growth will be found among non-anglo whites.

Over the short run California may actually experience a labor shortage, or at least a shortage of adequately trained workers, as larger and larger shares of the population reach retirement years throughout the 1990s. This will probably help us weather the coming defense industry downturn, but it could also cost us some basic industries that won't be around when we need them.

In the first decade of the 21st Century, today's immigrant population, with its younger families, may well flood the labor market. Our immigrant population comes in two distinct forms: low skilled workers, mostly from Latin America; and highly educated immigrants, mostly from Asia.

Nearly 44 percent of adult Asian immigrants hold college degrees, compared with just 16 percent of the general adult population, according to Joel Kotkin, in his new book, *The Third Century*.

Does this suggest a two-tiered economy in the next century, with highly educated whites and Asians dominating information-age industries while everyone else works in "third world" style manufacturing? Some people see the outlines of this today in the growth of apparel, hotel and restaurant jobs filled by immigrant laborers, especially in Southern California.

Yet other evidence suggests that Hispanic immigrants are moving into the middle class in the second and third generation no differently than earlier European immigrants did. Others note that capital flowing into older urban areas through Asian immigration is reinvigorating inner city neighborhoods.

"Vision 2010" holds that we must build "an economically competitive state in an increasingly international economy, one that remains on the cutting edge of new technology and innovation, and one that successfully assimilates immigrants into the mainstream of society."

We will have the opportunity to achieve all this in the context of a multicultural, multiracial society located at the heart of a Pacific-oriented global economy. It should be fun.

L ike a lot of commercials these days, it is hard to figure out what the latest Lottery television ad is selling. Filmed in black and white with splashes of sporadic color, it features pages of a novel flipping in the wind, a woman laughing on a seesaw, an archer taking aim, a man approaching a house with flowers hidden behind his back and a cherry red ladybug crawling on a pair of gray hands. A cross between a Calvin Klein commercial and an MTV video, the ad could be selling anything from jeans to toothpaste, beer to candy bars. But a wispy male voice gives it away at the end: "Play Lotto and imagine."

A tasteful and subtle ad.

But the California Lottery needed more than subtle ads to revive its sagging fortunes. It needed a jolt. And a jolt is just what it received on November 14th when Lottery Director Sharon Sharp presented the Lottery Commission with a program for infusing new life in to the games. Of the current games, only

Michelle Quinn is a writer with the California News Service, a project of the U.C. Berkeley graduate school of Journalism.

THE LOTTERY LEMON

Have Californians soured on their games of chance?

By Michelle Quinn

Reprinted from *California Journal*, December 1991

"Scratchers" will remain; "Lotto" and "Little Lotto" will end in mid December, and "Disco" will end in April 1992. In their place will come "Super Lotto," where players who correctly choose six of 51 numbers can win multi-million jackpots; "Keno," where players can win million-dollar jackpots by correctly choosing combinations of numbers; and something called "Fantasy 5," where players pick five of 39 numbers and win jackpots that average up to $200,000. The goal of this revamp is to craft the games to appeal to all kinds of lottery players - from those who seek the big jackpot to those who like the small but instant prize.

Why the huge change? Because the California Lottery is in deep trouble.

In the Lottery world, where directors say without irony that they are in the business of selling dreams, sales have dropped below what anyone could have fantasized. Everything from the Persian Gulf War and the recession to changes in the Lotto game and governmental barriers unique to California have been blamed for the Lottery's plummeting sales. Public schools are bracing for a record low contribution to education during a time when money is already tight. And along with the sales, Californians' opinion of the Lottery has taken a nose dive.

In the fiscal year that ended June 30th, revenues were down 14 percent from $2.479 billion to $2.133 billion. Compare that to lotteries nationally, where the $20 billion dollar lottery industry increased sales 2.7 percent, according to Bill Bergman of the North American Association of State and Provincial Lotteries. But in contrast to an 8 percent growth rate in fiscal 1990 and 20 percent in fiscal 1989, the lottery business nationally is clearly feeling the recession, said Terri Fleur, senior editor of *Gaming and Wagering Business* magazine.

Still California's drop in sales has surprised everyone, La Fleur said. So far this year, sales are only at 74 percent of where they should be, according to the Lottery's own admittedly conservative goals. That is especially bad news for education, which was supposed to be the Lottery's *raison d'etre*. Under the initiative voters approved in 1984, education receives 34 cents of every dollar taken in by the Lottery.

If purchases of Lottery tickets continue to slump, sales could drop to $1.47 billion. That translates to $500 million for

education or $78 per student — a $300 million drop from last year's contribution of $804 million for education, or $129 per student. Taking into account that state education didn't receive a statutory 4.6 percent inflation adjustment this year — a whopping $1 billion dollars — the Lottery nose dive takes on a greater magnitude.

Enter Sharon Sharp, the Lottery's new executive director, and her plan to increase the number of prizes and retool the games to attract more players.

The problem with the Lottery is that, except for the ticket and machine vendors, everyone who is supposed to be happier because of its existence, isn't. There is so much dissatisfaction that Sharp eventually may have to figure out what she can change and what is beyond her control. Education leaders, prepared to get less, say the Lottery's existence works against their efforts to raise needed money. Retailers are upset with their declining sales, the awkwardness of the machinery and their commission on tickets sold. Democratic Assemblyman Richard Floyd of Carson, the Legislature's only outspoken Lottery fan, criticizes the bevy of complicated games, the expensive marketing and the bureaucracy, which he calls the "Lottery's empire."

A bove all this, the "playing public" has shown with its pocketbook that the games have lost their appeal. And the public in general has shown its discontent. In a recent California Poll, 49 percent of California's adults say they have a good opinion of the Lottery, a plunge from 1985 when 75 percent said they liked what was then a new Lottery.

Whether Sharp will be successful in boosting Lottery sales has yet to be seen. She is not just battling sales records and bleak quarterly reports but the Lottery's history in California, which is at the heart of the problems.

The story of the California Lottery's development is about the marriage of convenience between business interests and citizens' education concerns. The Lottery initiative was born out of the education crisis of the early 1980s caused partially by Proposition 13 reductions in property tax. It was oversold as a simple and effective financial solution to school funding, according to both Lottery officials and Lottery critics. In the ballot argument, the Lottery was supposed to provide $680 million to education annually, a goal which it has hit every year except the second year.

Business interests, which failed in a previous lottery campaign in 1964, pushed through the 1984 initiative. At least one business did. The 1984 Lottery initiative, Proposition 37, was virtually bankrolled by Scientific Games. A subsidiary of Bally Casino and makers of lottery tickets, Scientific Games made $2.1 million dollars 0n California lottery tickets last year, and G-Tech, a Providence, Rhode Island-based international lottery empire, made up to $23 million last year off of the machinery involved in the California Lottery.

But as the ugly step-child of state politics, the Lottery was never fully embraced by California's elected officials. The Legislature and the controller's office retain a large degree of control over the nature of games and winnings that can be earned.

Despite governmental barriers, the Lottery has to make the games and, more important, make them fun. "Scratchers" games, which provide instant prizes, are regenerated every six to eight weeks. A player scratches off the latex to find out if he or she has won money or the grand prize to play the Big Spin on television, which could give you from $25,000 to $2 million. "Decco" is a daily draw game based on playing cards. Pick one from each suit and match cards drawn by the Lottery to win from $5 to $5000. "Decco" is being phased out next year.

But the big game, the game everyone cares about, is "Lotto." Players pick six numbers, and if the numbers they pick are also picked by the Lottery, they win the jackpot. The big jackpot. If no player picks the correct six numbers, the jackpot expands for the next Lotto game. And since Lotto is played twice a week (Wednesdays and Saturdays), the jackpot can grow enormous. Last April, for instance, it reached $119 million before 10 different people picked the correct numbers.

But to get big jackpots like this one, the Lottery, in a controversial move in June 1990, changed the game and nearly doubled the odds to win. Instead of picking six numbers out of 49, a player had to pick six numbers out of 53. Thus, a player had a one-in-23 million chance to win, as opposed to the previous odds of one-in-14 million. Not only did the change make players less likely to win, but it made them frustrated with Lotto, said Floyd.

"These idiots increased the lottery almost double. You can play the thing but you can't get your lousy five dollars. People say to hell with this game," Floyd said. A bad feeling about Lotto trickles down to other games, he said. Lottery officials dismissed the notion that the changes in Lotto are the reason for decreasing sales. The new version, unveiled as "Super Lotto" and due to start on December 15th, is a compromise, with players picking six of 51 numbers. Odds for a jackpot are one-in-18 million.

One way to understand the Lottery is to look at where a dollar spent on a ticket goes. By law, 50 cents goes back to players in the form of prize money, 34 cents goes to education and no more than 16 cents may go to running the Lottery and paying retailers. For fiscal 1990, that 16 cents translated to $330 million. Of that 16 cents, about 6 cents ($131 million) went to retailers' commissions, 2 cents ($42 million) to ticket and machine manufacturers, 2.5 cents ($57 million) for advertising costs and 3 cents ($68 million) for administrative support.

Hoping to regenerate interest in the Lottery, Sharp wants to increase the 50 cents given back to players for Scratchers only, an idea former director Chon Gutierrez had been working on when he left. Compared with the other 33 states that have lotteries, California is among states with the lowest amount paid back to players for Scratchers. "Every other state has done this, and sales have increased 36 percent," McNabb said.

How does Sharp propose to give players more money? Although her November proposal did not call for it, she eventually aims to cut into the 34 cents going to education, as well as cutting one-fifth of the Lottery's operating cost by cutting advertising, performing staff layoffs and, as a last resort, slashing retailer commissions. Sharp wants to see $25 million phased out to make sure the Lottery stays within the 16 percent spending gap.

The cut puts educators in a peculiar position. On the one hand, they are furious at the prospect that their percentage of the big pie may be cut.

"Tell the Lottery to cut it out of their percentage," said Susie Lang, spokesperson for Superintendent of Schools Bill Honig. On the other hand, school officials have never been comfortable about having their programs used to entice what they see as gambling. Leaders such as Honig and Maureen DiMarco, Governor Pete Wilson's education ad-

viser, say that the Lottery creates a misconception that schools are rich, making it harder to generate public support for more money for education. "We will never overcome our need for money as long as the Lottery is around," Lang said.

While overall spending on education has gone up 13 percent since 1983, according to DiMarco's office, schools still find themselves hurting for money. "They started the decade under-funded and have not caught up yet," according to Jim Wilson, director of fiscal policy at the Department of Education. Money from the Lottery, which makes up 3 percent of education costs, was supposed to be just the frosting on the cake, for extras such as computers and after-school programs. However, educators say Lottery money has been used for teachers' salaries, making the schools even more vulnerable to the rise and fall of Lottery sales.

"Like a drug habit, the school districts are hooked on it," said Democratic Senator Ralph Dills of Gardena about the Lottery. A former school teacher, Dills is the chairman of the Senate Committee of Governmental Organization, which oversees all bills meant to change the Lottery. "To assume that the Lottery is going to help the schools is to fool the public and make them mad at the school," he said.

"It takes the proceeds of 1450 Lottery tickets to buy one microscope for a high school chemistry class," said Honig.

Retailers also are unhappy with the Lottery. Cissy Shinn, manager of Oakland's Merritt Restaurant and Bakery, said she has the Lottery in her store "as a convenience to customers." She hasn't seen any difference in her sales, even on big jackpot days, she said. Ray Chow, part owner of Ping Yuen Drug Store in San Francisco, said he's happy with the Lottery, but he attributed his success to his store's high volume on the extra promotions and prizes he gives out on top of the Lottery's prizes.

"We went into the Lottery as a competitive factor," said Don Beaver, president of the California Grocers' Association. But Beaver says it's hardly been worth it, considering how the arithmetic works out.

According to Beaver's calculation, the Scratcher games cost a store owner 9 to 12 cents for every dollar spent, but the store only gets back 7 cents. With the Lotto games, played on employee-activated terminals, a store gets 6 cents on every dollar spent, though it cost them 8

to 9 cents, Beaver said. Games played on consumer-activated terminals cost 7 cents, he said. To add insult to injury, Beaver said, crowds drawn to stores for a big Lotto jackpot end up hurting business. "It plugs up the lines and parking lots, and regular customers can't get in."

Lottery officials say that they are working closely with retailers to reduce the handling of the tickets. "These are tough times," said McNabb. "Nobody is going to get more money."

If Sharp plans to correct any of the problems that are keeping down the Lottery, she'll need help from the governor and from friends in the Legislature. In addition to limiting prizes to 50 percent of sales, Lottery laws also prohibit Scratcher games with themes such as sports, slot machines, blackjack or bingo. Sharp wants to change all this to make the games more enticing. Furthermore, she wants to increase the maximum amount of money that can be paid to a winning player in a retail store. As prescribed by the controller, payments of prize money over $25 for Scratcher games and $100 for on-line games take six to eight weeks.

Sharp will have to move quickly. "Each week sales go like this, it makes it increasingly difficult to make up," Sharp said.

But moving with any speed will be difficult. She has the Lottery Commission and the Legislature to contend with before making any drastic changes. She'll meet up with governmental barriers, said Gutierrez, the outgoing director. "In her state [Illinois], she didn't have these handcuffs. She didn't have those hurdles," Gutierrez said, adding that it may take an outsider to do what he couldn't do. "She will force a discussion on those points because for her they are unnatural."

For some, there's nothing left to discuss. The Lottery has proven itself to be a mistake, they say. "The best thing you can do with the Lottery is get rid of it," said Dills. "It's a poor man's sales tax. It's a fallacy. It's a fraud. The Lottery has done nothing for education [other] than create the idea that we don't have to do anything for schools." 🏛

THE JUSTICE SYSTEM

California has often been praised for the excellence of its state and local government — relatively free of scandal, with high-quality civil servants, nationally respected governors (Hiram Johnson and Earl Warren among them) and a Legislature that at least once ranked first in a national survey (although the caliber of the legislators and the quality of legislation were not considered in the ratings). But perhaps the state's greatest gift to the nation was the leadership of its Supreme Court. Under a series of forceful chief justices — among them Phil Gibson, Roger Traynor and Donald Wright — the state's highest tribunal had often shown the way for the United States Supreme Court. The California Supreme Court built a reputation for activism and independence with decisions that struck down the death penalty (People v. Anderson, 1972), outlawed the state's system of financing public education (Serrano v. Priest, 1971) and invalidated an anti-fair housing initiative approved by the electorate (Mulkey v. Reitman, 1966).

The judiciary may be the most powerful of the three branches of state government because the Constitution is so detailed and because the Supreme Court has the power — which it had not been hesitant to use — to strike down acts of the Legislature or initiatives that conflict with the state and federal constitutions. The court also uses its power to void acts of the executive branch that violate either a statute or the constitution.

An activist Supreme Court has often been viewed as a second Legislature — more powerful than the first. Governor Ronald Reagan sought to reduce the activism of the court through his appointments, but one of the big disappointments of his eight years as governor was that his appointee for chief justice, Donald Wright, turned out to be another activist rather than the conservative Reagan had thought him to be.

In 1977, Democratic Governor Edmund G. Brown Jr. had an opportunity to recast the court and by 1981 his appointees comprised a majority on the court. He appointed the court's first woman, Chief Justice Rose Elizabeth Bird; first black, the late Wiley W. Manuel; and first Latino, Cruz Reynoso. Bird was a highly controversial figure when she was appointed and throughout her tenure on the court. While there were many criticisms of the Bird court by conservatives, the most critical was the court's failure to allow any executions during her tenure as Chief Justice. (Polls indicate that over 80 percent of California citizens favor the death penalty.)

In November 1986, in an unprecedented election, three of the Brown-appointed liberals, Justices Bird, Reynoso and Joseph Grodin lost their confirmation elections. This enabled Governor George Deukmejian to appoint three more conservatives to the high court (Justices John A. Arguelles, Marcus Kaufman and David N. Eagleson). These three combined with two previous appointments — Chief Justice Malcolm Lucas and Justice Edward A. Panelli — gave the Deukmejian court a conservative majority. In April 1989 Joyce L. Kennard was appointed to replace Arguelles. In 1990, Armand Arabian was appointed to replace Kaufman and in 1991 Marvin Baxter replaced Justice Eagleson.

Ronald George was appointed by Governor Wilson in 1991 to replace Allen Broussard, the only remaining Jerry Brown appointee, who retired. The seventh and most senior justice is liberal Stanley Mosk, appointed by Pat Brown in 1964.

Lower and appellate courts

The Supreme Court sits at the apex of the California judicial system. There are three lower levels — the justice and municipal courts, the superior courts, and the district courts of appeal.

Members of the Supreme Court and the district courts of appeal are appointed by the governor subject to confirmation by the Commission on Judicial Appointments (consisting of the chief justice, the attorney general and one appeals-court justice). In recent years, the commission has called for public hearings on controversial appointees. Bird was approved by a 2-1 vote following a heated public debate. Incumbent judges' names appear on the ballot at the first general election following their appointment and again at the end of each 12-year term. If the incumbent receives a majority of "yes" votes for retention, he or she has another 12-year term.

- *Municipal and justice courts.* These local courts hear misdemeanor cases, preliminary hearings on some felony charges, small-claims actions and civil cases involving relatively small amounts of money (less than $25,000 in both municipal and justice courts).

- *Superior courts.* These countywide courts hear juvenile criminal cases, felonies, appeals from justice and municipal court decisions, and civil cases that cannot be tried in the municipal courts.

- *Courts of appeal.* These are divided into six districts (based in San Francisco, Los Angeles, Sacramento, San Diego, Fresno, and San Jose). Each division within each court contains three or four justices, with three justices normally sitting on each appeal. The court has jurisdiction over appeals from superior-court actions and decisions of quasi-judicial state boards.

- *The Supreme Court.* The state's highest court handles appeals from the district courts of appeal, although some cases can be taken directly from the trial court to the Supreme Court. In death-penalty cases, for example, appeals automatically go from the superior court to the Supreme Court. The high court also reviews orders of the Public Utilities Commission and has some appointive powers.

Judges of the municipal, justice and superior courts are elected by the people for six-year terms. Vacancies in justice court positions are filled by the county supervisors; the governor fills vacancies in the municipal and superior courts. On occasion, there is a wide-open race for a judgeship, but usually the post is filled by appointment and the incumbent retains the judgeship at the ensuing election.

A judge may be removed or otherwise disciplined by the Supreme Court — but only upon recommendation of the Commission on Judicial Performance, which is composed of five judges, two attorneys and two lay people. Judges are also subject to impeachment and recall, but the more common disciplinary procedure is through an investigation by the commission and action by the high court.

The state Judicial Council is a 21-member board charged with the overall administration of the court system. It is headed by the chief justice, who in turn appoints most of the members. The Administrative Office of the California Courts is the staff agency charged with carrying out the council's policies and conducting research for the council.

California uses the standard jury system. Grand juries (19 citizens in most counties, 23 in Los Angeles) investigate public agencies and have the power to hand down criminal indictments. However, the state Supreme Court ruled in 1978 that preliminary (probable-cause) hearings must be held, whether or not a suspect is indicted. Trial juries usually consist of 12 registered voters, but both sides in a case can agree to a smaller panel or waive a jury and submit the case to a judge. A unanimous vote is needed for acquittal or conviction in a criminal case. 🏛

California's Court System

JUDICIAL COUNCIL

Makes rules on judicial procedure; surveys and expedites judicial business.

COMM. ON JUDICIAL PERFORMANCE

Recommends to Supreme Court censure, removal or retirement of judges.

COMM. ON JUDICIAL APPOINTMENTS

Confirms or rejects appointees of Governor to Supreme Court and Courts of Appeal.

U.S. SUPREME COURT

CALIFORNIA SUPREME COURT

Original jurisdiction: writs of mandamus, prohibition, habeas corpus, certiorari.

Appellate jurisdiction: discretionary power to review and decide cases transferred from courts of appeal; appeals from superior court involving death penalty.

DISTRICT COURTS OF APPEAL

1ST DISTRICT	2ND DISTRICT	3RD DISTRICT	4TH DISTRICT	5TH DISTRICT	6TH DISTRICT
San Francisco	Los Angeles	Sacramento	San Bernardino San Diego	Fresno	San Jose

Appellate jurisdiction: appeals from superior courts. Original jurisdiction: habeas corpus, mandamus, certiorari, prohibition.

SUPERIOR COURTS
(one in each county)

Original jurisdiction: Civil-amount in controversy exceeds $15,000, mandamus, habeas corpus, equitable relief, probate, family law and juvenile court matters. Criminal-felonies.

Appellate jurisdiction: appeals from municipal and justice courts.

The constitution of the State of California provides that judicial power of the state is vested in a Supreme Court, Courts of Appeal, Superior Courts, Municipal Courts, and Justice Courts (Article VI, section 1). Provision is also made for a Judicial Council (Article VI, section 6), a Commission on Judicial Appointments (Article VI, section 7), and a Commission on Judicial Qualifications (Article VI, section 8).

MUNICIPAL COURTS
(one in each judicial district of more than 40,000)

Civil jurisdiction: amount in controversy, $15,000 or less. Criminal: lesser misdemeanors, preliminary hearings for felonies, infractions.

JUSTICE COURTS
(one in each judicial district of 40,000 or less)

Civil jurisdiction: amount in controversy, $15,000 or less. Criminal: misdemeanors, preliminary hearings for felonies, infractions.

Recommendations, advice, confirmation.

Lines of appeal or review.

The death penalty in California

Closing in on the first execution

By Rebecca LaVally

Reprinted from *California Journal*, July 1990

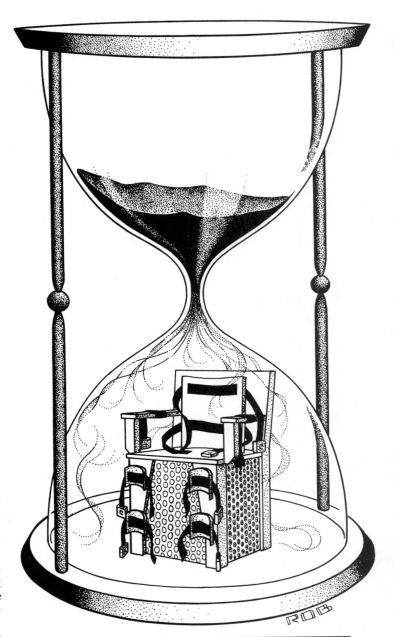

Governor George Deukmejian, usually not a publicly passionate man, was livid during a hastily called news conference a few hours before Robert Alton Harris had been scheduled for an escorted walk into San Quentin's gas chamber.

Deukmejian told reporters that he and most of the state's other citizens were dismayed that the U.S. Supreme Court had just refused to lift a judge's stay of the execution on grounds that Harris had had inadequate psychiatric assistance at his trial.

"I know that I share with most Californians great disappointment and frustration," Deukmejian declared. Delaying Harris' death would "only result in the denial of justice," he complained, branding the federal appellate system "incompetent."

The Republican governor was on safe ground in championing the execution of triple-murderer Harris under a law that Deukmejian himself had carefully crafted while serving in the state Senate 13 years ago. His long campaign to send convicts to their deaths has been consistently endorsed and aided by California voters, who paved the way for Deukmejian to reconstitute the California Supreme Court in

Rebecca LaVally, former Sacramento bureau manager for Gannett News Service and United Press International, works for the Senate Office of Research.

UPDATE

On April 21, 1992 Robert Alton Harris, having exhausted all his appeals, was executed in the San Quentin gas chamber. One of the last appeals was that execution by lethal cyanide gas was cruel and unusual punishment.

a conservative cast early in his second term.

Execution of California's first Death Row inmate since 1967 was just what most voters had in mind when they dumped Chief Justice Rose Bird and Associate Justices Joseph Grodin and Cruz Reynoso from the high Court nearly four years ago. A single issue dominated that historic revolt against the three appointees of Democratic Governor Jerry Brown, himself a foe of capital punishment. Voters were infuriated and justices kept reversing death sentences.

In a shift that legal scholars are calling dramatic and remarkable, the state Supreme Court, now dominated by Deukmejian appointees, has swung away from throwing out most death sentences to upholding most of them. And the pace of review has quickened (see previous story).

Statistics say it all: Within two years of Bird's departure, the Court's rate of affirming capital cases moved from third lowest among the 50 states to eighth highest. The Bird Court reversed 58 death sentences and upheld just four during her decade on the bench. Under her successor, Chief Justice Malcolm Lucas, the Court affirmed 64 of the 89 capital appeals it reviewed in just three years. Among the few who lost an appeal before the Bird Court was Robert Alton Harris — a fact the governor was quick to point out to reporters as evidence of the appropriateness of his death in the gas chamber.

Deukmejian made capital punishment an issue in both of his successful gubernatorial campaigns, repeatedly pledging to appoint "common sense judges."

In the aftermath of the purge of Bird, Grodin and Reynoso, he could mold the seven-member Court in his own image. It went from a 5-2 liberal majority in 1986 to 5-2 conservative domination in March 1987.

"Rarely has a high Court undergone such a dramatic change in so short a time," wrote Gerald Uelmen, dean of the Santa Clara University School of Law, in last November's Loyola of Los Angeles Law Review.

In a case-by-case comparison of the Bird and Lucas courts on death-penalty rulings, Uelmen concluded: "One is haunted by the sensation that two remarkably different institutions are at work, and the animus driving these two institutions is as different as night and day."

The Bird Court tended to resolve doubts in favor of reversing death sentences; the Lucas Court does not.

The new Court promptly struck down a controversial Bird Court ruling — responsible by itself for a spate of death-sentence reversals — requiring that murderers be shown to have had "an intent to kill" before the death penalty could be imposed.

Capital cases, most often involving first-degree murder, are elaborate. Separate phases determine guilt, whether the crime qualifies for the death penalty and, finally, whether death will be imposed. In each phase, troubles and errors can surface: the competence of the defense, the competence of a defendant to stand trial, jury selection, admissibility of evidence, jury instruction.

The Lucas Court has been more likely than the Bird Court to rule errors harmless, with no effect on the outcome of a case, in upholding verdicts and penalties.

Deukmejian's 1977 law was enacted by the Legislature over Jerry Brown's veto and was expanded 15 months later by voter approval of an initiative authored by ultra-conservative state Senator John Briggs, an Orange County Republican.

Uelmen, who publicly supported Bird, Grodin and Reynoso in 1986, said the Bird Court, in dissecting ambiguities in the Briggs initiative, sought to encourage prosecutors "to use the death-penalty law cautiously and selectively." The Lucas Court, he wrote, "has rejected a supervisory role, and the number of new death judgments is spiraling upwards."

Says Briggs: "I used to get the hell beat out of me for drafting a bad initiative, but it wasn't a bad initiative. We had some bad judges interpreting it. The judges that replaced [Bird, Grodin and Reynoso] agreed with the people and me, and it's nice to be right, after all these years," said Briggs, who is now a lobbyist in Sacramento.

Others who fought the three justices are applauding the new Court's penchant for directing more convicted murderers toward the gas chamber. Alameda County District Attorney John Meehan, who has studied the Bird Court's decisions, says it dragged its feet in reviewing capital cases and would "reach" for reasons to overturn them.

"We had in California a death penalty that was almost a joke," recalls Meehan, former president of the California District Attorneys Association, which targeted the three justices for defeat. "You'd do everything possible to have a clean trial but, by that time, the California Supreme Court was looking for any basis to reverse it. The Bird Court created law retroactively, causing cases to be reversed. It had a tremendous amount to do with their philosophical beliefs about the death penalty itself. We found ourselves as prosecutors trying cases on what we thought the law might be by the time it [the case] reached the California Supreme Court, which is an outrageous position."

Meehan says the Lucas Court has served justice by stepping up the pace of reviewing death cases, usually making its decisions within four months of hearing oral arguments.

But some defense attorneys suggest the new Court, mindful of voter sentiment in 1986, seems to sway with the political wind.

"Statistics are the black and white of it," says Elisabeth Semel, president of California Attorneys of Criminal Justice, the state's largest group of criminal defense lawyers. "The meat of it is the lives of the various defendants affected by this enormous swing the Court is taking."

She and others say errors ruled "harmless" by the Court could have enormous consequences for the men on Death Row.

San Francisco capital defense lawyer Robert Bryan, chairman of the National Coalition to Abolish the Death Penalty, complains: "What scares me is ... the arbitrariness of the whole process. A lot of their decisions are shocking. They recognize error, but they say, well, it's harmless."

Justices Lucas and Grodin, in remarks published in the Los Angeles Times more than a year before the 1986 election, revealed their stark differences in reviewing death cases for troublesome flaws. Their comments, in a larger sense, define the difference between the courts of Jerry Brown and George Deukmejian.

Lucas said: "I personally do not apply 'tougher' standards to capital cases ... Assuming proper and careful attention is given to reviewing these cases, the law should be uniformly and consistently applied without regard to the penalty selected in a particular case."

Said Grodin: "... the very fact that the penalty is final and irreversible makes it necessary for each judge, no matter what his or her personal views, to be exceedingly careful. Once the sentence is carried out, it is too late to correct mistakes." 🏛

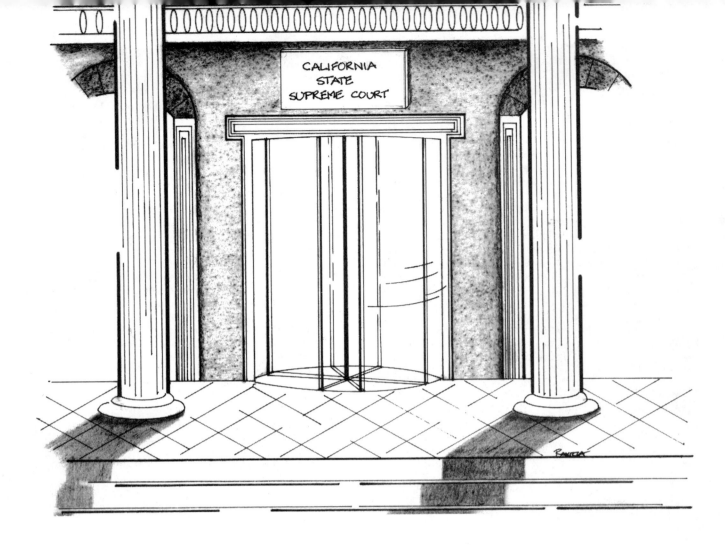

The Supreme Court's revolving door

Is all the turnover good for the high Court?

By Robert Egelko

Reprinted from *California Journal*, July 1990

It took an $11 million campaign in 1986 to get Chief Justice Rose Bird and Justices Cruz Reynoso and Joseph Grodin off of the state Supreme Court. Getting their three successors to leave was a lot cheaper: $86,371 a year, apiece — the price of a pension.

Justices John Arguelles, Marcus Kaufman and David Eagleson, the veteran jurists appointed by Governor George Deukmejian when he remade the Court in 1987, announced their retirements with little fanfare or emotion after two, three and four years' service, respectively.

The departures prompted one commentator to talk gloomily of a "turnstile Court." They also were a sign that the death penalty, the

Robert Egelko covers the state Supreme Court from the San Francisco bureau of the Associated Press.

downfall of the Bird Court, continues to serve up an intractable problem for the state's judiciary.

Arguelles, 61 when he retired, and Kaufman, 60, later outlined their reasons to reporters — reasons that were predictable. (Eagleson, 65, is keeping mum until he steps down officially next January.) The two had each spent more than two decades on the bench, done their part to get the Court back on its feet, and wanted to spend more time with their families. The workload was rewarding but arduous (Arguelles) or "overwhelmingly tedious" (Kaufman), yet they might have stayed if they hadn't been confident the Court was in good hands, and if they weren't newly eligible for

Bird

Lucas

maximum pension benefits.

Speaking separately from one another, Arguelles and Kaufman explained how the judges' pension system discouraged them from remaining on the bench. (Both are now associated with large Southern California law firms, where they no longer work most nights and weekends and presumably make more than the justices' $115,161 annual salary.) They wouldn't have been penalized for staying a little longer — only a judge who remains past 70 suffers a cut in future benefits, from 75 to 50 percent of salary — but once a judge has 20 years on the bench the maximum pension eligibility is reached at age 60. After that, judges must keep contributing 8 percent of their salary to the pension fund.

"It's almost like working for nothing," Arguelles said. Besides, he observed, Deukmejian had been good enough to appoint him, and, "I decided that with the Court stabilized, and with the awareness that [Deukmejian] would name my successor — and I had confidence in his abilities to select a very able person — I felt that I could leave ...The Court has continued to function in my absence."

In other words: no big deal. Judges come and go, but the Court endures — at least the current, stabilized court. Joyce Kennard, 48, has replaced Arguelles, Armand Arabian, 55, has taken Kaufman's spot, and Deukmejian will shortly name another of his appellate justices to succeed Eagleson, who leaves two months after his 20th anniversary on the bench. Only the faces change, getting younger and further from early retirement incentives.

Kaufman even speculated that Deukmejian had deliberately picked three judges who were close to retirement age in 1987, intending them to be "interim appointees."

That was denied by Marvin Baxter, who was Deukmejian's appointments secretary in 1987 and now is a justice on the Fifth District Court of Appeal in Fresno and a candidate to succeed Eagleson. "I don't know of any way anyone can ever predict the tenure of a judge," Baxter said. Kaufman disclaimed any inside knowledge, but his sugges-

tion had a certain plausibility, based on the premise that Deukmejian was familiar with his judges' thinking.

It is perhaps unfair to imply that these are peculiarly the actions of Republican appointees, who think of the Court as a stepping-stone to a comfortable corporate practice. Justices of all political stripes have resigned over the years for reasons both profound and mundane; Justice Otto Kaus, a Jerry Brown appointee, quit in 1985 after four years with much the same explanation as the recent retirees; and Justice Frank Newman, another Brown appointee, left after an even briefer stay in 1982 to return to teaching. It may also be only an historical irony that membership on the Court is treated as relatively inconsequential less than four years after an election in which it was seen as holding the balance of power in California.

The three defeated justices, however, who spent over $2.5 million trying to keep their jobs, could be forgiven for viewing their successors as insufficiently devoted to the Court, although they have not said so publicly. Grodin, now a law professor, refused to criticize the new retirees, commenting only in the abstract that it hurt the Court's reputation and prestige "to regard it as a place where people can come and go casually."

"If someone of the U.S. Supreme Court were to resign because they thought they didn't have anything more to

Grodin

Reynoso

gain in pension by staying on and they could make a lot of money by private practice or private judging, I think we would be quite astonished," the former justice said.

This is not the U.S. Supreme Court, of course — there is no life tenure, and the rulings bind no one outside of California — but not long ago it was generally placed in the top rank of the nation's state courts. That image took a battering during the 1986 election. One who saw it as further harmed by the recent retirements was J. Anthony Kline, Governor Jerry Brown's former legal affairs secretary and chief judge-screener and now a Brown-appointed presiding justice on the 1st District Court of Appeal in San Francisco.

"I think what these departures are doing is reinforcing a diminished image of the California Supreme Court and an increasing view that it is not as much the apex of a legal career," Kline said. "The most ominous message ... is that the [state] Supreme Court is no longer seen as the best job that a lawyer or judge could have."

The "turnstile Court" label came from Gerald Uelmen, dean of the Santa Clara University Law School, who has become a kind of unofficial statistician of the Court as well as one of its foremost commentators. One of his studies showed that the average stay on the Court between 1936 and 1986 was 13 years.

"I think the days of long tenure on the Court may well

be over," Uelmen said. Rapid turnover, he said, is "very disruptive," and hurt the Court's "long-term stability and predictability." Grodin had a similar view: Great state courts are usually those whose stable memberships give them "a kind of institutional coherence."

But words like "prestige," "reputation" and "stability" may mean one thing to a law professor or the legal community, and quite another to the general public.

However the Bird Court may have been regarded in academic circles — a matter of considerable debate — it was rejected by the voters after a campaign that subjected the Court to an unprecedented level of public scrutiny. Californians may no longer know who their justices are, but their esteem for, or at least acceptance of, the Court has evidently been restored; all five Deukmejian appointees are to be on the ballot this November, and it would be astonishing if any encountered substantial opposition. As for stability and continuity, as Arguelles noted, one set of Deukmejian appointees has replaced another; the character of the Court — the majority's background and overall outlook, and the kinds of decisions that can be expected — remains the same.

Why, then, should anyone outside of a narrow circle of Court-watchers and appellate lawyers care about the resignations on the state's highest Court?

There are a few reasons.

First, the Court has severely curtailed its role as the arbiter of civil law in California — the area of its work that affects its constituents the most, as homeowners and renters, employers and employees, insurance buyers, injury victims and taxpayers. Turnover is an important contributor to the slowdown, though not the only one.

According to Uelmen's latest study, the Court issued only 105 written decisions in the 12 months ending March 31st — down from a normal pace of 140 the previous year. Just 28 rulings were in civil cases, compared to 43 in routine lawyer discipline cases, with the rest in capital and other criminal cases. The decline was even more drastic in the number of cases accepted for hearing — the Court's mech-

Arguelles

Kaufman

anism for determining its docket: just 80, compared with a 10-year average of 268.

The downturn coincided with the debut of Kennard, who is by all accounts a hard worker and a fast learner. She wrote only two majority opinions during the year. A similar initiation period can be expected for Arabian, appointed this year, and for Eagleson's successor next year.

"It takes at least a year for somebody to break in on the Court, particularly in the death-penalty cases," said Grodin, who served for four years. "A judge who has served on the Court of Appeal [which doesn't handle capital cases] hasn't had any exposure to that stuff. Even after you've broken in,

you don't really hit full stride till you've been there for a few years."

"The justices appear to be working harder than ever, with less to show for it," Uelmen said in his study. (Some

Kennard

Arabian

current and former justices have complained about regularly working six or seven days a week.)

The impact of the drop-off can be striking in individual cases. As the state's high Court accepts fewer cases, the last word on more and more of them belongs to the six appellate courts, each with judges of varying views and abilities and extremely low public profiles. And when a case is accepted for Supreme Court review, it can languish undecided for years.

The most notorious current example is a dispute over the power of the state Fair Employment and Housing Commission to award damages to discrimination victims for emotional distress and other types of harm they suffer, aside from loss of pay. The lawsuit, based on events that took place in 1980-81, was granted a hearing by the Bird Court in 1986 but has never been calendared for oral argument. Meanwhile, the commission has continued to award damages for emotional trauma — the largest single element of many of its cases, such as sexual harassment suits — but the awards are routinely appealed and tied up in lower state courts, which have issued conflicting rulings on their legality. The Legislature has twice passed bills to declare the commission's authority to award limited damages, but Deukmejian has vetoed them, saying the issue was before the Court. No one knows what the law is.

Instead of issuing rulings, the Court has turned to the arcane and much-criticized practice of "depublishing" appellate decisions as its most common method of shaping the law (see "Depublication," *CJ*, April 1985).

Only about 10 percent of Court of Appeal rulings are certified by those courts to be published in books of reported decisions, which can be cited as precedent by other judges and lawyers; once final, they become binding on trial courts statewide. ("Unpublished" appellate rulings are binding only on the parties.) However, the state Supreme Court, when deciding not to accept a case for review, can order a published appellate ruling erased from the books, leaving the result of the case unchanged but destroying its status as precedent. Depublication, unique to California, is supposed to indicate dissatisfaction with some aspect of the lower court's reasoning, but the high Court is not required to state its own reasons and never does. As a result, while it may remove some unwanted language from the casebooks, the process usually leaves everyone in the dark as to the Supreme Court's view of the law.

Abuse of the depublication process was one charge

leveled by prosecutors against the Bird Court, although Bird herself disliked depublication and usually dissented from it. The current Court under Chief Justice Malcolm Lucas is depublishing about 130 cases a year — twice the Bird Court's rate, and last year depublished more cases than it decided.

Depublication casts the Court in the inapt role of censor rather than interpreter of the law and "injects a real

---

UPDATE

Governor Pete Wilson made his first appointment to the state Supreme Court when he named Ronald George, former Associate Justice of the Court of Appeal in Los Angeles. Confirmed in September 1991, George replaced Associate Justice Allen Broussard, who retired.

---

mystery into the law," said Uelmen. But the justices have accepted the practice as a necessary evil to keep their caseload under control, as long as they lack the time to decide all pressing legal disputes themselves.

The chief reason for the lack of time is the death penalty — the grim omnipresence of California law and politics. It undid the Bird Court and has disrupted — perhaps even dominated — the Lucas Court. Bird, Reynoso and Grodin were unseated largely because the Court upheld only four of 68 death sentences — a rate that proved politically unacceptable in a state that had not ousted a Supreme Court justice in 50 years. The current Court has affirmed more than 70 percent of its death sentences and decided the cases three times as fast, solving the political problem but creating a logistical mess.

Lucas, promoted to chief justice by Deukmejian in 1987, faced a backlog of 170 capital cases that had grown to 200 by the time Arguelles, Kaufman and Eagleson completed their shakedown year. He decided to make those cases the Court's top priority; in one dizzying year, the justices produced a record 56 death-penalty rulings but succeeded only in whittling the backlog down to its earlier size. The pace has slowed markedly since then due to turnover, reordering of priorities and the disruption, although about three-fourths of the cases are in early paperwork stages and not yet ready for Court arguments.

Arguelles, who usually voted with the majority to affirm death sentences, recently lent support to suspicions voiced by defense lawyers but denied by prosecutors — that the Lucas Court, by upholding death cases regularly, had encouraged prosecutors around the state to file more death-penalty charges, increasing still further the number of appeals the Court will have to review in the future.

The death cases, which the Court is required by law to review directly from the trial courts, occupy between 25 to 40 percent of the justices' time, by different members' estimates. The trial transcripts run thousands of pages, lawyers are required to raise every conceivable argument, and few important legal issues remain after 12 years of wrestling with the state's last death-penalty initiative.

The capital cases, though, are a response to the public's demand for the death penalty. The public also demanded a stiffening of the State Bar's disciplinary system, and the result has been an upsurge of routine lawyer misconduct cases, which also must be reviewed directly by the Supreme Court, and which occupy an increasing portion of the justices' time. They have far less time than they need to tackle everything else on their plate, including issues of civil law that affect millions of people and offer the kind of intellectual challenge the Court is supposed to provide.

Kaufman said the excessive time spent on death cases was one reason, among many, for his retirement. Arguelles called the cases "cumbersome" but said they didn't hasten his departure. Eagleson, in a speech last year, denied that capital cases or "judge burnout" were serious problems for him or his colleagues. Uelmen said the response sounded like a "party line," and he was not alone in his doubts.

Gideon Kanner, a Loyola University law professor and a conservative counterpart to the liberal Uelmen, pointed critically to the 77 percent of the Court's opinions last year consisting of capital cases, other criminal cases and lawyer discipline.

Calling the Court's turnover alarming but understandable, Kanner wrote in a recent op-ed piece, "Few sensible men and women of great professional achievement are willing to spend the rest of their active lives poring over mountains of verbiage, responding to routine demands of society's dregs."

"It's hard not to conclude that the burden of death-penalty cases is wearing the justices down and burning them out," said Stephen Barnett, a UC Berkeley law professor.

The Court is likely to rid itself soon of automatic review of lawyer misconduct cases. A far more substantial and daring step would be to transfer initial review of capital cases to the Court of Appeal. Supreme Court review would still be required of all affirmed death sentences, but the idea is that appellate courts could weed out some of the flawed cases, distill the factual record and spread the workload around.

The longstanding proposal, which would probably require a state constitutional amendment, was endorsed recently by Arguelles and Kaufman. Bernard Witkin, a prominent California legal commentator, has said it's the only way the Court can get its caseload under control. But the present prospects are doubtful.

For one thing, Lucas said several years ago that the plan would only add another layer of delay; without his support, there would be little chance of legislative approval. Also, most appellate justices are opposed, for good reason: Their job carries the closest thing to guaranteed life tenure of any elected state office — a status that might change quickly for anyone with a record of death-penalty reversals. In fact, even if the transfer took place, it probably would only defer most of the high Court's death-penalty burden temporarily; relief seems possible only by either abolishing capital punishment, eliminating most of the defendants' constitutional safeguards, or adopting Justice Stanley Mosk's equally problematic proposal to split the Court into civil and criminal divisions.

For the moment, the Court's turnstile may slow down. Justice Edward Panelli, who has complained about the workload, isn't eligible for maximum retirement benefits until 1992. Lucas has been the subject of occasional retirement rumors, which he's denied; Mosk and Justice Allen Broussard have also disavowed any plans to leave, although that could change if a Democrat is elected governor.

But the latest defections could be a warning that the Court, which appeared to regain its health after the convulsions of 1986, is still ailing. 🏛

Picking Justice's pocket

Are state courts becoming tax collectors?

By Michael Trihey

Reprinted from *California Journal*, September 1991

In post-Proposition 13 California, the state and its budget-strapped counties quietly have turned to an unlikely and unsuspecting source to build courthouses, finance fingerprinting and emergency medical programs and to support retired judges.

Speeding motorists pay hundreds of millions of dollars a year in "penalty assessments" that frequently have little to do with driving violations but have been an increasingly important source of money for the criminal justice system and, now, the state's general fund.

It is a politically expedient hidden tax, say some legislators and judges, who see the assessment process as a fundamentally dishonest system that threatens to turn honest citizens into fugitives, police into bounty hunters and judges into state revenue agents.

At its worst, the system requires dangerous criminals be set free when traffic violators, unable to pay large assessments, are sentenced to overcrowded jails. At the very least, it is a

Michael Trihey is assistant city editor of the Bakersfield Californian.

bureaucratic nightmare to court clerks who must administer it.

"It was a nice program when it started in 1953," said Republican Assemblyman Charles Quackenbush of San Jose. "But it's turned into a monster."

"Penalty assessments have just gotten out of hand," said John Burton, the San Francisco Democrat who chairs the Assembly Committee on Public Safety. "They're horrendous."

The assessment system is a mammoth, increasingly controversial program that affects millions of Californians each year, but it is little known to the general public.

The assessments are fines on top of fines — surcharges added in criminal and infraction cases. Bit by bit, the payments have grown proportionately with state and local budget difficulties, culminating in June 1991 when, as a part of AB 1297, they were increased dramatically to help balance the state budget.

After that increase, the surcharges are expected to pull $480 million a year from lawbreakers, the vast majority of them motorists and parking violators.

The basic assessment for the state is now $17 for every $10 of fine — a 170

percent increase that turns a $100 infraction into a $270 violation and, said judges, turns courts and law enforcement into a government collection agency.

"The basic problem here is that the state is in financial trouble," said Richard Stanford, presiding judge of the Central Orange County Municipal Court. "They're looking to the courts as a revenue source. And that's not what the courts are meant to be."

Judges have been concerned for years that the assessments were creating a growing disparity between crime and punishment. Now, with an assessment schedule that puts total payments for some of the most common traffic violations into the hundreds of dollars range, judges are saying there may be a backlash: Judges may reduce the basic fine for less-than-wealthy miscreant motorists, cutting the fine-plus-assessment to a total the judge believes more appropriate for the offense and the offender.

"There may be a subtle mentality on the bench here to lower the fines to lessen the hit," Judge Stanford said. "That kind of defeats the whole purpose of the thing ... but when it starts interfering with our ability to do justice, in general, the mentality around here is, 'We're not just a taxing agency. We're not just here to make money.' We like to believe we have a little higher calling than that."

"The question comes down to whether it is really too much of a penalty in relation to the actual offense," said Ronald Quidachay, presiding judge of the San Francisco Municipal Court.

Legislators have been concerned about the level of assessments, too. As late as May, when the surcharges varied from county to county (ranging from $9.50 to $14.50 per $10 of fine and averaging $11.50), lawmakers were saying the penalties were becoming too high. Some, like Burton, said they would approve of new assessments only in extraordinary circumstances. That's what happened, he said, when push came to shove on the $14 billion budget imbalance. "We were forced into doing a lot of stuff we didn't like," he said. "We had to do it."

Tucked in Assemblyman Phil Isenberg's AB 1297 and overshadowed by the enormity of the budget crisis, the increase in assessments received little notice in the media. But that's the way it always has been with the surcharge program. Legislation raising the price for running a stop sign never got much press. For one thing, it's very complicated and rarely has been controversial because it is so politically safe. Increases of 5 or 10 percent at a time are enacted through county-specific bills, usually introduced by the lawmaker representing the affected county. An assemblyman or senator rarely was called upon to raise the assessment in his or her own district.

Since the enabling legislation began with a local resolution by the affected county's board of supervisors, the introducing legislator couldn't be held fully responsible for the increase in the assessment. Traffic offenders have little representation in the legislative process and rarely know about the increase until they get a ticket — and then they're angry with police and the courts, not with the lawmaker who helped enact the assessment.

"These are viewed in Sacramento as district bills," said David Scharlac, the legislative counsel for the Automobile Club of Southern California. "Typically, Trice Harvey will say, 'Why are you messing with me? This is down in my district, it doesn't apply to the whole state. Don't give me a bad time.'"

Harvey, the Republican assemblyman from Bakersfield, introduced legislation in February that would have raised Kern County's assessment 10 percent to what then would have been the highest in the state: $15.50 per $10 of fine. His bill, which would raise $700,000 a year for 10 years to build a new crime lab, is still alive but, after the assessments were raised statewide to $17 by AB 1297, doesn't have much of a chance of becoming law.

"The board of supervisors and the D.A., who wanted me to do this, don't feel the people would want to vote to give a general tax increase of any sort for this, but would support having those who are violating the law pay," Harvey said. "It's much easier to let those who may be getting ticketed and so forth for law infractions pay it, instead of the general populace."

"It's a good political shelter," said Quackenbush. "Drunk drivers and speeders don't have much of a lobby. And you can always say you're not voting to raise taxes, you're just getting tough on lawbreakers. I can understand that feeling."

Alison Harvey, Assemblyman Isenberg's chief of staff, said using assessments was appropriate in balancing the budget because drivers cost the state much more than they pay.

"We're an auto-related society, and we're going to absorb that within our tax structures," she said. "It costs the courts about $350 million a year to handle motor-vehicle infractions. Of the 17 million annual filings in the courts, 13 million are auto-related. In fact, the motorist doesn't pay his fair share in society at all. Across the board, roads or parking or the impacts of automobiles, they just aren't paying their own way. So there were no particular feelings of guilt about going after motorists. In fact, it was quite to the contrary."

The assessments were first imposed at 5 percent in 1952 to reimburse the state school fund for driver-education programs. They gradually increased as "abuser fees," with the assessment directly related to violation on which it was based. But after 1978 — and Proposition 13 — the number and size of assessments grew dramatically and in many cases the nexus between violation and assessment was non-existent. An assessment of 100 percent goes to the state, some of it for specific projects, some of it to the general fund. The remaining 70 percent goes to the county in which the crime or infraction was committed, where boards of supervisors can allot it to projects specified in state law — such as courthouse or jail construction, fingerprinting systems or emergency medical facilities.

"In the last five years the penalty assessments have changed drastically," said John Korach, of the State Controller's Office. "It used to be $3 assessment for each $10 of fine at the state level."

In Sacramento County, "in 1984 it was $7 [per $10 of fine], total," said Sherman Moore, accounting manager for the Sacramento Municipal Court. "In '87 they changed it to $9, and in '88 they changed it to $11, then in '89 they changed it to $11.50, then in '88 they changed it again, to $13.50."

"These numbers just keep growing," said Karl Jaeger, presiding judge of the Los Angeles Municipal Court. "And the Legislature, instead of funding things or not funding them, tacks it on as a penalty assessment and leaves it to us to explain it to the defendant. And there are so many things that are so remote to the operation of the court and the court system, that judges find it mind-boggling."

The one-two fine-plus-assessment punch frequently hits those who least can afford it — motorists in run-down cars cited for equipment deficiencies the driver couldn't afford to fix in the first place. The poorer the violator, the larger his fine and assessments are likely to be: A farm worker driving an uninsured car with bald tires and emitting too much smoke can face a final court bill of thousands of dollars. The combination sometimes is more than the value of the car.

"A lot of times, people who get these citations have limited resources," said state Senator Don Rogers, a Bakersfield Republican. "They may be out of work and then they get thrown in jail and can't work."

Honest drivers, judges said, sometimes are so shocked by the amount of the combined penalties — penalties they know they cannot pay — that they simply don't come to court. That results in a warrant, additional fines and penalties and, usually, an eventual arrest.

"Quite a few" motorists end up in jail because of unpaid fines and assessments, said Judge Stanford in Orange

County. "We already have overcrowded jails. Now we have to put people in jail for things that, if we didn't have this penalty assessment, they would be more likely to pay it than go to jail."

That's the "double whammy" said Quackenbush, the assemblyman. "You have to pay all the costs of incarceration, and you don't get the fine or the assessment."

In some counties with severely overcrowded jails, when someone goes to jail, someone else must be released. That's why most judges try to find alternatives to jailing traffic offenders, even if they can't pay their fines or assessments.

"I always try to find a way to avoid incarcerating these guys," said Bakersfield Municipal Court Judge Frank Hoover. "If I've got some poor person who doesn't have $400 to pay for a cracked windshield, I don't want to put that person in jail and have to release an habitual drunk driver or habitual drug user to make room."

That kind of scenario and administrative problems have prompted the California Judicial Council to oppose increasing assessments, said the council's Sacramento counsel, Stephen Birdlebough. "The minute the level of your fines gets up to where there is any substantial number of people who elect to serve it out instead of paying it, it becomes very counterproductive. Court time is very expensive. It becomes counterproductive if the assessment and fine become so high people come to court to argue they should get a lighter sentence," he said.

And the whole business cheapens the justice system because it increasingly is becoming, judges say, a business.

"We have ceased to recognize the courts as a fully independent branch of the government that the legislative and the executive simply have to pay for," said Judge Hoover. "They just have to pay for it, and hope we don't screw it up. They should not expect us to do anything but make sure the state and federal constitutions are adhered to. They should not look to us to raise money. If we impose fines, we should impose them as a punishment and deterrence, and we should collect them in the same fashion. If we raise money, good. But our purpose should not be to raise money."

The system gives police officers the same problem, said Quackenbush.

"I think everyone has always had resentment for the police officer sitting behind the billboard, waiting for people to roll through some convenient stop sign. This is the kind of thing we're getting into when you've got to put pressure on your police officers to go out and wring money out of people. That isn't what they're all about.

"I'm not any kind of soft-on-crime person," he said. "I'm always right down the line, jacking up sentences and things like that. But I'm not sure this is really good budgeting procedure. Do we want our cops being pressured to go out and write tickets on parking violations or do we want them busting crack houses and going after murderers?"

Another big concern is the pure mechanics of levying the assessments.

"It's a nightmare," said Laura Hankins, senior consultant to the Assembly Committee on Public Safety, which considers assessment legislation. "It's absolutely crazy."

Payments to the court must be divided between the fine and the assessment, each of which must be divided among the state and local governments. The county's portion of the assessment then must be allocated to the various projects designated by the board of supervisors.

And those are just the basic assessments. Many crimes carry additional flat fees. In each traffic case in many counties, for instance, a $1 assessment is added to pay for night court. In some counties, drivers convicted of not wearing seat belts pay a $2 fee for a brain injury clinic in addition to the 20 percent assessment they pay for emergency medical services. In cases where narcotics are involved, the defendant in some jurisdictions must pay a $50 lab fee — in addition to the 20 percent assessment for construction of the criminalistics laboratory. Other assessments contribute to a non-victim restitution fund and pay for crime prevention.

The fines and assessments frequently add up to more than the motorist can pay immediately. When the defendant is permitted a payment schedule, each payment must be divided into its various parts so that each account will get a partial payment.

Everyone wants to get tough on drunken drivers so, in some counties, as many as 32 state and local assessments are added to the basic $390 fine, bringing the total due to nearly $2500. That's getting tough on court clerks, too, who must divide each payment by each drunken driver 32 times.

"And it depends on when the violation was committed," said Moore of the Sacramento Municipal Court. "Some people take a while to get through the court system. If the offense took place in 1988, the fines and assessments in place then are charged. If it happened in 1989 or 1990, there are different penalty schedules."

"And almost none of it comes from people who commit crimes that were crimes in 1910: rape, robbery, burglary— the people who are the reasons we have prisons and armed policemen," said Hoover, the Bakersfield judge. "These aren't the people this deals with.

"These assessments come from the people who drive unregistered cars and have bald tires and crappy engines that can't get smogged," Hoover said. "And if that's the group of taxpayers the Legislature thinks is going to balance the budget, they're nuts." 🏛

Justice for sale

Faster justice for those who can pay

Reprinted from *California Journal*, October 1991

After more than 15 years of litigation, four of the nation's top oil companies — Chevron, Mobil, Shell and Texaco — settled a lawsuit brought by the State of California for allegedly fixing the price of crude oil.

Rather than face another 15 years of legal maneuvering in an already overcrowded justice system, the two parties agreed in August to reach a private resolution with the help of a hired judge. The case, which put about $220 million into state coffers, was just one of the many civil matters that have been settled through the increasingly acceptable — and lucrative — business of private judging, or "alternative dispute-resolution."

Over the past decade, there has been an unprecedented boom in for-profit, alternative dispute-resolution businesses, or ADRs. The business is built around individual judges and professional arbitrators selling their knowledge and expertise to frustrated litigants, as well as to big business firms, tailoring proceedings for parties willing to pay.

And not coincidentally, that growth has paralleled an equally dramatic rise in demand on the state courts system, prompting litigants who can afford it to find other sources of judicial remedy.

"Litigation takes so long and costs so much," said Richard Birke, associate director of the Center on Conflict and Negotiation at Stanford Law School. "There are more cases out there than courtroom time. Because of the incredible needs of criminal cases, a lot of civil cases may never get to be heard."

Enter dispute-resolution and private judging firms, which offer a quicker, easier and often cheaper solution.

ADR is a broad category, encompassing everything from non-profit neighborhood mediation centers resolving small-claims disputes between neighbors and family members to the high-powered firms that boast a choice of distinguished retired judges to hear cases whenever and however the parties choose, for a fee.

continued on next page

By Mariel Garza

Mariel Garza is a freelance writer in Southern California.

It is this business aspect of the ADR industry, the so-called justice-for-sale, that has drawn wary looks from skeptics.

Parties pay around $300 and $400 per hour for judicial arbitration services, which allows them to pick their judge, pick their hearing date and stipulate all the other details of the hearing.

"The essence of ADR is that you put the control of the dispute in the hands of the disputants and take it out of the hands of the court," said Richard Chernick, president of the Los Angeles County Bar Association and a partner at Gibson, Dunn and Crutcher.

But that is exactly what some fear: that too much will be taken from the courts and the public, and that private-sector cases will end up decided behind closed doors.

"My view is that any case the resolution of which judges use and that stands the possibility of being precedent-setting should be heard in public," said Sacramento Municipal Judge Rudolph Loncke, who has publicly voiced his concerns about the private judging industry growing unchecked. "Any case that affects the people of California should be resolved by the people accountable to the people of California."

Loncke agrees that judicial arbitration has done good things. However, he warns that without a thorough examination of the ADR businesses, there is a potential for problems ranging from a loss of talent on the bench to sitting judges posturing for the private firms to discrimination in the choosing of private judges.

"The checks and balances aren't there," Loncke said. "I'm not saying any of this is happening. But it is something we should avoid."

Chernick disagrees with the assertion that important public cases could end up in a private hearing. "No one in their right mind would take a case like that," he said.

Still, the fledgling industry remains unregulated by an overseeing body.

However, that may change since both the Judicial Council and the State Bar have begun to study the ADR industry and to develop guidelines.

"I think there is the beginning of some overseeing of ADR through the courts and the bar, " said Sheila Purcell. As a dispute program developer for the State Bar Association, Purcell provides technical support to ADR groups serving middle- to low-income clients. Purcell said she has recently been appointed to the Judicial Council's advisory committee on dispute resolution that will review and make recommendations on how the courts refer cases out to ADR.

Few dispute that the court system is jammed, making it harder for the average litigant to access justice. This in turn makes ADR a much more attractive option than taking one's chances with the courts.

The story goes, according to Chernick, that in 1978 two lawyers working a case through the backlogged Los Angeles Superior Court decided they had waited long enough. The two apparently contacted a retired judge who agreed to hear the case. When the lawyers discovered how helpful the alternative process was, they spread the word. Thirteen years later, private judging and ADR firms are disposing of tens of thousands of civil cases annually.

Orange County-based Judicial Arbitration and Mediation Services was one of the first firms to mine this rich judicial vein. Begun in 1979 by retired Orange County Superior Court Judge H. Warren Knight, JAMS now employs 160 retired judges and has heard 11,000 cases throughout the country.

"Basically, my thought after eight years on the bench was that there must be an easier way to do this," Knight said.

The firm, which mediated the settlement between the four oil companies and the State of California last month, will set up just about any arrangement for a dispute hearing that the involved parties want.

Although in the long run firms such as JAMS may save hundreds of thousands of dollars in legal fees and court time, some regard private judging as an elitist form of justice.

James Ford, presiding judge in the Sacramento County Superior Court, said recently in a commentary in the *Daily Journal*, a Los Angeles legal newspaper, that "the perception and reality will always be that [private judging] is a vehicle for the well-to-do."

That perception may be true, but Chernick said that the broader growth of the industry has and is creating more resources for everyday disputes and less-affluent litigants.

For example, he cites Los Angeles County's dispute-resolution program, which began as a small neighborhood justice center. That effort has grown to a thriving mediation program that has resolved "tens of thousands of cases that might have found their way into the courts."

"I think everybody is equally able to participate in the private resolution process," Chernick said. "It's not like the private hospital/public hospital, private school/public school dichotomy."

Though relatively new to the business arena, private dispute resolution itself is not. Centuries before the institutionalization of the legal system, tribes and villages would bring disputes to the wise elder for resolution. However, with the creation of justice systems, people increasingly looked to the courts for answers.

But now that court dockets are close to reaching critical mass, many legal associations and justices and government officials are looking toward ADR to catch the runoff and to assist the system in providing justice for all.

Since 1926 the American Association of Arbitration, a non-profit resolution organization, has worked in conjunction with the country's courts to clear up civil cases. The arbitration association also has seen a jump in cases with a national high in 1990 of 65,000, said Jerry Murase, regional vice president in Los Angeles.

In his speech to the American Bar Association in August, Vice President Dan Quayle advocated the use of a "multi-door courthouse," which would provide accessible alternatives for disputants. "This idea will, of course, empower people with disputes, and it'll help unclog the courts," he said.

However, only civil cases benefit from alternative dispute resolution. And if the governments want to unclog the courts, it should focus instead on criminal cases, Judge Ford said.

"The government has to abandon the idea that the criminal-justice system is the answer to the war on drugs," Ford said. "Because it is the drug cases causing the delays in the courts."

The urgency of criminal cases, when often a defendant is being held in jail until trial, gives them priority over civil cases. And as criminal cases keep pouring in, civil matters are often pushed aside, Ford said. But if the flow of the criminal cases subsided, civil litigants could once again be guaranteed their day in court. 🏛

THE LEGISLATURE

California's Legislature is not much different from Congress and legislative bodies in other states in overall power and structure. It is, simply stated, the policy-making arm of government, restricted only by the federal and state constitutions and the governor's veto. Like Congress, it can also conduct investigations into almost any issue of public concern and impeach public officials. It also can ratify amendments to the United States Constitution. In recent years, there has been a trend toward the Legislature's appropriating for itself some of the appointive power traditionally given to the executive. Thus, it is not uncommon now to have a commission consist of both gubernatorial and legislative appointees.

Seats in both the 40-member Senate and 80-member Assembly are apportioned on the basis of population. (Until 1966, the Senate was apportioned by geography, like the United States Senate.) Assembly members serve two-year terms; Senate terms are for four years, with half the terms expiring every two years. Under the provisions of Prop. 140 of November 1990, term limits are now imposed on state legislators (3 terms, 6 years in the Assembly; 2 terms, 8 years in the Senate). The Senate and Assembly are organized differently, with power diffused in a committee of the upper house but centered in the office of speaker in the Assembly.

The Senate

The lieutenant governor is the president of the Senate, but he has virtually no power. He is entitled to cast a vote to break a 20-20 tie, but this situation almost never develops. If the Senate can be said to have a single leader it is the president pro tempore, and he is elected by a simple majority of his colleagues. The pro tem is charged with overall administration of the house, but the real power — committee appointments and assignment of bills to committee — rests with the five-member Rules Committee. The president pro tempore is chairman, and the other four seats are traditionally divided between the two major parties. Between 1969 and 1975, there was an almost-constant battle for the leadership post between two factions sometimes referred to as the Old Guard and the Young Turks. However, in recent years the divisions in the Senate have tended to be along party lines. There has been stability in leadership, at least among Democrats, since 1980 when David Roberti became president pro tempore.

Aside from the Rules Committee, the two most important panels in the Senate are the Appropriations and Budget and Fiscal Review committees. The Budget and Fiscal Review Committee handles the budget. The Appropriations Committee hears any other bills with direct or implied state cost. Thus it can kill almost any major bill.

The Assembly

The Assembly has a form of government that might be called self-inflicted dictatorship. The speaker is elected by at least 41 votes (a simple majority) and thereafter wields tremendous power; this officer appoints all committee chairs and names all committee members except for the Rules Committee. Control over committees amounts to the power to kill any bill. A bill defeated in committee can be brought to the floor by a majority vote of the full assembly, but this occurs very infrequently. A vote to withdraw a bill from committee would be tantamount to a vote of no-confidence for the speaker. The speaker's control over legislation probably makes him the second-most-powerful official in state government next to the governor. However, on occasion, the speaker has had difficulty leading. Battles within majority Democratic ranks in 1979-80 between then-Speaker Leo McCarthy and challenger Howard Berman, each with his own faction, led to legislative paralysis in the lower house. In 1988 the "Gang of Five" (anti-leadership Democrats) openly feuded with Democratic Speaker Willie Brown over legislative matters in the Assembly. Though the five were punished by Speaker Brown (losing chairmanships, committee assignments, staff and office space) they refused to back down. For a time, the "Five" combined with the Republican caucus had a majority in the Assembly. However after the November 1988 elections, Democrats had 42 seats plus the rebellious "Gang of Five" who were no longer needed for a majority. The "Five" returned to the Democratic fold, and their punishments forgiven.

The Rules Committee in the Assembly is primarily a housekeeping group, assigning bills to committees, setting salaries for legislative employees, purchasing supplies, and handling routine resolutions.

Speakers come to power in two ways — by the members of the majority party or by coalition. Speaker Willie Brown formed a coalition with members of both parties in 1981.

In the Assembly the key committee is the Ways and Means Committee. It is the general clearing house for most bills before they reach the floor. This is because no measure with fiscal implications — most important bills — can go from a so-called policy committee directly to the floor.

Both houses have become more partisan in recent years. The Senate only a few decades ago paid little attention to party conflict, but the caucuses have become stronger and it is not unusual now to see party-line votes. Partisanship increased in the Assembly during the conservative Reagan and Deukmejian governorships. Further fomenting partisanship, party caucuses are active in campaigns for legislative seats, and their staffs are always at work digging up issues that could prove embarrassing to the opposition.

Legislation

There are three basic types of legislation: bills, constitutional amendments and resolutions. These measures can only be introduced by legislators. The governor cannot introduce a bill, but he can ask a friendly member to put it in the hopper. Even the governor's budget carries the name of a lawmaker. In fact, however, very few bills are the direct inspiration of a legislator. Most bills come from interest groups, staff members, constituents, government officials, and a variety of other sources.

A bill is simply a proposed statute. It can be enacted by a simple majority vote in both houses unless it is an urgency measure or carries an appropriation, in which case a two-thirds vote of approval is required. Constitutional amendments are proposed changes to the state Constitution; a two-thirds vote of each house will place one of these measures on the ballot for voter consideration. Resolutions are merely statements of legislative viewpoint. They may be addressed to other governmental agencies, describe state general policy, or commend or memorialize someone. They are

California's Legislative Process

Initial steps by author

IDEA

Sources of bills: legislators, legislative committees, governor, state and local governmental agencies, business firms, lobbyists, citizens.

DRAFTING

Formal copy of bill and "layman's digest" prepared by Legislative Counsel.

INTRODUCTION

Bill submitted by senator or Assembly member. Numbered and read for first time. Assigned to committee by Assembly or Senate Rules Committee. Printed.

Action in house of origin

COMMITTEE

Testimony taken from author, proponents and opponents. Typical actions: Do pass; amend and do pass; no action; hold in committee (kill); amend and re-refer to same committee; refer to another committee; send to interim study.

Bills with any fiscal implications, if approved by policy committee, are referred to Appropriations Committee in the Senate and to Ways and Means Committee in the Assembly.

SECOND READING

Bills given do-pass recommendations are read a second time and placed on file for debate.

FLOOR DEBATE AND VOTE

Bills are read a third time and debated. A roll-call vote follows. For ordinary bills, 21 votes are needed in the Senate and 41 in the Assembly. For urgency bills and appropriations measures, 27 and 54 votes are required. If these numbers are not reached, the bill is defeated. Any member may seek reconsideration and a second vote. If passed or passed with amendments, the bill is sent to the second house.

Disposition in second house

READING

Bill is read for the first time and referred to committee by the Assembly or Senate Rules Committee.

COMMITTEE

Procedures and possible actions are identical to those in the first house.

SECOND READING

If cleared by committee, the bill is read a second time and placed on the daily file (agenda) for debate and vote.

FLOOR DEBATE AND VOTE

The procedure is identical to the first house. If a bill is passed without having been amended in the second house, it is sent to the governor's desk. (Resolutions are sent to the secretary of state's office.) If amended in the second house and passed, the measure returns to the house of origin for consideration of amendments.

Resolution of two-house differences (if necessary)

CONCURRENCE

The house of origin decides whether to accept the second-house amendments. If the amendments are approved, the bill is sent to the governor. If the amendments are rejected, the bill is placed in the hands of a two-house conference committee composed of three senators and three Assembly members.

CONFERENCE

If the conferees fail to agree, the bill dies. If the conferees present a recommendation for compromise (conference report), both houses vote on the report. If the report is adopted by both, the bill goes to the governor. If either house rejects the report, a second (and even a third) conference committee may be formed.

Role of the governor

SIGN OR VETO?

Within 12 days after receiving a bill, the governor may sign it into law, allow it to become law without his signature or veto it. A vetoed bill returns to the house of origin for possible vote on overriding the veto. It requires a two-thirds majority of both houses to override.

Urgency measures become effective immediately after signing. Others usually take effect the following January 1st.

normally passed by voice vote. Constitutional amendments and resolutions, unlike bills, are not subject to gubernatorial veto.

Legislative process

When a member introduces a bill, its title is read and it is printed. Then it is assigned to a committee by the Assembly or Senate Rules Committee. The committee hearing is the most crucial stage in the legislative process, for it is at this point — not on the floor — that the fate of most legislation is determined. Following public hearing, the committee can kill the measure or send it to another committee (usually the fiscal committee) or to the floor as is or with recommended amendments. When it reaches the floor, the bill's title is read a second time, amendments are often made, and the legislation is placed on the agenda for debate. After debate, a roll call is taken. If the bill is passed, it is sent to the other house, where the same process takes place. If the bill is amended in the second house, it must return to the house of origin for acceptance or rejection of the amendments. If approved at this point, the bill goes to the governor for signature or veto. If the amendments are rejected, a conference committee of three members of each house is formed to compromise differences. This procedure is always followed on the budget and often used at the end of a session to speed the last-minute rush of bills (because a conference committee report can be produced more rapidly than a revised printed version of a bill). For the first time, the budget conference committee was opened to the public in 1974, and it was only a year later that conference-committee secrecy ended completely, as was inevitable once budget doors were opened.

A bill goes to the governor if both houses approve a conference committee recommendation.

In the Senate, roll calls are taken orally by the secretary of the Senate and aides. Once a roll call is concluded, members may not change their votes, and absent members cannot add their votes. The Assembly uses an electronic vote counter. Members push switches, and lights shine on a board — green reflecting aye; red, no. With the unanimous consent of the membership, members are allowed to change their votes the same day or add their votes if their actions do not alter the outcome.

Legislative modernization

Until 1966, the Legislature met for general sessions in odd-numbered years and for short budget sessions in even-numbered years. Legislators then received $6,000 a year, and their elective positions were not considered to be full-time occupations. In 1966, the voters approved Proposition 1a making each year's session unlimited, raising the pay to $16,000 and allowing lawmakers to give themselves cost-of-living increases of five percent a year. In the June 1990 primary election voters approved Prop. 112. While some of the provisions of this constitutional amendment established new ethics regulations, perhaps its key feature was the creation of a new Citizens' Compensation Commission. The reason this amendment was proposed was because the Legislature antagonized many votes when they would vote to increase their salaries. To deflect this criticism the commission was launched. In December 1991 the new commission raised salaries of state legislators from about $40,816 a year to $52,500. In addition, legislative leaders received extra compensation: floor leaders,

$57,750 each; and the Speaker and Senate President Pro Tem, each receive $63,000.

In 1972, the people approved another constitutional amendment. This one put the Legislature on the same two-year schedule as Congress, with bills remaining alive for two years. The Legislature now is in session year-round, with breaks for Easter, Christmas, half the summer and during statewide elections. In addition to their salaries, legislators receive $100 a day for expenses, use of leased automobiles, credit cards and district offices.

In addition to the standing committees, which consider the merits of bills, the Legislature also establishes two-house joint committees and one-house select committees to study specific problems (often of special concern to only one legislator, who becomes chairman of the committee). These committees can submit recommendations to the Legislature but have no direct power over legislation. Many of these select committees have been eliminated under the new budget strictures of Proposition 140.

Legislative staff

Each member of the Legislature has a personal staff plus the assistance of specialists assigned to committees and to the party caucuses. There are also three major independent bureaus with significant influence on the legislative process — the legislative analyst, the legislative counsel and the auditor general.

• *Legislative analyst*, Elizabeth Hill, provides advice to the Legislature on anything with a fiscal implication, which can cover virtually every major bill. The analyst annually publishes a detailed analysis of the governor's budget, which becomes the basis for legislative hearings on the fiscal program.

• *Legislative counsel*, Bion Gregory, has a large staff of attorneys to provide legal advice to lawmakers and draft their bills and proposed amendments.

• *Auditor general*, Kurt R. Sjoberg (acting), conducts investigations of state agencies to determine whether they can be run more economically and efficiently, he reports directly to the Joint Audit Committee and to the Legislature as a whole.

In all, a staff of some 2,000 served the Legislature until the passage of Prop. 140 in November 1990 which mandated term limits for members and budget reductions for the Legislature. The Legislature's staff is being reduced to comply with the measure. In addition to the analyst, auditor general, and counsel, there are sergeants-at-arms, secretaries, political aides, and committee consultants. The consultants are the most important element of the staff; they provide specialized knowledge for committees, gather information and provide independent evaluation of information obtained from interest groups, the governor and others.

Reapportionment

Almost nothing stirs the juices of a legislator — either at the state or federal level — as much as the prospect of his or her district being reapportioned. Whether as a result of court order or the federal census, redistricting has the potential of throwing many legislators out of office. The census is conducted every 10 years at the beginning of a new decade, and every congressional, Senate and Assembly district in California must be redrawn after each census to eliminate population differences.

California's Assembly districts have always been apportioned by population, but the state Senate has been apportioned under two systems. Prior to 1926, the Senate was also apportioned by population, but in that year the voters approved a "federal plan" devised by Northern Californians to keep control of the Senate from rapidly growing Southern California. This plan provided that no county could have more than one senator and that one senator could represent no more than three counties. As a result, the senator from Los Angeles at one time represented 440 times more people than the senator from Alpine, Inyo and Mono counties. This was the most severe apportionment imbalance in the nation. Such discrepancies were eradicated in 1966, when the U.S. Supreme Court's "one-man, one-vote" edict went into effect.

Redistricting is usually fairly simple if both houses of a legislature and the governor are of the same political party. The party in power merely divides the state to suit itself and gives the opposition party the scraps. The usual procedure is to offer some members of the opposition good deals so that a nominally bipartisan reapportionment bill can be passed. Actually, it is impossible to create good districts for one party without fashioning some just as good for the other. But the legislators doing the redistricting can usually pick and choose whom to favor among members of the opposition.

Under the state Constitution, the Legislature is empowered to reapportion all seats (52 in Congress, 40 Senate and 80 Assembly districts), subject only to a gubernatorial veto. Thus, when a governor is of a different party than the Legislature's leadership an impasse is apt to develop. In this case, either a bi-partisan plan is drawn favoring the incumbents of both parties, maintaining the status quo, or the matter ends up in the courts.

Republicans tried repeatedly in the 1980s to modify or change the way that reapportioning was to be determined. Their objective was to shift the decision making away from Democratic legislative leaders:

1) In 1982 Republicans joined with Common Cause and qualified Prop. 14 to establish an independent districting commission to do the reapportioning. Voters defeated the proposal.

2) In 1983 then Assemblyman Don Sebastiani qualified a new initiative which provided, he claimed, "fairer" districts than the one the Democrats had devised. This initiative was declared unconstitutional by the state Supreme Court prior to its being voted upon. The court ruled that reapportioning could take place only once each decade.

3) In 1984 Governor Deukmejian authored an initiative to have reapportioning handled by a panel of retired appellate judges. Voters rejected this proposal.

4) In June 1990 two Republican-backed reapportionment proposals qualified for the ballot. Prop. 118 would have required the reapportionment bills to be passed by a two-thirds (not simple majority) vote in each house. Prop. 119 was designed to establish an independent reapportionment commission appointed by retired appellate judges which would review plans presented by various citizen groups and choose the "best" plan. Both propositions lost.

Reapportioning for the 1990s was done by the Legislature — as usual. Democratic legislative leaders argue that the elected representatives of the people should make the reapportioning decisions — not an "independent" commission. Critics contend that allowing the Legislature to devise its election districts is like "putting the fox into the chicken coop." However the 1991 reapportionment plans passed by the Democratic-controlled Legislature were vetoed by Republican Pete Wilson with the result that districts were drawn by the state Supreme Court with the help of "special masters." The results will probably prove devastating to the Democrats in November 1992. 🏛

The luster is off the California model

By Richard Zeiger

Reprinted from *California Journal*, June 1990

I n the 1960s the late Jesse Unruh was in the forefront of a movement to "professionalize" state legislatures. The tenets were simple: Provide state lawmakers with more staff, better working conditions and adequate salaries. They then would be free from dependance on special-interest lobbyists or governors and become a truly co-equal branch of government.

California led the way, and the Legislature, under Unruh, produced a flurry of progressive laws that were the envy of statehouses throughout the nation. The reforms Unruh instituted, known as the "California model," were widely copied elsewhere.

But the changes also had unintended consequences, and California — still farther along the track than other states — is no longer viewed as a shining example. Now what light we shed is viewed more as a warning beacon: Go that way and you will crash upon the rocks.

The sins of the California model, as outlined at a recent conference of state officials sponsored by Rutgers University's Eagelton Institute of Politics, are many. All, however, are rooted in the notion that as legislatures became more professional, the legislators themselves became professionals. The notion of "citizen-lawmakers," who would perform a stint of public service in the capital and then return to their homes and their real jobs, was replaced by individuals who were making a career out of holding political office.

In a paper prepared for the conference, Burdett Loomis, a professor at the University of Kansas, notes that legislatures are "increasingly being populated by full-time, professional politicians whose well-being is directly tied to their success in their legislative careers." He notes that the number of state lawmakers who identify themselves as "full-time legislators" has increased four-fold in the years between 1976 and 1986, and even that figure "seriously underrepresents the number of full-time legislators."

The jobs have become valuable sinecures, and office-holders are preoccupied with keeping themselves in office. It's a task that comes before worrying about passing laws. As a result, legislators gradually transformed the tools called for in the California model into devices that could help win elections. Their staff mutated from non-partisan policy experts into political operatives whose real expertise was furthering the political ambitions of their bosses. Lawmakers spent more time worrying about elections, and less about the job of passing laws. They discovered they would raise money for campaigns from the groups that came to lobby at the Capitol, and the cost of running for office quickly expanded when they figured out that the person with the most money to spend, more often than not, would be the winner.

The advantage of incumbency made it easier for sitting legislators to hold on to office. But even though turnover dropped, the lack of serious challengers did not free lawmakers to vote their consciences. Rather, it resulted in a lack of political courage on the part of legislators who were nonetheless preoccupied with retaining their positions and were unwilling to take risky stands that might offend voters or big contributors. Furthermore, they were unwilling to risk a run for higher office, if that might jeopardize their current position. To run and lose meant to become unemployed.

Legislative leaders found their ability to control the process diminished as individual legislators learned to develop their own power bases, raise their own money, and reduce their dependency on the weakening political parties. They could no longer use their political muscle to force recalcitrant colleagues to go along with leadership's policy decisions.

Furthermore, as "careerism" becomes more dominant among legislators, lawmakers are looking for ways to distinguish themselves from their colleagues so that they may advance through their chosen profession, which can include putting pressure on legislative leaders to provide them with plum committee assignments and staff that can be used to increase their own viability.

Lawmakers discovered that while they may be individually popular in their own districts, the Legislature as a whole was not popular with voters. They could follow the example set by Ronald Reagan and others and run for election by complaining about the very institutions of which they were a part.

And in states like California that have the initiative process, lawmakers even moved outside the legislative arena, joining those who saw more hope of passing legislation by going directly to the voters rather than dealing with a fractionalized and uncertain legislative process. At the same time, sponsoring initiatives became a way for individual lawmakers to further distinguish themselves from their colleagues and perhaps advance their political careers.

Use of the initiative became a vicious cycle. It was needed because the Legislature refused to act. But lawmakers were unwilling to act, particularly if that entailed political risk, because divisive issues were headed for the ballot anyway. The increased use of the initiative further eroded the ability of leadership to shape state policy, and as the leadership becomes weaker, it is still harder to gain consensus on important issues.

The failure of state legislatures to come to grips with difficult problems has been reflected in opinion polls, which have shown a steady erosion of public confidence in state legislatures. In California, for example, the percentage of people having a favorable opinion of the Legislature has declined from 65 percent in 1968 to 36 percent last year.

Karl Kurtz, of the National Conference of State Legislatures, argued to the Rutgers symposium participants that maintaining confidence in legislatures is important.

"If legislatures do not have a certain minimum level of public support, laws will not be obeyed; the institution will be bypassed routinely by executive fiat, court order or voter initiative .... In short, public support provides legitimacy to the institution."

But if the public is unhappy with legislatures as institutions, that apparently does not extend to the lawmakers individually. Most polls continue to show members of the public happy with their own representative.

Kurtz explains, "The legislator has a friendly face, a human identity. Most legislators provide services to their constituents and community, and all of them are past masters at hiding or explaining their unpopular votes and taking credit for popular legislation. The legislature, on the other hand, is a faceless institution that raises taxes or cuts back services. The legislature, an anonymous abstraction, can be blamed for everything."

Participants in the symposium also blamed the news media for creating some of the problems. Reporters focus only on the problems and the scandals, participating legislators argued, and rarely for long on honest, but complicated attempts to solve problems. As a result, the public is exposed only to state legislatures that appear inept at best and corrupt at worst.

For the larger states, the "professional" legislature is a reality. And these states tended to look for reforms in the election process to ease the worst sins of the fully-evolved system.

Quite a bit of attention was focused on public financing of elections as a way to ease the burden of lawmakers who feel they must constantly raise money in order to be prepared for the next election. In addition, a substantial number of participants felt that longer terms would eliminate some of the pressure.

Also, lawmakers were urged to consolidate money-raising in the hands of legislative leaders, who could then distribute it where needed during election season. This would eliminate the need of most lawmakers to worry about raising money and strengthen the hands of leaders in dealing with the emerging entrepreneurship of individual legislators.

Ironically, that is precisely the system that had developed in California, but was dealt a setback by voters who approved Proposition 73 in 1988. That measure outlawed the transfer of money from one politician to another. The argument made by backers of the measure — three members of the state Legislature — was that leaders were exercising too much power and were dominating the process. If legislators raised their own money, they could vote their own consciences, the argument went.

Smaller states were urged to approach steps toward the California model with caution. Those which had a short legislative session were encouraged to keep them in order to make it easier for legislators to maintain their original occupations.

Staff should be kept under the control of legislative leaders, and preferably kept non-partisan, as a way of reducing temptations to have staff perform political tasks. In Connecticut, for example, all legislative staff is under the direction of a single, non-partisan executive director.

To boost public confidence in the legislative process, codes of ethics should be established and full disclosure should be made of all campaign contributions and lobbying expenses.

While representatives from the smaller states sometimes found it hard to believe they would end up going the way of California, they were often warned that the changes were inevitable unless specific steps were taken to stop the changes. Representatives from larger states warned that the changes would take place for one simple reason: In the political arena, winning elections comes first. And all the tools created for the full-time, professional legislature make winning elections easier. The temptation to use them that way is great, and incumbent lawmakers may find — as they have in California — they are impossible to resist. 🏛

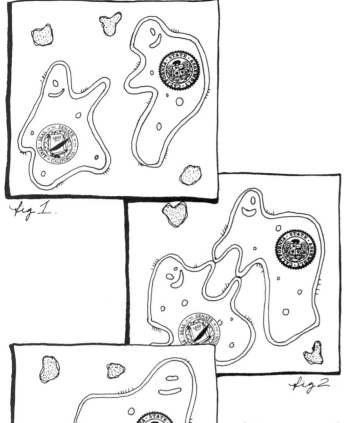

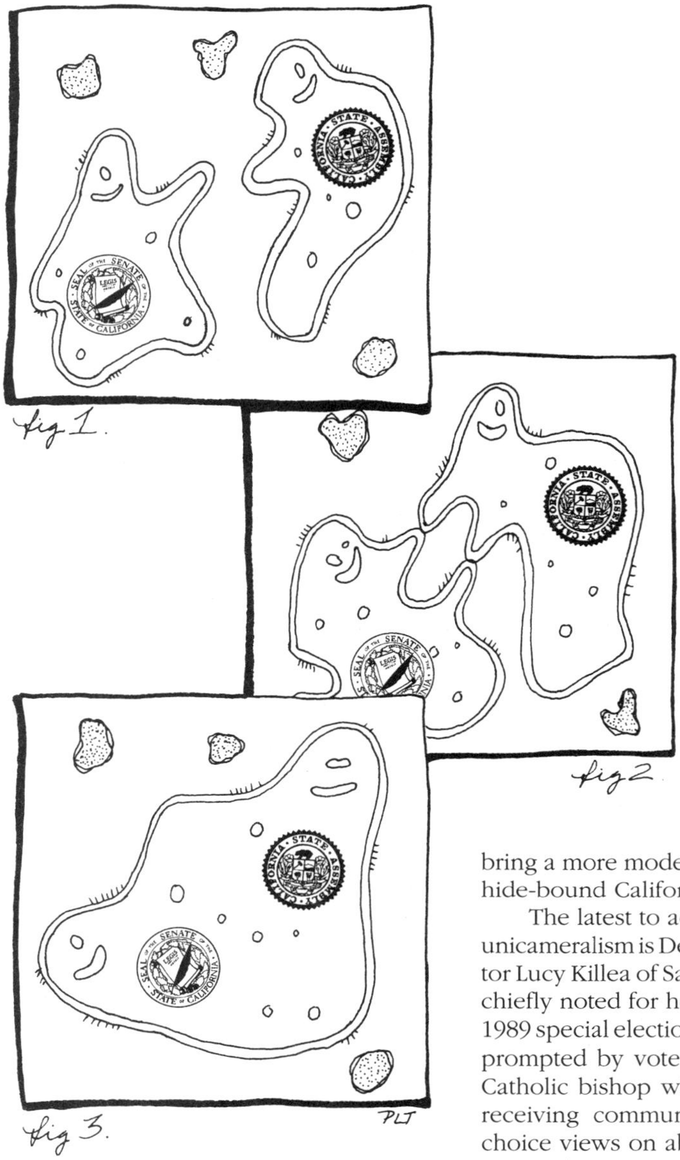

fig 1.

fig 2

fig 3.

PLT

The unicameral legislature

New look at an old idea

By Jim Richardson

Reprinted from *California Journal*, May 1991

Aunicameral legislature in California is an idea whose time probably has not come. But amid the ruin that is the California Legislature in the early going of the 1991-1992 session, that age-old idea has surfaced yet again — and not just among the political scientists who find the subject sport, but among the more cynical breed of lawmakers as well.

The outcome of their dialogue likely will not be a one-house Legislature in the foreseeable future, even its more candid proponents admit. But the discussion, some lawmakers believe, could

Jim Richardson is a reporter in The Sacramento Bee *Capitol bureau.*

bring a more modest *perestroika* to the hide-bound California Legislature.

The latest to advance the cause of unicameralism is Democratic state Senator Lucy Killea of San Diego, heretofore chiefly noted for her upset victory in a 1989 special election — an event in part prompted by voter reaction against a Catholic bishop who barred her from receiving communion over her pro-choice views on abortion.

In the spring of 1991, already frustrated in her new job, Killea busily stumped service clubs and lined up political scientists behind unicameralism. Killea proposes establishing a state constitutional revision commission to work out the details. She took a well-publicized trip to Nebraska, the only state with a unicameral legislature. Killea got a fair amount of news coverage on the issue, particularly in her hometown newspapers (where, perhaps not coincidentally, she has been floating the idea of running for mayor later this year).

"We have certainly ended up with gridlock rather than checks-and-balances," said Killea.

But the last thing some of the Legislature's weary leaders want to think

about is a major reform of their institution at a time when they are grappling with a $12 billion budget deficit and have district reapportionment looming just around the corner. Nor have legislative leaders recovered from the legal confusion of Proposition 73's campaign contribution limits, overturned after a long legal wrangle. They are still trying to get used to Proposition 112, a measure they successfully put forward — with varying degrees of enthusiasm — that drastically restricts gifts and bans honoraria for speeches. And legislative leaders are still in deep shock over term limits and accompanying severe budget cutting required by Proposition 140, approved by voters in November 1990.

"The Legislature can only take so much major restructuring," lamented Democratic Senate President pro Tempore David Roberti of Los Angeles, in an interview on Killea's unicameral proposal. "If every time you turn around there is another proposal to restructure the Legislature, quite frankly we'll never get anything done. At some time we have to concentrate on substantive issues."

Killea's argument is that the Legislature has not focused on substantive issues partly because the two houses are so different. Among the contributing factors to the paralyzing budget impasse of 1990, when the Legislature left the state without authority to spend money for nearly a month, was that the two houses could not reach agreement. Each house became consumed in its own politics. At one point, the Senate passed a budget and left town, leaving a fuming Assembly. One Assembly member had choice words for the Senate's action, calling it "dog doo" left on the front porch.

The idea of a unicameral legislature has a certain appeal — doing away with duplicative legislative functions, consolidating dual committees, bringing forth a degree of efficiency and accountability — to lawmaking. Killea maintains that the only thing stopping a unicameral legislature are "artificial reasons" for having two houses and institutional resistance to change.

"I think the sense of crisis around here is causing people to look at it more closely," said Killea. "What we have isn't working. There are a tremendous number of major issues we haven't been able to deal with even in a minor way."

She got a boost to the cause from no less than Republican John Larson on his way out the door as chairman of the state Fair Political Practices Commission. "You can hide too many things with the two houses here," he said in a newspaper interview endorsing unicameralism. "One house will give you anything you want, knowing the other is going to throw it right in the river."

Killea is not the first to push the unicameral idea. Between 1913 and 1937 there were no fewer than 15 proposed constitutional amendments on the subject put forward by California legislators. The idea was revived in the 1970s by the most successful legislator of the modern era — the late Assembly Speaker Jesse Unruh. But 11 such proposed amendments got nowhere.

"The present two-house system is a costly and inefficient anachronism that thwarts the popular will, caters to private interests and hobbles responsible and responsive decision-making," Unruh said in a widely quoted speech. "Unless unicameralism is made central to the present efforts to reform and modernize state legislatures, I do not believe that increased salaries, new facilities, and professional staff will be more than temporary pal-liatives for the ills that it is hoped they will cure. These reforms in themselves only make a more efficient horse and buggy. I take little comfort from the fact that legislatures can be the fastest horse and buggy in the jet age."

Picking up the mantle, Democratic Assemblyman Tom Bane of Tarzana, now the powerful chairman of the Assembly Rules Committee, tried pushing a unicameral legislature in 1975. His bill was approved by a committee dominated by rebels to then Speaker Leo McCarthy. But it went no further. "Some of the people voted for it just because they wanted to have fun," Bane recently recalled.

The current majority and minority leaders of the state Senate, Democrat Barry Keene of Benicia and Republican Kenneth Maddy of Fresno also pushed unicameral bills in the 1970s and early '80s. Keene and Maddy have signed on as co-authors to Killea's bill.

"There's no reason to have two houses," said Maddy, adding he sees "no chance" for Killea's bill (a reality making it easier to support).

In advancing her bill, Killea took a different approach than in earlier efforts. She proposes increasing the size of the Legislature — although she has not suggested exactly to what size. In effect, Killea proposes giving legislators smaller districts, an idea attractive to many who are otherwise loath to a single-house legislature.

Smaller districts are harder to gerrymander. The cost of getting elected theoretically would be less and serving a smaller number of constituents would be easier. Also, the argument goes, with so many more representatives in the Legislature, it would be harder for a narrow special interest to buy or influence enough votes to dominate an issue.

"There is some logic to that," said Senator William Leonard of Red-lands, the second ranking Republican. Although he calls unicameral-ism a "stupid idea," Leonard likes the idea of a bigger Legislature with smaller districts. However, he points out, smaller districts could be achieved without a single-house legislature. Leonard suggested increasing the size of the Assembly by a three- or four-to-one ratio with the Senate instead of the current two-to-one ratio.

Leonard said that despite predictions to the contrary, the Assembly and Senate have each maintained a distinctive character even after court decisions put Senate districts on the same one-person, one-vote basis as Assembly districts. "Here, theoretically, we should all be duplicates of each other. We're not. And I think that's healthy. That means each of us is looking through different eyes at these same bills to see if they read the same way to each of us."

Maddy, however, said that in reality, the Legislature has killed few bills. Roughly 5000 bills per session landed on then-Governor George Deukmejian's desk and there is no sign the number will be appreciably smaller for Governor Pete Wilson. "There is really not a 'check-and-balance' between the two houses," said Maddy. "The trial lawyers are just as strong over there as they are here. They're not checked-and-balanced."

Lawmakers maintain publicly that they have an open mind toward Killea's proposal. However, many say privately — and a few will say publicly — that the real value to her proposal is in spurring a discussion of the Legislature's unwieldy rules.

Roberti and many Democrats have long argued that the single largest impediment to lawmaking is not the dual-house system but the rule that the state budget must be approved by a two-thirds vote in each house. The rule has allowed a small minority of Republicans — sometimes only in one house — to thwart the will of the majority.

The two-thirds vote rule, however, has been next to godliness and the line-item veto in sanctity with Republicans, who have been in the minority in both houses of the Legislature for 20 years. However, some Republicans have begun to change their minds, partly spurred by the discussion over the unicameral proposal. The two-thirds vote has fostered a mentality of being a permanent minority, and in their view, allowed Democrats to escape responsibility for their actions.

"I think we lose in the public relations image every year," said Leonard. "We say we are holding out for something to fill in the blank. The public doesn't buy it. I'm almost of the opinion of saying, 'Look-it, you Democrats, there's a $12 billion problem — you want to run it? Here, you put it out by majority vote. Don't count on me to vote aye."

Then, Leonard suggests, Republicans will be in better position to run for office and become the majority party. "Do you like this? If not, vote for me."

And that suits Roberti fine. "Right now everybody can legitimately confuse the issue as where responsibility lies," said the Senate's top leader. 🏛

EXPORTING DISCONTENT

Term limits: California's gift (?) to the nation

**By Charles Price
and Helen Neves**

Reprinted from *California Journal*, December 1991

"Restriction upon the succession of incumbents serves a rational public policy. This may deny qualified men an opportunity to serve, [but] as a general rule the overall health of the body politic is enhanced by limitations on continuous tenure. ... [The state has a legimate interest in] protecting against an entrenched, dynastic legislative bureaucracy."

— Chief Justice Malcolm Lucas, writing for the majority in *Legislature of the State of California v. March Fong Eu*, October 11, 1991.

I f those words were noise, they would be the brief hiss of a candle flame being snuffed out against a damp thumb. If they were an episode of "The Twilight Zone," they would be an unthinkable nightmare become reality. For with those words, a six-to-one majority of the California Supreme Court upheld Proposition 140. With those words, the best hope of lawmakers for political life everlasting flickered out; there would be no judicial reprieve from career-ending term limits imposed by voters in November 1990.

The Court's sweeping decision validated nearly every provision of Proposition 140, the brainchild of former Republican Los Angeles County Supervisor Pete Schabarum:

• It upheld term limits, with members of the Assembly limited to three terms or six years; senators, constitutional officers and Board of Equalization members limited to two terms or eight years.

• It agreed that Proposition 140 imposes a lifetime ban; once an elected official has "maxxed out" in a particular office, he or she may never again run for that same position.

• It upheld a provision that slashed the Legislature's budget by 40 percent.

Charles Price is a political science professor at California State University, Chico, and a frequent contributor to California Journal. *Helen Neves is a doctoral student in public administration at the University of Southern California. This article is a shortened version of a paper presented by Professor Price at the National Term Limits Conference, September 1991, hosted by the Rockefeller Institute, State University of New York at Albany.*

In fact, the Court only overturned that part of Proposition 140 that eliminated the state legislators' pension system.

Legislature v. Eu was the nation's first judicial test case of state legislative term limits, and the California Court's decision adds impetus to similar efforts in other states. Although the decision will be appealed to the U.S. Supreme Court, the odds that a conservative U.S. Supreme Court will overturn a decision of the conservative California Supreme Court seems unlikely.

Term limits are not new to American politics. Some states limit the number of terms their governors may serve, and the 22nd Amendment to the U.S. Constitution has limited every president since Dwight Eisenhower to two terms. But until 1990 term limits had never been imposed on state legislatures. Last year, however, first in Oklahoma and later in California and Colorado, term-limit advocates were able to qualify ballot initiatives later approved by state voters. The California ballot boasted two different term-limit initiatives in November 1990.

With the success in California, term limits became more than a local cause; it became a movement that threatened to stride colossus-like across the country. Just last month, however, the movement suffered its first setback as Washington state voters defeated what would have been the toughest term-limit measure yet. Speaker of the House Tom Foley helped spearhead the drive to defeat Washington's initiative, arguing that term limits on members of Congress would permanently eliminate the state's ability to amass seniority — and, therefore, power — and put Washington at the mercy of other states. Opponents also played upon Washingtonians' dislike for things California, pointing out that term-limits was just one more Golden State import they could do

Legislative wanna-be

Sitting legislators weren't the only ones whose futures were changed by the recent California Supreme Court ruling on Proposition 140, the term-limits initiative. The political aspirations of many legislative wanna-bes also may have ended when a six-to-one majority of the Court upheld the constitutionality of Proposition 140 last October.

In recent years, many of those wanna-bes have come from the ranks of legislative staff and others with years of behind-the-scenes training in Sacramento. Many of them intended to parlay their insider knowledge of state government into long-term careers as Assembly or Senate members.

But with Proposition 140 now firmly in place, with its limits on both legislative terms and budgets, that career path is rapidly losing its luster.

"Now," said David Takashima, chief of staff for Democratic Assemblyman Steve Peace of Rancho San Diego, "it doesn't make any sense to run for elected office."

That sentiment runs to the heart of Proposition 140, which was designed to evict incumbents and prevent would-be candidates from regarding a seat in the Legislature as the political equivalent of university tenure. Barring a successful appeal to the U.S. Supreme Court blocking term limits, 80 members of the Assembly and 40 members of the Senate will find themselves displaced in less than a decade.

While the Court has ruled that current lawmakers may keep their pensions, those elected in the future won't get that pork. That, says Takashima, is a financial burden too heavy for him to bear. "I have two young children to support, and eventually I want to send them to college," says the 41-year-

old, 15-year veteran of the Legislature's staff. "Without a pension, I wouldn't be able to do that."

Lobbyist Bruce Pomer, a former candidate for the Sacramento City Council, says he also has changed his mind about vying for a seat in the Legislature. Pomer, 42, who represents the Health Officers Association and is a community college trustee, last year considered launching a campaign for the Sixth Assembly District in Sacramento, now held by Democrat Lloyd Connelly. Pomer has since abandoned the idea.

"Proposition 140 wipes out any interest I'd have in running for office," he said. "I thought by some time in my career I could devote my life to public service. But you don't get good at something unless you're there for a while."

In ruling Proposition 140 constitutional, the California Supreme Court declared that it sought to "protect against entrenched, dynastic legislative bureaucracy." Sacramento consultants, however, say the Court may have inadvertently slashed the pool of qualified candidates, abandoning the Legislature to those wealthy enough to dabble in politics as a hobby.

Eventually, these consultants predict, California's Legislature — made up of the marginally employed and retired — will resemble the one that existed before 1967, when Proposition 1A created a paid, fulltime governing body.

Chris Elliott is a writer with the California News Service, a project of the U.C. Berkeley graduate school of Journalism.

---

without. Thus, the defeat in Washington may not have stopped the term-limit movement, merely slowed it down.

Oklahoma, Colorado, California and Washington are in the vanguard of the term-limits movement because they are initiative states, four of the 23 mainly Western states where adopting laws and/or constitutional amendments is not the exclusive province of the legislature and governor. But the movement has not caught fire everywhere. Not surprisingly, it has exhibited little clout in non-initiative states or at the federal level since few legislatures would impose term limits on themselves. It also has not fared well in initiative states where there is no provision for putting constitutional amendments on the ballot, or where initiatives rarely qualify for the ballot. Elsewhere, however, the movement is full steam ahead, and term-limits proposals soon may appear on ballots in Oregon, Montana, North Dakota and Arizona. Once again, for good or bad, California is on the cutting edge of the latest political "reform."

Why the sudden interest in term limits?

For one thing, voter frustration appears to be at an all-time high, thanks to what seems like an endless chronicle of less-than-upstanding behavior by elected officials over the last several years. At the federal level, voters have endured the Iran-Contra hearings, the savings-and-loan and banking scandals, bounced checks and other congressional "perks," finessed pay raises, negative political campaigns and the

sordid Clarence Thomas Senate confirmation hearings, among other things. At the state level, voters have been deluged with FBI sting investigations in a number of states that have uncovered considerable official corruption. In addition, partisan gerrymandering has produced professional state legislatures that are often wasteful and overstaffed. In California, the Legislature frequently is gridlocked by free-spending special interests unwilling to compromise. Thus, an increasing number of complicated issues are presented to voters via ballot initiatives. All this has helped to produce a growing anti-incumbent mood among the electorate.

Sensing this mood, national organizations such as Americans to Limit Congressional Terms, Citizens for Congressional Reform and Americans Back in Charge have taken an active role in promoting term limits as a viable reform. While these groups strive to present a bipartisan image, conservative Republicans are often their mainstays. Term limits, Republicans believe, is their best hope to wrest control of Congress and other state legislatures from Democrats.

Thus far, the impact of term limits in Oklahoma, California and Colorado has varied. In Oklahoma, political scientist Gary Copeland says that most Oklahoma legislators have given little thought to their term cap because they may serve up to 12 years, which means they may stay in office until 2002. Also, the Oklahoma Legislature is part-time and non-professional, so most lawmakers serve only a few terms

say, "No, thanks!"

By Chris Elliott

"It's asking a lot of these candidates to take six years off, and then to have them rebuild their business after that," said Jon Kaufman, executive vice president of Solem and Associates, a San Francisco-based consulting firm. "I think Proposition 140 will discourage interest in public service and good government."

Maybe yes, maybe no. But the possibility that the pipeline of Sacramento-savvy candidates could run dry has some insiders worried.

"Where will tomorrow's legislators come from?" said Bob Schmidt, a public relations consultant in Sacramento. "It's a legitimate question, and it's a cause for grave concern."

One theory holds that local office will once again become the most important route to the Legislature. "You're not going to have the youngish, 30s, Sacramento-trained people running for office any more," says Tony Quinn, a political consultant for Braun Ketchum Public Relations and a former Republican legislative staffer.

In addition, Quinn and other consultants say, members of school boards, city councils or supervisorial boards — particularly women — who never aspired to more ambitious office before term limits are now likely to see a stint in Sacramento as an option.

Anecdotal evidence suggests, however, that neither local officeholders nor legislative staffers who want to take advantage of the legislative housecleaning are prepared to commit themselves just yet. Their reluctance, of course, is only compounded by uncertainty about reapportionment as the courts and the Legislature struggle over where new district boundaries will be drawn.

"Proposition 140 might give me a reason not to run now and see what comes up in the future," said Hunt Braly, 36, chief of staff for GOP state Senator Ed Davis of Chatsworth. In 1990 Braly challenged incumbent GOP Assemblywoman Cathie Wright but lost in the June primary.

Because term limits give would-be candidates a fighting chance against the better-established incumbents, Braly says Proposition 140 is healthy in principle. At the same time, he adds, "It makes it easier for someone in my position not to run now because I know the opportunity will be there again."

Kim Mueller, a member of the Sacramento City Council, says she is in no hurry to trade her council seat — which is not subject to term limits — for one in the Assembly.

"At this point, I'm going to wait," she said. "If I were to run, I'd take a good, long look at it."

Mueller, 34, a former volunteer and member of the city's toxics commission, says she does not regard politics as a way to pay her bills and, as a result, is not dissuaded by Proposition 140.

"I don't dream of being in office all of my life," she said.

Nor does Sacramento City Councilman Josh Pane. After his first term on the council ends, he said, he may seek a seat in the California Senate regardless of Proposition 140.

"If you're successful before you go in, you'll be successful when you get out," said Pane, 32. "The system needs revitalization. It needs new blood. I think Proposition 140 is worth it." 🏛

---

anyway. Colorado (and Washington, had it passed) limits not only state elected officials but congressmen as well. Moreover, in Washington term limits would have applied retroactively. Thus, House Speaker Foley could have run for only one more term (1992-94) before being forced to retire. That provision gave Foley and other opponents plenty of ammunition in their successful battle to defeat the initiative. One legal question that federal courts may someday be asked to resolve regarding term limits involves congressional seniority. Since seniority is critically important in Congress, do congressional term limits in some states violate citizens' equal protection?

In California, the impact of Proposition 140 is already being felt even though term limits themselves will not take effect on present incumbent legislators until 1996. A number of legislators have been scouting out other occupations. For example, former Assembly Speaker pro Tempore Mike Roos of Los Angeles left last spring to head up an education-reform consortium in his home city. Others are casting covetous eyes toward Congress. To that end, for the first time in several decades Democratic legislative leaders did not allow senior Democratic congressmen to draw the lines of congressional districts. Legislators reserved that right for themselves, mostly to suit their own ambitions rather than protect incumbent members of Congress.

"It would be naive to think that many are not eying new congressional seats [to escape] term limits," said veteran state Senator Bill Craven, a Southern California Republican.

In addition, the legislative budget reduction of nearly 40 percent has already meant that scores of staff have been eliminated or have retired early in order to receive a generous severance payment. According to some observers, legislative staff has been seriously compromised by the exodus. As Senate Republican leader Ken Maddy noted: "It is my opinion that the political hacks on the staff of legislative leaders should have been the first to go. They would not be missed." Unfortunately, political operatives remained on staff for the most part. Those who left tended to be nonpartisan technical staff.

Proposition 140 also affected all constitutional officers except for the new elective position of insurance commissioner and state judges. For the most part, Proposition 140's limits on these officials will have a relatively minor impact on governor, lieutenant governor, attorney general or controller because there has always been an unofficial two-term tradition for these offices. Only rarely has an incumbent in one of these postions served more than two terms. (An exception is Lieutenant Governor Leo McCarthy, re-elected to a third term in 1990). However, less-visible officials such as the secretary of state, treasurer or members of the Board of Equalization will be affected because incumbents in these offices sometimes hold office for extended periods. For instance, Secretary of State March Fong Eu has held office since 1974.

In order to better understand the future impact on the California Legislature of Proposition 140, legislators were surveyed on their attitudes toward this initiative. In all, some 34 legislators (about 30 percent) responded. Whether the 34 legislator respondents were representative of the general membership generally is problematic. It is probably true that those who despised the initiative were more likely to respond than supporters of the measure. Nevertheless, the size of the sample assures a diversity of views on the subject.

• In the November 1990 general election did you support, oppose or remain neutral on Proposition 140?

	Supported	Opposed	Neutral or ?
Democrats	0	19	0
Republicans	2	7	1
Independents*	0	5	0
Total	2	31	1

(* Senator Quentin Kopp is the only independent in the Legislature, although he may be joined by Senator Lucy Killea, who has left the Democratic Party and will be running as an independent in the 1992 election. Several other legislators returned their questionnaires anonymously and did not want to be identifed personally or by party. They have been listed as independents.)

Not surprisingly, the overwhelming majority of California legislators opposed Proposition 140 and campaigned actively against it. Several legislators did not publicly oppose it because they were afraid voters would take it out on them at the polls or because, as Senator Kopp put it, "It would have been self-serving to [publicly] oppose it."

Republican Craven opposed the measure, saying that it was vindictive. He said that Proposition 140 "places legislators in the same category as felons. In their case, they have a prohibition from running, and we are prohibited for life for running for the same office."

Democratic Senator Mike Thompson said Proposition 140 was not needed because California already had term limits — "elections." Veteran Republican Assemblyman Stan Statham argued, "[under Proposition 140] you'll have two kinds of legislators: those who are learning and those who are leaving." Taking the opposite view, Republican Assemblyman Chris Chandler contended, "The only way we have of moving away from a fulltime, life-term Legislature is by the artificial means of term limitation."

Most legislators surveyed were convinced that Proposition 140 would lead to considerable internal turmoil because members will lack experience, and the massive constant turnover will make it impossible for the Legislature to work effectively.

Said Democratic Assemblyman Sal Cannella, "If we have nearly 80 new people showing up in the Assembly on the 6th of January 1996, nobody will know what they're supposed to do. There will be no continuation of government. There will be no understanding of policy or legislative tradition. What are the rules? Who is going to be the speaker or the committee chairs?"

Many legislators emphasized that it take time to learn the legislative job. Maddy stated, "It takes four to five years in the

Senate before you become a truly effective senator."

Echoing this theme, Democratic Assemblyman Rusty Areias noted: "This is a pretty complicated place — a $55-billion dollar budget, 128 different departments and agencies. [New legislators] may be able to get a few things done in their second term, and then in their third term they'll be looking around for another job."

Added Assemblyman Statham, "Only legislators who have been here awhile can stand up to the special interests."

Democratic Assemblyman Ted Lempert noted: "One of the first things I did when I first came up here was to look for members I could trust on certain issues....I wonder if I were coming here in 1996 as a new legislator, who could I turn to in the Legislature? Would I have to turn to someone in the administration?"

However, Chandler felt that expertise was overrated. "I think if we had more legislators listening to what the people want, we'd be a lot better off. Name one thing these expert legislators have come up with over the last 10 years."

Proposition 140 wasn't the only term-limit proposal last November; there was also the less-Draconian Proposition 131, a campaign-finance/term-limits initiative authored by former Democratic Attorney General John Van de Kamp.

• Did you support, oppose or take no position on Proposition 131?

	Supported	Opposed	Neutral or ?
Democrats	4	11	4
Republicans	3	7	0
Independents	2	1	2
Total	9	19	6

While there was greater support for Proposition 131 among legislators, most were strongly opposed to it as well. Its only senatorial proponent, Senator Killea, stated, "I wasn't seeking a lifelong career." While agreeing with the concept of term limits, Killea felt those imposed by Proposition 140 were too short.

"Term limits of 10 to 15 years would allow enough time for sufficient experience and would provide for more gradual changes in the members of the legislative body," Killea said.

• If Proposition 140's term limits had been in effect when you first ran for the Legislature, would you still have run?

	Yes	No	Neutral or ?
Democrats	9	7	3
Republicans	5	4	1
Independents	4	0	1
Total	18	11	5

Most legislators conceded that even if Proposition 140 had been in effect when they first ran for the Legislature, they would have run anyway. However, a substantial number indicated they wouldn't have sought legislative office.

"It was hard for me to leave the security of the attorney general's office," said Democratic Assemblyman Xavier

Becerra, who was elected in 1990.

Said Democratic Assemblywoman Delaine Easton, "I was working for a large corporation, and it would have been difficult to sacrifice the benefits and ladder-climbing opportunites for a dead-end job."

Blue collar legislator Sal Cannella noted: "I worked in a factory for 30 years before I came here. I had to give up everything when I was elected. I don't go back and pick up the 30 years of seniority I had in that job... People who own businesses or are in the professions can put those positions on hold and go back to them after they leave the Legislature. Those who favor Proposition 140 keep talking about bringing back a citizen-legislature. That's baloney. The citizen is the blue-collar person working in a factory, driving a bus or teaching school and they can't just go back to their jobs again after serving in the Legislature."

- Do you think that term limits will mean a reduction in the quality of people running for the state Legislature?

	Yes	No	Neutral or ?
Democrats	9	6	4
Republicans	2	3	5
Independents	1	1	3
Total	12	10	12

While there was sharp disagreement whether there would be fewer quality legislators in the post-Proposition 140 Legislature, many lawmakers were convinced that, as Senator Thompson put it, "There will be more wealthy people running for office because they can afford it, or retired [people] because they have the time."

Democratic Senator Barry Keene thought there would be fewer lawyer-legislators. However, Maddy predicted that private institutions such as utilities, banks, labor unions and possibly law firms will furlough people to run, thus having "their representative" in office. On the other hand, Republican Senator Marian Bergeson, who opposed term limits, said, "It would give more women a chance to get elected."

- Under Proposition 140, will the Legislature have more difficulty being a co-equal branch with the governor?

	Yes	No	Neutral or ?
Democrats	18	0	1
Republicans	7	3	0
Independents	2	1	2
Total	27	4	3

Most legislators were convinced that the Legislature would have greater difficulty standing up to the governor under Proposition 140. A few disagreed. Kopp, for instance, argued that "both legislators and governors face term limits under Proposition 140. Power will not inevitably flow to the governor and his administration." Several legislators contended, however, that to be effective as a co-equal branch, the Legislature must speak with a collective voice. But, they warned, this will be difficult with virtually no experienced legislators.

- Under Proposition 140, will the Legislature be more dependent on lobbyists?

	Yes	No	Neutral or ?
Democrats	18	0	1
Republicans	7	2	1
Independents	5	0	0
Total	30	2	2

Clearly, legislators were convinced that lobbyists who comprise the "third house" would become more influential under Proposition 140. As one legislator put it, "There are no term limits on lobbyists." And, because the Legislature is short-handed on staff, some lobbyists are already stepping into the breech by assuring legislators who "carry" their bills that the lobbyist will do all the mundane details — contacting members of the appropiate committees, furnishing expert witnesses at hearings and resolving conflicts. Although senior lobbyists will be forced to get to know the new "revolving-door" legislators, Craven noted: "Absent competent, experienced staff, the members of the Legislature must depend more heavily upon third-house information to get a grasp on the matters at hand. We will have less opportunity ... to give total analysis and research to the issues in an objective manner."

However, Chandler disagreed, saying, "This all fits into this terrible, trite, knee-jerk, business-as-usual mentality that is unfortunate. If every legislator voted as if this were his last term, this would be a better and more responsive place."

- Was reapportionment complicated this year by Proposition 140?

	Yes	No	Neutral or ?
Democrats	17	1	1
Republicans	5	3	2
Independents	2	1	2
Total	24	5	5

Most legislators agreed that Proposition 140 complicated reapportionment this year because so many state legislators were interested in running for Congress to avoid term limits. Statham noted, "For the first time in California's history, assemblymen and senators are more interested in drawing congressional lines than state legislator lines." Clearly, too, all elected officials higher up on the political foodchain will have to be warier in coming years. The ambitious below them — who, in the past, may have been content to move up the legislative ladder — may now feed their ambitions by challenging incumbents.

Craven summed up legislators' views of Proposition 140's impact by quoting Alexander Hamilton: "Nothing appears more plausible at first sight, nor more ill-founded upon close inspection." Added Craven, "When you limit a term, you also limit the interest and the feeling of responsibility in the elected official. I believe the public is best served when they hang the proverbial Sword of Damocles immediately above the legislator's temple. Legislators, in turn, then very obviously recognize that if they do not perform appropiately, the electorate will cut the cord." 🏛

Senate President pro Tempore David A. Roberti, the son of an Italian immigrant tailor, has survived at the pinnacle of power in California for more than 11 years. A shy, introspective liberal, Roberti has fought off challenges from Republican foes and Democratic rivals alike.

Now, however, a court-ordered reapportionment plan and voter-approved term limits are conspiring to bring his Senate career to a sudden end.

By an odd twist of fate, the Senate's most powerful politician has been forced to run a special election in a new district in order to retain his job for another two-and-a-half years. If he wins, the Los Angeles senator may very well be the first legislator forced out of office by the term limits of Proposition 140.

At the age of 52, the rumpled, pragmatic Roberti has spent nearly half his life in the California Legislature representing the Hollywood district where he grew up. Often underestimated by his foes, he has battled governors, helped shape the state budget and pushed through major legislation to aid the homeless, care for children and ban assault rifles.

Yet despite his tremendous influence over the lives of Californians, Roberti is hardly a household name. His power rivals that of Assembly Speaker Willie Brown, but Roberti has been overshadowed for years by the flamboyant San Francisco Democrat who leads the lower house.

"He has always smarted from standing in the shadow of Willie Brown," said Republican U.S. Senator John Seymour, who, as a state senator, often tangled with Roberti. "Willie's style is so flashy. David is not that kind of leader. He is soft-spoken, quiet and consider-

Richard C. Paddock is a reporter for The Los Angeles Times *who spent eight years covering the state Capitol. He is now based in San Francisco.*

DAVID ROBERTI FACES THE END

The mixed legacy of a practical politician

By Richard C. Paddock

Reprinted from *California Journal*, March 1992

ate. He works to build consensus."

Roberti took power in the Senate in a 1980 coup when he put together a slim majority of Democratic senators to elect him president pro tem. In recent years, however, the coalition Roberti built has been tainted by scandal as three of his original supporters have been snared in a federal corruption probe.

Former Senators Alan Robbins, Joseph Montoya and Paul Carpenter — all Los Angeles County Democrats who held important posts under Roberti — have been found guilty or confessed to using their Senate positions to extract money from citizens seeking legislative action.

Despite the fall of his three allies, Roberti has remained aloof from the scandal. Rather than admitting any share of responsibility, Roberti points to the limits of his power and the fragile nature of his leadership position.

"There are only so many people you can treat as pariahs," he said. "If you don't get their votes and can't put majorities together, that gets heavy criticism, too—or the loss of my job."

Now Roberti's job is in jeopardy and, ironically, it is the corruption scandal that has given him the chance of saving his post, at least temporarily.

Under the 1992 reapportionment plan approved by the California Supreme Court, Roberti's Senate seat will vanish with most of its residents divided up among three other districts. By chance, one of the new districts housing some of Roberti's former constituents will be the seat that Robbins vacated last fall in disgrace. A special election will be held in April to fill Robbins' term, and Roberti is running for it.

Should he win, however, Roberti will become the first victim of the state's new term limits. Although the seat will be up in 1994, it will count as his second term under Proposition 140, forcing him to leave the Legislature two years ahead of any other lawmaker.

"Proposition 140 has made us all face our mortality," Roberti said.

In many respects, Roberti is a paradox in power. He is a very private person, yet he has chosen a career where he is constantly in the public eye. A lawyer, he has succeeded in a cutthroat business, but he is a soft-hearted man who stops his car to help injured animals he sees on the road. He is one of the most liberal members of the

Legislature, but he has subordinated his personal views to maintain his position as leader of the fundamentally conservative Senate—a body so traditional that men are not even allowed in the door without a coat and tie.

Short and heavyset, with a prominent nose and beady eyes, Roberti looks more like a large, lumbering teddy bear than a power broker. He has none of the polish or boyish good looks of politicians in the television age. Roberti describes himself as "the world's most unphotogenic person."

"He certainly would not be central casting's pick for president of the Senate," said former Senator Robbins before he pleaded guilty to corruption charges. "The reason David is pro tem, and stays pro tem, is that he is a superb strategist and an excellent mediator."

The key to Roberti's success is his willingness to seek compromise among the members of his house.

"He's the ultimate pragmatist," said one former staff member who asked not to be identified. "I think for him it's maintaining power that motivates him. I think getting something for his political agenda is definitely secondary. It's the first thing that goes when times are tough."

U nlike the Assembly, where Brown often exercises unilateral authority, the Senate is governed by a five-member Rules Committee chaired by Roberti. Such a system nearly always dictates that he exercise leadership by building consensus among his colleagues.

"The whole business of government, " Roberti says, "is creating majorities."

Senators, by virtue of their longer terms and large districts, are a diverse group of lawmakers who like to maintain their independence. To describe the challenge of leading such a group, one legislator offered his Theory of Senators as Walruses:

"They each sit on top of their own rock, protecting their turf," the lawmaker explained. "They don't run around much, but they roar when anybody gets close. David has figured out a way to move all these mighty walruses off their rocks on occasions."

Roberti sees it as his job to forge agreements even if he does not personally agree with the final result. For example, in last year's tumultuous budget negotiations, Roberti helped put

together a deal that included an historic cutback in welfare benefits. Although Roberti personally opposed the cuts, he argued that it was the best compromise that could be reached. He pushed the bill through his house and voted for it himself.

"It's a vote I'm sure that he cast with a lot of bile in his mouth," said June Roberti, his wife, longtime supporter and social conscience.

Roberti is aided by a low-key personal style that other members of the Senate seldom find threatening. He is mild-mannered, even humble, and he has a sense of humor about himself that keeps him from taking his job too seriously. A loner by nature, he often seems awkward and detached. But when he cares about an issue, he can be a surprisingly powerful orator.

"People underestimated him," said Los Angeles City Councilman Michael Woo, a former aide to Roberti. "There's almost a change of personality he goes through when you see him sitting in his chair on the Senate floor, then he stands up and gives an exciting, charismatic speech."

In the Senate, he rarely presides over meetings and seldom rises to impose his will on his colleagues. Instead, he sits quietly at his desk in a back corner of the Senate floor, often deep in thought or talking quietly to senators who stop by his desk seeking favors or support.

Roberti is skilled at understanding what his members want and giving them enough to keep them from getting restless.

"I think he is a master of inside politics, the politics of 40 personalities," one former staff member said. "I don't think he's distracted by the large picture. He studies each member and understands what they want. Once he understands what they want, it's not too hard to make sure they get it."

Often that can mean something as simple as assignment to a particular committee or, more important, a chairmanship. Roberti has made that easy by establishing 30 separate standing and select committees, ensuring that there are plenty of plum positions to go around. He also has succeeded in placating his membership by doling out new staff positions to those who are disgruntled.

"I think his leadership is characterized by acceptance of diversity, the assertion of strength at the right time, a very finely tuned political acumen," said Senate Majority Leader Barry Keene of Benicia. "He recognizes the individual political needs of senators who come from districts that are different from his. And yet, when it's necessary to put together that consensus, he can be very forceful."

During his tenure as leader, Roberti has had some success in pushing his personal agenda. He has won passage of legislation creating after-school child housing assistance to the homeless. He played a key part in battling the National Rifle Association and winning passage of a measure to ban assault rifles.

However, he has not done as well with other matters that are important to him, such as prohibiting abortion — an issue on which he disagrees with many of his fellow Democrats. But he is philosophical about what he can accomplish.

"I can do an awful lot here, even if it's just building consensus," he said, "because even in building consensus you can move the world a little bit in the right direction."

Despite his liberal leanings, Roberti has worked well with Republican members of the Senate, developing a particularly close association with GOP Senate Leader Ken Maddy of Fresno.

"We have obviously developed a good working relationship in the Senate over the last several years," Maddy said. "David is a very conscientious and hard working pro tem with a strong desire to show the Senate as a responsible, working group."

The biggest stain on Roberti's tenure as Senate leader is the corruption scandal that led Robbins to resign from the Senate last year and plead guilty to extortion and tax-evasion charges. Former Senators Montoya and Carpenter were convicted by federal juries in 1990 on extortion and racketeering charges.

Roberti acknowledged that he could not have been elected president pro tem in 1980 without the support of the trio. After taking power, he rewarded all three with key positions in the Senate hierarchy. Montoya became chairman of the Business and Professions Committee, a post he used to extort honoraria and campaign contributions from people seeking legislative action before his committee. Roberti named Carpenter Democratic caucus chairman, the number three position in the Senate. Carpenter was responsible for raising campaign money for Democratic legislators and used his post to extort money from interest groups pushing for passage of legislation in the Senate.

And until Robbins resigned from the Senate, Roberti kept him in the post of chairman of the Senate Insurance, Claims and Corporation Committee, where he wielded influence over a wide range of important bills. Robbins also served on a pivotal two-house conference committee responsible for writing the state budget.

All three lawmakers had reputations for heavy-handed fund-raising and sleazy back-room deals long before the FBI caught up with them. But Roberti took no action to limit their power. Roberti declined to discuss the cases of the three senators. But rather than having dictatorial powers over the members of the Senate, he argued, he is beholden to a large extent to the members who elected him leader.

"You have to put together a majority, let's be honest about it," he said. "You have to deal with the membership as they're sent to you. The underlying presumption is that I picked the membership. Not only have I not picked the membership, but the membership has picked me."

Unlike Speaker Brown, who moonlights as a lawyer and accepts controversial clients, Roberti does not practice law outside the Legislature. There are no signs that he has become a wealthy man in office. He and his wife, June, own just two pieces of property — their house in Los Angeles and their house in Sacramento — Roberti said.

The Senate leader does have a penchant for taking free trips at the expense of various groups — a practice he defends on the grounds that foreign travel broadens the outlook of legislators.

Stung by the corruption scandal, Roberti sponsored Proposition 112, a constitutional amendment that banned the acceptance of honoraria by legislators and restricted the gifts and free trips they can receive.

Roberti also argues that over the past two decades, the Senate has gradually made its operations more democratic and accountable to the public. No longer, he said, can a committee chairman sit down privately with a lobbyist and decide the fate of special-interest legislation. Committees can no longer meet in secret to decide the fate of bills and detailed analyses of bills must be available to the public before the Senate can vote on them, he added.

"It was worse, so much worse," he said. "Things have improved vastly... We've opened up the system."

At the same time, Roberti remains close to many of the special interests that dominate decision-making in the Capitol. As the Senate's chief fundraiser, he has raised more than $10.6 million since 1985 through 18 separate campaign committees he controls. Roberti received huge donations from such groups as labor unions, the California Trial Lawyers Association and the California Medical Association.

"The whole idea that David Roberti is on the high ground is overstated," a former staff member said. "It's a very carefully protected image. Lobbyists know they can come in and work around him. David doesn't stand in front of any moving trains."

A rarity in modern politics, Roberti grew up in the same district he now represents. His father, Emil, who came to the United States as a young man, and his mother, Elvira, the daughter of immigrants, created a noisy, close-knit environment for David and his older brother, Mario.

"Our father is a very out-going person," said Mario Roberti, an oil company attorney in Hawaii. "Our mother was very likeable and quite competitive. These qualities translated into certain goals for their children."

They instilled in their sons the values of hard work, humility and high personal standards, as well as faith in the Catholic church, labor unions and, of course, the family. In fact, David Roberti lived with his parents until he was elected to the Assembly at the age of 27. Some years later, they came to live with him.

As a child, Roberti's mother hoped her sons would become entertainers, and she made sure they took dance, singing and piano lessons. "When I was a little kid, my mother dressed me in a little army suit and I would have to perform," David Roberti recalls. "I hated it."

Later, his parents signed him up for lessons in public speaking to help him overcome his shyness, and the skill he developed as an orator has helped him throughout his life in politics.

The Robertis' Hollywood neighborhood was filled with people who worked on the back lots of the studios, but movie-making was not part of David Roberti's life. Even though his father worked every day making costumes for actors and actresses, young David never set foot in a studio until he was a legislator.

The two brothers attended Catholic schools and were diligent students. David developed a love for reading that sometimes drove him to great lengths. At the age of 12, when he was trying to find a quiet place to study, he rode the streetcar all the way from Hollywood to the end of line in Vernon and back again. Mario Roberti recalls that his panic-stricken father searched everywhere for David. "My brother was totally oblivious to what was going on," he said.

Later, the youngest Roberti developed the habit of reading while walking down the street. When he was studying for a big exam, he would walk for miles through the streets of Hollywood with his nose in a book.

Roberti vividly remembers the day the priest gave him last rites. He was nine years old and there was snow on the ground in Los Angeles. He had developed an obscure fever from mosquito bites, contracted blood poisoning from a major case of poison oak and suffered a severe reaction to the medication he was given. He was in and out of a coma for several days. A priest was summoned to his hospital room and administered the rites as his parents stood by crying. But soon after, to everyone's surprise, he made a miraculous recovery. Nevertheless, Roberti's brush with death left its scars.

"It gives you a fatalism that sticks with you," he said. "You've got to do the best you've got without worrying too much about what's going to happen two or three or four years from now."

Roberti's career in politics was shaped by one campaign he never waged. As a senior at Loyola University he toyed with the idea of running for student body vice president but decided against it because he was afraid of losing. The winner ran unopposed, and Roberti still feels bad that he did not run.

"I'm probably the only person left who remembers the event," he said. "It was a wonderful lesson: Regrets are worse than losing." It was a moral he kept firmly in mind as he decided to run for the Assembly and later for the Senate, the post of Senate majority leader and ultimately, president pro tem.

But Roberti's entrance into Democratic politics was as much an accident as anything. He was a young law student — and a Republican — when he attended his first meeting of the Young Democratic Club in Hollywood. To his surprise, he was elected president — and changed his registration shortly afterward. It was the easiest election he ever had.

In 1966 he ran for the Assembly. He was one of 11 Democratic candidates in the primary. Aided by June (his wife-to-be), his parents, his brother and friends, he ran as an anti-Vietnam War candidate, walked precincts and mounted a grass-roots campaign.

"We were young and very idealistic," June Roberti recalled. "We were into the peace movement and farmworker issues. We had a cause."

David Roberti was as startled as anyone when he beat the front-runner in the race. He won a paltry 20.7 percent of the vote, but it was enough to guarantee his future in politics.

After winning his Senate seat in a 1971 special election, Roberti held a series of increasingly important leadership positions. He launched a short-lived campaign for lieutenant governor in 1974, but abandoned it when he found little support.

While Roberti has had great success in winning Senate elections for himself and his allies, he is far from a political kingmaker. His endorsement has carried little weight in other races, including Assembly contests in communities that overlap his own district. In fact, in the last three such races, he has endorsed losing candidates. His only protege to win elective office has been Los Angeles City Councilman Woo.

From time to time, Roberti has considered the possibility of running for mayor of Los Angeles. But despite his power in state affairs, he has been unable to build much of a political base — or even much name recognition — in the city that is his home.

When the time comes to leave the Senate, Roberti said, he might run for another office. Or he might travel, or teach history. But for the time being, he is looking ahead to his next race — and remaining in the Senate.

"Hey, I'm as ambitious as the next person, believe me," he said. "Otherwise I would not be holding this position. But it would be a terrible shame to have spent my time here worrying about what I was going to do next." 🏛

LOBBYING & INTEREST GROUPS

The Political Reform Act of 1974 helped reshape relations between lobbyists and legislators. Prior to enactment of this proposition, legislative advocates spent a great deal of time and money entertaining lawmakers and thus winning their favor (and their votes). But the 1974 act prohibited a legislator from taking more than $10 a month from a lobbyist, barred lobbyists from "arranging" for campaign contributions from their clients (this provision has since been invalidated by the courts), established extensive and detailed expense and income reporting requirements, and established the Fair Political Practices Commission to implement the law. The measure has been reasonably successful in cutting the entertainment tie between legislators and advocates and began modifying the way of life in the Capitol. Actually, the system had started to change in 1966 when the Legislature became a full-time body. Many lawmakers and lobbyists brought their families to Sacramento, reducing time available for socializing.

The system today is a far cry from the 1930's and 40's when the late Artie Samish boasted: "To hell with the Governor of California! I'm the Governor of the Legislature." And the state's archetypical lobbyist then was probably right. In his long reign, hardly a bill passed the Legislature without Samish's approval. He raised about $1 million over a six-year period from a nickel-a-barrel levy on beer provided by his biggest client, the Brewers Institute, and spent it getting legislators "elected and un-elected," as he liked to put it. Over a long period ending in 1953 with his conviction for income-tax evasion, Samish was the second-most-powerful person in state government; the rest of the state's lobbyists were virtually powerless by comparison. Samish's downfall began when he was interviewed for Collier's magazine and posed with a ventriloquist's dummy he called "Mr. Legislature." The resulting embarrassment prodded the Legislature to pass a mild "reform act" technically banning lobbying and regulating "legislative advocates" in Sacramento. But if the activities of lobbyists are not as blatant as in Samish's day, their power — and the influence of campaign money — continues unabated. Indeed, the increasing costs of running for election — campaigning for a hotly contested Assembly seat can cost more than $1 million — has made lobbyists and the firms that employ them more important than ever. Moreover, the Legislature in recent years has been plagued with a new round of scandals set off by a "sting" operation run by the FBI and the U.S. attorney's office. One state Senator, Democrat Joseph Montoya of Whittier, resigned his office after being convicted of taking $3,000 to help secure passage of the FBI's phony legislative proposal, a bill that would have subsidized a shrimp-packing plant on the Sacramento River. Several other lawmakers and lobbyists have had their offices raided by the FBI and remain under suspicion. State Board of Equalization member Paul Carpenter, a Los Angeles Democrat and former Senator, has also been convicted in the "sting." And a third Senator, Alan Robbins, resigned and plead guilty to corruption.

Types of lobbyists

While a few big-name lobbyists who represent stables of clients receive most of the publicity, the corps of advocates includes almost every interest group in the state. In 1992 nearly 900 advocates are registered. They fall into several different categories:

- *Contract lobbyists*. These advocates will work for almost any client willing to pay their fee. The most successful of them charge high prices, have made substantial campaign contributions over the years and get results.

- *Corporation and trade association lobbyists*. These advocates work for one company and represent only the interests of their firms, although they often work in tandem with other lobbyists trying to reach the same goal.

- *Public agency lobbyists*. Aside from the associations representing public agencies, numerous cities, counties and special districts maintain their own representatives in Sacramento. And most state agencies have "legislative liaisons," though they are not required to register.

- *"Brown-bag" lobbyists*. These advocates represent interests seeking reforms in a variety of so-called public-interest fields. They include the League of Women Voters, the National Organization for Women, the Planning and Conservation League, the Sierra Club, Common Cause, the Friends Committee on Legislation, and numerous organizations with budgets sufficient only for brown-bag lunches.

Lobbying process

Lobbyists operate in several ways. They provide information and arguments on pending legislation in an attempt to win legislators to their point of view. (Advocates claim that this information function is a vital part of the Legislature's work because it helps define the public interest.) They also establish friendships with legislators. In addition some lobbyists represent groups that contribute substantial amounts to campaigns and entertain lavishly. Finally, many lobbyists orchestrate appeals from their membership at the local level such as letter-writing campaigns and political participation. Lobbyists also lobby the governor, the bureaucracy, regulatory commissions, the courts and the public.

Lobbyists can succeed because there are a great many bills considered each year about which lawmakers have relatively little knowledge or interest, and a good word from a lobbyists friend may tip the balance. A smart lobbyist knows he or she is wasting time trying to persuade a legislator who has a firm philosophical commitment to one side or another on an issue, and so focuses on the uncommitted lawmaker.

All legislators are susceptible to persuasion by representatives of interest groups. But some are more attuned, for example, to corporate spokesmen, while others are more apt to go along with a representative of an environmental organization. Unlike the Samish days, when the public did not get a clear picture of the happenings in Sacramento, the pleading of teams of the Capitol's most powerful and persuasive advocates now occasionally fall on deaf ears when legislators got a clear message from their constituents. While lobbyists tend to come from within government ranks — i.e., legislators and ex-staff — members retiring from the Legislature because of Proposition 112 of June 1990 must wait one year before going into lobbying. 🏛

Lobbying has been an accepted part of the legislative process for years, its practicioners known as the "third house" of the Legislature. But in recent years, due mainly to the ever-increasing cost of political campaigns, the role of the lobbyist has changed. They have always influenced the legislative process, but with the escalating costs of campaigns, they've become the major conduit for money that politicians need to be reelected. This issue of *California Journal* examines aspects of the lobbying industry, including its most

successful firms, a handful of prominent lobbyists and the expansion of lobbying's underground and the way government lobbies itself.

If lobbying is the art of persuasion, it just may be the healthiest art form in Sacramento. The number of groups and firms employing paid persuaders has nearly tripled in the past 10 years so that nearly 1700 organizations now have some form of representation in Sacramento. The amount spent on lobbying has increased even faster, probably exceeding $70 million for 1985. In 1975 only $20 million per year was spent on lobbyists.

In part this reflects the growth of state government itself; the California state budget has almost tripled during that same period. But it also reflects an increased recognition that decisions made by the state — in the Legislature and in a myriad of state agencies — have substantial impacts on a growing number of businesses and professions. Even other government agencies now find the need for a Sacramento advocate to protect their share of the state's largess. This aspect of lobbying's growth doesn't alarm most observers. Indeed, it can be seen as a healthy participation in the governmental process.

Warping the system

However, the growth of the lobbying industry has also coincided with another phenomenon — the rapidly escalating cost of election campaigns. And the connection between the two, in the view of many, has become so pervasive that it is beginning to warp the system with an unholy alliance between private interests, who view lobbying expenses

and campaign contributions as business investments, and legislators, who see in lobbyists and special interests a ready source of the campaign cash needed for reelection.

In recent years the trend has produced the "bag bill" — a measure introduced and perhaps pursued solely to leverage campaign contributions out of special interests. Proposals that often start out with a noble purpose end up, conveniently, as a kind of Brinks truck filled with campaign cash.

The most notable current example is a proposal to change the state's "uni-

THE PERSUADERS

LOBBYING — AN ART FORM FLOURISHING IN SACRAMENTO

Reprinted from *California Journal*, February 1986

By RICHARD ZEIGER

LOBBYING TOTALS: 1975-1991

YEAR	#LOBBYISTS	#EMPLOYERS	TOTAL $ SPENT
1975-76	630	795	40,018,666
1977-78	582	760	49,656,908
1979-80	613	857	59,023,150
1981-82	638	1041	58,345,176
1983-84	753	1338	112,519,158
1985-86	838	1695	137,594,247
1987-88	825	1544	158,498,208
1989-90	817	1537	193,578,059
1991-92	886	1455	116,465,129

tary" method of taxing foreign corporations that operate in California. Many corporations, both foreign and domestic, found they had something to gain or lose from this proposal and thus unleashed an army of lobbyists armed with the promise of campaign riches. Indeed, the proposal has proved so lucrative for lawmakers' campaign accounts — not to mention the bank accounts of the Capitol lobbying corps — the suspicion is widespread that the matter is unsettled because no one wants to give up an easy source of money.

A part of the process

Even those who deny that contributions matter — most notably Assembly Speaker Willie Brown, who has been accused by some of allowing the bag bill to flourish — concede they are expected from those who can afford them. In a recent *California Journal* interview, Brown maintained that the vast amount of money given by special interests "cancel each other out," adding that he could not remember a single instance when contributions made the difference in the outcome of a bill. But Brown noted that his Assembly members "have to get reelected. They've got to get the dough from someplace." The logical source is those who want to play the legislative game.

The change has affected not only legislators, but the business community as well. Businesses have accepted that campaign contributions are just another part of the process. According to one lobbyist, there used to be a time when at least some businesses resisted contributing "under the gun." That has almost disappeared. Furthermore, the amount of money involved is going up.

"Once, if you contributed $20,000, spread among a number of legislators over two years, that was a lot. Now, it's $70,000 or $80,000 per year for one person," the lobbyist added.

Walter Zelman, lobbyist for the consumer group Common Cause, believes the mining of campaign contributions from lobbyists "has tainted the process" and that the problem lies with the system and not with so-called corrupt individuals.

But campaign contributions are becoming a relatively blunt instrument; just about everyone expects them and, at least for the Legislature's biggest fund raisers, they no longer leave a lasting impression. As a result, lobbyists have begun developing more sophisticated ways of reaching legislators.

Lobbyists, of course, are more than conduits for campaign contributions (although for some, the ability to influence how, when and where a client contributes creates an enormous amount of leverage with legislators). Lobbyists also devise strategies for moving bills through the legislative process, work with clients and/or employers to influence bills through grass-roots efforts in lawmakers' districts, manage professional associations and public-relations campaigns for clients and develop a diverse set of contacts in all branches of state government.

In the past few years, businesses have also begun hiring platoons of lobbyists to push for a measure. Although one individual or firm may be in charge, it is not uncommon to subcontract out some of the lobbying work to specialists who might have good contact with one crucial legislator. This has created new opportunities for former legislators or staff members to enter the lobbying profession where they can take advantage of the personal friendships — all to the benefit of their new employers.

Also emerging in recent years is the combination firm employing both lawyers, lobbyists and even public-relations specialists. These firms offer a "complete service" to their clients. The changes needed in the law can be researched, lawmakers contacted and a publicity campaign mounted if necessary.

The combination of an increasingly professional lobbying corps, backed by the money to fuel election campaigns, is proving to be almost overwhelming. At times it threatens to unbalance the governmental system. Although legislative staff is large enough to provide an objective look at pending legislation, there is little in the way of political balance.

Zelman notes that his type of public interest lobbyist can have some impact, even without campaign contributions. "But we can't compete in sheer numbers. In some fields there are 30 or 40 private-interest lobbyists for every public-interest lobbyist," he said.

This imbalance, in recent years, has resulted in the Legislature regularly appearing to be at the beck-and-call of special interests. Indeed, the only time you see a good old-fashioned fight these days is when two large special interests square off.

Zelman and other reformers — most of whom favor some form of public campaign financing — see the solution in reforming the campaign financing system so that lawmakers will not have to turn to special interest lobbies for money. "The solution is to make it easier to raise money, not more difficult. Then they can worry about the things they are supposed to worry about," Zelman offered. 🏛

How tobacco courts California

By Charles Price

Reprinted from *California Journal*, August 1991

For all you anti-smoking fanatics out there, here's the good news: Tobacco is not grown in California.

Here's more good news: Tobacco products are not manufactured in California.

Here's even more stupendous news: Poll after poll after poll on top of survey after survey after survey show that your fellow Californians don't like tobacco smoke. Any tobacco smoke. They are bothered by the fumes, worried about breathing secondhand smoke and adamant that those under the age of 18 be denied access to cigarette vending machines. They want to pun-

Charles Price is a political science professor at California State University, Chico, and a frequent contributor to California Journal.

ish those who sell tobacco to minors and ban all tobacco advertising.

But wait! There's more good news! In 1988 all those don't-tax-me Californians voted to increase cigarette taxes (Proposition 99). Plus, Californians seem more health conscious than their brethren east of the Sierra: Only 20 percent of Golden Staters smoke, compared with 30 percent in the rest of the country.

Yup. California isn't exactly Marlboro Country.

Yet, tobacco use continues to foster a statewide plague of sorts. The American Cancer Society estimates that 42,000 Californians will die from tobacco-related deaths this year. Each day, 300 California teenagers become regular smokers. The annual burden to the state's economy caused by tobacco use is more than $7 billion dollars.

Based on all of this, one might guess that the tobacco industry would have relatively little clout in Sacramento.

Guess again.

With only two exceptions, bills aimed at restricting tobacco use introduced in the current legislative session have either been killed or sidetracked into two-year bills. And it wasn't for lack of trying by anti-tobacco lawmakers. Among some of the more significant tobacco-restriction bills that lost out:

• AB 16 would have prohibited smoking in public places — locations where the public is invited or permitted;

• AB 49 would have banned smoking in state buildings;

• AB 402 would have created the Smoke Free Air Act and banned smoking in public and privately owned buildings open to public;

• AB 452 would have increased

the tax on cigarettes;

• AB 1305 would have limited youth access to cigarette vending machines;

• AB 1667 would required stores selling tobacco to be licensed;

• AB 3865 would have done away with tax deductions for tobacco ads;

• SB 93 also would have prohibited smoking in public places;

• SB 468 would have banned sales of candy, gum or snack foods packaged to resemble any tobacco product;

• SB 1099 would have licensed and regulated tobacco sales by a Tobacco Control Division and a license fee would be required.

While all of these bill languished, another measure (AB 496 by Democratic Assemblyman Dick Floyd) supported by the tobacco lobby and opposed by health groups rumbled through the process. AB 496 lowers the fine for selling to an underage person and requires a certain number of hours of community service. But Floyd's bill also prevents any local government from adopting its own — perhaps more strict — regulations on the subject. It recently passed the Assembly and is pending in the Senate.

This is not to say that the tobacco lobby has been able to quash or derail every piece of legislation. Two bills supported by health groups have cleared their houses of origin and are awaiting action in the other house. AB 1574 would prohibit the Department of Corrections from selling or supplying tobacco products to incarcerated 16- and 17-year-olds, even if parents or guardians consent. And SB 1100 would prohibit giving away those freebie sampler packages of cigarettes or chewing tobacco.

Republican state Senator Marian Bergeson, sponsor of SB 1100, said her bill emerged from the Senate because she was able to shoot holes in tobacco-industry claims about who actually got those free samples (teenagers) and how many free samples were given away (more than 97 million a year).

Still, the fate of Bergeson's bill is instructive of the clout enjoyed by the tobacco industry — despite all polls and evidence. After her bill unanimously passed out of the Senate Judiciary Committee, it went to the floor where tobacco interests lobbied for its referral to the Senate Appropriations Committee. Legislative counsel agreed because the bill had fiscal implications.

According to Bergeson, delay is a favorite tobacco tactic when confronted by hostile legislation. Her bill passed Appropriations and was approved on the Senate floor, 27-2.

Unfortunately, there was another house to deal with — the Assembly. Bergeson wanted her bill assigned to the Assembly Health or Judiciary committees, whose members might have been sympathetic. Instead, it was referred to the Governmental Organization Committee. Chairman of that committee is Floyd, a Gardena Democrat. Floyd, an implacable foe of anti-tobacco health groups, is an in-your-face smoker who often paces the Assembly floor puffing away on a mammoth cigar. His committee has long been regarded as a graveyard for many tobacco restriction bills. According to Capitol observers, no anti-smoking bill has passed from the "GO" Committee in years.

Yet Bergeson was able to massage her bill out of Floyd's committee just before the Assembly recessed for its summer vacation. It will proceed to the Ways and Means Committee when the Assembly resumes its schedule in August. But clearly, the Government Organization Committee was Bergeson's biggest hurdle, and sponsors now are optimistic that the bill eventually will pass the Assembly and be signed into law.

Still, the strategy employed on behalf of Bergeson's bill points out the tobacco industry's clout. Bergeson downplayed the fact that her bill was an anti-smoking measure and instead emphasized that it was designed to keep cigarettes out of the hands of teenagers who have easy access to freebies passed out on street corners. Thus, committee members were able to record a pro-kids vote — not an anti-tobacco vote.

The tobacco lobby has had long practice battling anti-tobacco legislation. Health problems (cancer, emphysema, heart disease) connected with tobacco use first surfaced in health and medical journals in the 1940s. And although the industry did (and does) dispute those claims, the U.S. Surgeon General declared cigarette smoking a health hazard in 1964. Despite this declaration, the federal government continues to subsidize tobacco farmers.

The American tobacco industry itself is composed of six large, diversified corporations that produce and sell over 95 percent of domestic tobacco prod-

ucts. Each of the six has expanded its corporate empire by acquiring other commercial enterprises, particularly in the foods sector. Philip Morris, the largest U.S. tobacco company, owns — among other ventures — Kraft Foods, Miller Brewing Company, Oscar Mayer and Jello. R.J. Reynolds, the second-largest American tobacco company, owns Nabisco Corporation and their varied food products. However, tobacco sales continue to be the most profitable enterprise for all six companies.

Bergeson

The tobacco industry lobbying isn't limited to lawmakers; it extensively "lobbies" the public as well through advertising — long an industry tradition. In the 1930s and '40s tobacco companies sponsored popular radio programs. Later, they advertised extensively on television. While radio and television tobacco advertising have since been banned, the industry continues to spend considerable sums advertising its products, or itself as a good corporate citizen in newspapers and magazines (including *California Journal*). Women, minorities and the poor are special targets and represent some of the industry's most loyal customers. Tobacco companies also advertise extensively on billboards, at ballparks and on public transit.

Cigarette companies also lobby minorities by sponsoring touring shows of Black and Hispanic artists and contributing to scholarship funds of Black colleges (Philip Morris). R.J. Reynolds' plans to launch a new cigarette designed for urban Blacks was derailed by U.S. Health Secretary Louis Sullivan's angry attack on the proposed new brand. Diane Kaiser, a lobbyist for the Heart Association, noted that the tobacco industry in California also has become very involved in Cinco de Mayo festivals. Additionally, Philip Morris is the official corporate sponsor of the Bill of Rights bicentennial this year, a not-so-subtle hint that the right to smoke stands alongside the right to free speech as guaranteed by the First Amendment.

The tobacco industry always has considered California a critical state because of its booming population, ethnic mix and reputation as a political and social trend-setter. Thus, the industry has been and is willing to spend whatever it takes to maintain the status quo.

In 1978, after repeated failures by anti-tobacco groups to pass legislation to place restrictions on smoking in public buildings and workplaces, health groups decided to bypass the Legislature and place an initiative on the ballot. It qualified as Proposition 5. It was defeated after tobacco companies shelled out $6.5 million to fuel the opposition. Health groups raised $654,000. Proposition 5 lost 47 percent to 53 percent. Two years later, health groups tried a new slightly revised initiative on the same topic, and lost a second time by nearly the same margin as in 1978. Once again, the tobacco industry contributed millions to defeat the measure. Although health groups lost, they came much closer to achieving their anti-smoking goal via the initiative than in the halls of the Legislature.

The next major ballot confrontation between health groups and the tobacco industry occurred in 1988 when, after repeated attempts to increase the tobacco tax in the Legislature (California ranked 43rd among the states in the level of its tobacco tax at that time), health groups succeeded in qualifying a cigarette tax increase initiative (Proposition 99). Health groups argued that by raising the tax on a pack of cigarettes from 10 cents to 35 cents, it would make tobacco more costly and perhaps discourage young people from starting smoking. In addition, money generated would be used to fund a massive and aggressive anti-tobacco advertising campaign.

In one of the most costly initiative campaigns in state history, the tobacco industry spent over $21 million fighting the initiative. And for the first time, they lost — despite a pro-initiative bankroll of less than $2 million.

The anti-Proposition 99 campaign war chest points out why the tobacco industry carries so much political clout when it seems to have such a small constituency.

Money.

The extent to which tobacco has become a key special interest at the Capitol over the past few years is highlighted in a recent study by two University of California researchers, Michael Evans Begay and Stanton Glantz, who examined political spending by the tobacco industry from 1986 to 1990.

Their study shows that tobacco's lobbying expenditures at the state level increased nearly 10-fold between 1986 and 1990 ($235,245 to an estimated $2,091,615 in 1990). Its contributions to legislators and constitutional officers nearly doubled, from $318,000 to $582,000. And this does not count the money spent to defeat or pass various initiatives.

The tobacco industry is represented by a who's who of influential contract lobbying firms, including heavy weight SJR Jackson-Barish & Associates (see "The new big daddy," *CJ*, February 1990). Jackson's firm was hired recently to organize opposition to SB 468 by Democratic Senator Mike Thompson. Thompson's bill would have banned candy cigarettes and bubble gum designed to resemble chewing tobacco. Thompson sponsored his bill after discovering that a University of North Carolina study concluded that kids who use imitation tobacco products are four times as likely to take up smoking or chewing tobacco as kids not exposed to them. SB 468 failed to get out of Senate Judiciary.

Representatives of various anti-tobacco health groups and lawmakers who carry anti-tobacco legislation agree that even though the tobacco industry's image has been tarnished over the last several decades, tobacco's power in the California Legislature remains formidable. As Heart lobbyist Diane Kaiser put it, "All the tobacco lobbyists have to do is walk into a committee room, and the message is clear to legislators: Don't vote against them."

However, the tide may be beginning to shift. In 1988 health groups pushed through legislation banning smoking on public transit within the state, and Assemblyman Trice Harvey's AB 1574 and Senator Bergeson's SB 1100 are still alive. But health groups have a long way to go before they can match the influence of the tobacco lobby.

Arrayed against the tobacco lobby are the Heart Association, Lung Association, American Cancer Society, Americans for Non-Smokers' Rights, the American Medical Association and the American Dental Association. Yet health groups remained hamstrung.

S ince medical and scientific research is so overwhelmingly against tobacco, the industry's lobbyists tend to focus on the economic consequences of particular bills.

"Tobacco lobbyists don't come up with a lot of hard data," said Velo. On a bill to license stores that sell tobacco, "we had ... people testifying how easy it is for kids to buy cigarettes. The tobacco industry came up and said that mom and pop will be put out of business; there would be too much paper work to get a license."

Tobacco lobbyists and Tobacco Institute officials declined to be interviewed.

The tobacco industry greases its access to political movers and shakers in Sacramento by being a major money-giver. Common Cause ranked them 10th among all state groups in contributions in 1986 and fourth in 1988. As with other lobbies, the tobacco industry provides campaign contributions almost exclusively to incumbent legislators, particularly legislative leaders or members on policy committees dealing with tobacco issues. Begay and Glantz report that the top legislator recipients of tobacco largesse between 1986 and 1990 were Assembly Speaker Willie Brown, $154,750; Senate Republican leader Ken Maddy, $55,000; Senate President pro Tempore David Roberti, $43,578; and Assembly Governmental Organization Committee Chairman Dick Floyd, $26,564. These figures do not include gifts and honoraria, such as Speaker Brown's 1990 trip to Louisville for the Kentucky Derby.

Tobacco always has contributed substantial sums of money to initiative campaigns — and not only to defeat anti-smoking measures. It has also been known to pump money into campaigns where it has no vital, direct interest. In 1990, among other contributions, the tobacco industry gave $151,000 to oppose Big Green (Proposition 128), $455,667 to help a timber-industry sponsored alternative called Big Brown (Proposition 135), $6000 to oppose both term-limit initiatives (Propositions 131 and 140) and $575,000 to promote conservative tax and initiative-reform measures (Propositions 136 and 137). Observers say tobacco got involved with other initiative campaigns to curry favor at the Capitol and to generally be supportive of the business community.

So, anti-smoking fanatics, even though you represent a majority of Californians, don't look for tobacco to fold up shop.

Even if most of California isn't Marlboro Country, the state Capitol is. 🏛

Government lobbyists

California spends millions to influence itself

By Curtis Richards

Reprinted from *California Journal*, August 1991

I n the final hours of the 1990-91 state budget stalemate — the one that took place a year ago rather than the one that took place last month — lobbyists for counties secured passage of legislation authorizing counties to assess other governmental entities fees for property tax administration and jailhouse bookings.

A creative fee-for-service solution to a serious local government funding crisis? Perhaps. But the new law, which some claim was unfairly sneaked into the budget compromise, sparked intensified battles between local governmental entities. Schools and community colleges sued the state. Individual cities sued their host counties. And the provision ultimately was repealed in this year's budget package.

This skirmish, which one lobbyist terms "crazy," exemplifies a way of life in the Legislature as governments lobby government to protect their interests, and especially to gain their share of the state budget pie.

Local government expenditures for lobbying ranked fifth out of the 20 major categories of lobbyist employers,

Curtis Richards is a Sacramento writer who once worked for the state Legislature.

according to a recent report issued by the secretary of state — the official repository for lobbyist disclosure statements. Outspending the oil and gas industry, local governments shelled out nearly $18 million worth of public funds to lobby the Legislature and various state agencies in 1989 and 1990. Two local governments (the immense Metropolitan Water District of Southern California and Los Angeles County) and one local government association (the County Supervisors Association or CSAC) each spent more than $1 million. This represents a large increase over the $8.6 million in local-government lobbying expenditures from 1983-84 (see "Government lobbyists," CJ, February 1986). More than 180 employers classifying themselves as "government" spent $17,821,550 in 1989-90 compared with 126 employers that spent $8,546,303 in 1983-84.

To fully understand how much public money is included in the $193 million spent lobbying in 1989 and 1990, however, one must look well beyond the official "government" category. This category generally does not include public utilities, governmental health-care organizations, publicly governed transportation systems and, most important, public schools.

Education employers fall in line immediately behind

government, with some 209 self-identified education interests spending a total of $12,485,131 in 1989-90, compared with 92 employers spending $5,210,776 in 1983-84. About 80 percent of this $12.5 million comes from public schools and community colleges.

And, several powerful public-employee unions, which collect dues from teachers, state workers and local-government employees, spent $7.6 million to influence legislation in 1989-90, compared with $4.6 million in 1983-84. Standing alone in this classification, the California Teachers Association, which locked horns this year with Governor Pete

Top Ten Governmental Entities

	1983-84	1989-90
Metropolitan Water District	227,425	1,515,713
County Supervisors Assn.	162,593	1,176,832
Los Angeles County	729,390	1,071,610
Orange County	344,168	799,854
Los Angeles City	605,267	707,118
League of Cities	607,247	604,936
San Bernardino County	187,045	602,326
San Diego County	322,091	452,318
Alameda County	207,085	365,834
Santa Clara County	156,270	348,988

Wilson over suspension of its voter-approved education spending guarantee (Proposition 98), spent $1,857,510.

Additionally, the state spends untold amounts of money to lobby itself. State agency lobbyists do not have to register with the secretary of state or file disclosure statements. Every state department has its own legislative unit, from the Department of Alcohol and Drug Abuse to the Water Resources Control Board. And the two publicly funded university systems — the nine-campus University of California and the 20-campus California State University — not only have central-office lobbying teams, they also have a "campus and community relations" officer, or some such lobbyist, assigned to each campus.

"I think this is an abuse and misuse of taxpayers monies," charged Lee Phelps, president of the 14,000-member Alliance of California Taxpayers-Involved Voters. "We pay taxes to support legitimate functions of government, not to have those who draw salaries to appear before committees, to buttonhole legislators and pick more money out of our pockets."

It is "absolutely not" proper for government to lobby government, according to Phelps, a retired military officer who volunteers his time to run ACT-IV. "I think it's totally wrong. If it isn't damned illegal, it should be. I believe in sweet reason and persuasion aimed at the people who bear the burden, not those who inhabit their governmental structure."

"Tax consumers — those who depend upon tax revenue for their income, such as public employee unions, teachers unions, local governments — outnumber taxpayers in committee hearings and lobbying activities by a factor of about 100 to one," continued Phelps, who sees a need to "severely limit the ability of the Legislature to do more than the

minimum necessary to serve the population collectively."

Not everyone shares this view.

"I think anyone who has an interest in the Legislature is going to try and lobby the Legislature," said Ruth Holton, California Common Cause lobbyist for the past two years. "Some raise the question, 'Should public dollars be spent on lobbying?' I don't think anything is wrong with it. Clearly, local governments and state agencies have a lot of interest. They have opinions that certainly need to be heard and expressed."

Common Cause, which has "an interest in ensuring that anyone who gets paid to advocate for specific legislation gets registered as a lobbyist," reported spending nearly $500,000 lobbying in the past two years. ACT-IV reported no lobbying expenses for the same period.

"There is a common idea of lobbyists as a sleazy group of people, smoking cigars, cutting deals in backrooms," Holton said. "Actually, lobbyists convey information, in this case for the interests of cities, counties, universities. They need someone to follow the issues and represent their interests. Lobbyists aren't all sleazy. Unfortunately, the term lobbyist has a sleazy connotation. Everyone has a message to get across. The more complex the issue, the more complex the message, the more likely that the entity will have to hire a lobbyist."

And the state's dealings with various other governments is complex.

Government lobbyists are "essential to the future well-being of the state," commented Democratic Assemblyman John Vasconcellos of San Jose. "They've got to be here."

Top Ten K-12 Associations and Districts

	1983-84	1989-90
CA School Boards Assn.	383,772	1,153,247
Los Angeles Unified Schools	434,960	1,005,094
Assn. of CA School Administrators	634,700	825,139
San Diego Unified Schools	228,745	363,097
Long Beach Unified Schools	80,788	351,375
L.A. County Office of Education	408,432	318,688
San Francisco Unified Schools	50,398	254,271
S.D. County Office of Education	191,327	246,872
Kern County Super. of Schools	66,886	230,456
Clovis Unified Schools	—	204,573

Noting that local-government issues "get complicated," he said that in 1990 the Legislature "debated whether to starve the schools or county mental health."

"We've starved the public sector," explained Vasconcellos, chairman of the Assembly Ways and Means Committee. "We were penny-wise and pound -oolish under the awful Deukmejian years, and now we're paying for it."

League of Cities lobbyist Dwight Stenbakken confirmed that "the budget has been the predominant issue" for his organization. "Generally cities have been left alone in that process, but in the last couple of years we've been dragged into it. It's been an important issue."

For schools "the bottom line is that Proposition 98 is only a thin guarantee of a total pot of money," said Kevin Gordon, chief lobbyist for the California School Boards Association. "What's not defined is how the pot is to be split. The challenge for local school districts now becomes a process

Top Five Community Colleges

	1983-84	1989-90
Los Angeles CCD	55,000	270,599
CA Comm. College Trustees Assn.	94,514	134,162
Association of CA Community College Administration	86,042	119,025
Faculty Association of CA Community Colleges	44,919	110,610
San Diego CCD	99,816	104,635

to see who gets the most amount of money." CSBA spent $1,153,247 to lobby the Legislature in 1989-90; Los Angeles Unified spent $1,005,094; and an association of school administrators another $825,139.

"We have a lot of local districts retaining people for the purposes of having input into the process," said Gordon.

"It is unfortunate that people feel pressured to hire a lobbyist to get their message across," Holton remarked. "You shouldn't have to."

Yet, for one East Bay school district (Richmond), retaining a lobbyist last year paid off. The lobbyist, with the assistance of a couple of influential legislators who represent the district, secured a special $6 million budget line-item for the district. Called a "Bridge Financing" program, this district was bailed out with an outright grant rather than the customary repayable loan.

"CSBA is concerned that if everyone goes in and tries to tweak the system around, pretty soon the cow has a third horn. Then, you get this weird offspring called school financing," Gordon said. "Because the formulas have been so adjusted and jerked around over the years that a budget like ours becomes vulnerable because no one understands it. It is so complex that it breeds contempt to the average voter and, frankly, a lot of legislators."

"The myth that education needs more money is exactly that, a myth," Phelps alleged. "They always demand more without any relationship to the quality of the product they are producing, which is decreasing."

Phelps cited the financial troubles of Richmond Unified School district as "one more case of educational bureaucracy spending itself into a bottomless pit, then demanding that the average taxpayer lower their standard of living to bail them out."

"It's not just the schools. The whole institution of government in California has become so bloated with fat," said Phelps, a co-author of Proposition 140. "They think they have some kind of divine right to start each year with the previous year's base point, no matter what conditions are in the private sector. That's fundamentally wrong."

Referring to the bankrupt Butte County, Holton explained that "if Butte didn't pay a lobbyist to represent them in Sacramento, there would be someone in Butte to look at this, trying to analyze the bills, to follow what's happening in the Capitol. They need to have a liaison. ...Butte can't

ignore what's going on in the Capitol. These things don't happen in a vacuum, they need to stay on top of it. Butte County, in the end, probably did better off since they have someone looking out for their interests."

"I think there is a conflict of interest if a lobbyist is representing two local interests which oppose each other," Holton emphasized. "But, if a lobbyist represents several bankrupt counties, that's fine. You just shouldn't be selling clients short. That would be a fundamental conflict of interest."

The number of individual cities hiring lobbyists has "probably gone up a little, but I'm not sure there's been a substantial increase," said League of Cities lobbyist Dwight Stenbakken, adding that his organization represents all cities in the state. "A lot of times communities will hire someone to lobby something unique to their city that may not affect all cities."

"It seems like school lobbyists — boards, districts, teachers, administrators — have grown the most," said Stenbakken, an 11-year veteran lobbyist. "I have always been kind of impressed by the numbers of school lobbyists in town."

"I think we're real strong advocates on behalf of education," Gordon said. "When they want to rip you off, that's when we're pretty effective. It's always easier to kill something than to pass something. Really great lobbyists are those who are passing things. We're probably some of the

Top Four Public Utilities

	1983-84	1989-90
East Bay Muni. District	170,379	546,368
CA Muni. Association	150,351	403,286
Sacramento Muni. District	56,392	287,122
San Diego County Water Authority	—	218,791

best lobbyists out there in terms of killing something. We're not that great at securing large budget increases to put California on a par with other states."

But not everyone agrees that government ought to spend taxpayer money to lobby itself. Activist Phelps, for one, thinks the effort has given too much importance to public employees. "We've created a new royalty called public employees and public officials," he said. "They should be servants of, not parasites on, the public."

But Assemblyman Vasconcellos took a different angle. "How much money is spent by private interests [to influence the Legislature?] Is that more important than the public interest —than feeding kids, than educating our population, than providing parks and clean environments?" 🏛

PARTIES, POLITICS & ELECTIONS

Political Parties

By both design and tradition, political parties in California are exceptionally weak — especially when compared to the machine politics prevalent in some eastern states. The weakening of the party structure was engineered by Hiram Johnson and the Progressives starting in 1911 as a reaction to the machine politics of the railroad interests and San Francisco boss Abe Ruef. Parties were explicitly forbidden from endorsing in non-partisan contests and implicitly from making pre-primary endorsements in partisan contests for much of this century. All local offices and judgeships were made nonpartisan, and a unique method of running, called cross-filing, was instituted. Numerous provisions were written into the law for the express purpose of reducing party power, and many of these restrictions remain in the law today. An independent spirit was fostered in California, and even now there are parts of the state where the electorate pays very little attention to a candidate's party. It is these areas — notably the San Joaquin Valley and the rural districts — that can hold the balance of power in state elections.

Under cross-filing, which lasted from 1914 to 1959, a candidate could file for the nomination of not only his or her own party but other parties as well (and until 1952, without any indication of party affiliation). This had the effect of weakening party structure and making pressure groups and the press more important. It also led to the election of popular candidates in the primary, when they won both the Republican and Democratic nominations. Generally, cross-filing helped Republicans more than Democrats, and it is probably significant that Democrats have done much better in elections since the system was eliminated in favor of traditional primaries.

California now has six official parties — Democratic, Republican, Libertarian, Peace and Freedom, American Independent, and as of 1992, the Green Party. A party can win official status by getting the signatures of one percent of the registered voters or by obtaining a petition signed by a number of voters equal to ten percent of the votes cast for governor in the previous election. To remain official, a party must get two percent of the vote for a statewide candidate and retain one-15th of one percent of registered voters. Loss of official status means that a party can run candidates by write-in only, a difficult assignment in an era of electronic voting.

Party organization

The party structure is spelled out in detail in state law, although some minor variations are allowed for Democrats and Republicans. These are the basic official elements of party structure:

• *National committee members.* These are elected by the delegation to the national convention and serve as the state party's representatives on the national committee of each party.

• *Delegates to national convention.* Slates are developed by supporters of each primary candidate, and winning delegates — with alterations and additions — cast the state's votes at the quadrennial convention. The winner-take-all primary is used by California Republicans. State Democrats use a proportional representation system of delegates elected from congressional districts.

• *County central committees.* These committees, elected directly by the voters, are charged with directing party affairs in each county. In fact, however, these committees are weak, and the real power is held by the office-holders in each county.

• *State central committee.* This committee is comprised of about 1400 members in the GOP and 2500 to 3000 members in the Democratic Party. This committee is charged with electing party officials, managing and operating the party, and selecting presidential electors. An executive committee of the state central committee handles the day-to-day operation of the party. The state central committee usually meets once a year. Republicans have a separate party meeting, the state convention, which comprises state central committee members and, in addition, 400 to 500 associate members who draft their state platforms (the Democrats entrust this task with their state central committee).

• *State chairman.* In theory, the chairman speaks for the party and develops election strategy in conjunction with the executive committee. With rare exception, however, the main leaders are the major office holders of both parties.

As noted, Progressive reforms weakened party organization in the state. However, several new developments may serve to strengthen California parties:

1) Because of court rulings in the 1980s, parties may now make endorsements in partisan primaries. (They are still prohibited from endorsing in non-partisan contests.) Democrats have established detailed regulations for their party on their endorsing rules and format. Republicans have decided, because of potential divisions, not to endorse. Since 1988, (the first year that endorsing went into effect), endorsing has not been a major factor influencing the nomination or election politics of the Democratic Party, but it could evolve into a significant factor in the years ahead.

2) Parties have democratized selection to State Central Committees. There are fewer appointments by office-holders, and more elections from the counties. Democrats have created Assembly District Caucuses in the 80 districts to choose 12 delegates per district.

3) Prop. 73 barred elected officeholders from transferring money to favored candidates. Prop. 73 was in effect in 1989 and part of 1990 until it was struck down in the courts only a few weeks prior to the November 1990 election. Even though the court struck down the initiative, elected leaders may be somewhat more circumspect in divvying up these funds. Voters have indicated they do not like the process. Finally, the California Republican Party has usually had more success in raising money for the party than have Democrats.

4) Lastly, election by Democrats of Jerry Brown (former governor and ambitious elective office seeker) symbolized the growing importance of the state chair's position. Current state chairs are Phil Angelides for the Democrats and Jim Dignan for the Republicans.

DEMOCRATIC and REPUBLICAN PARTY ORGANIZATION

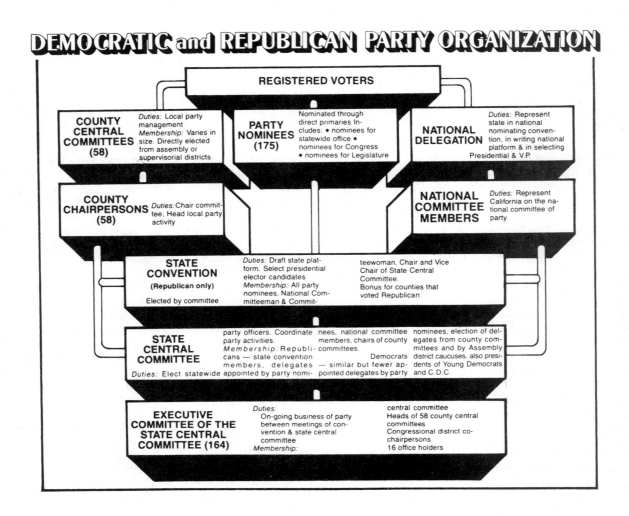

REGISTERED VOTERS

COUNTY CENTRAL COMMITTEES (58)
Duties: Local party management
Membership: Varies in size. Directly elected from assembly or supervisorial districts.

PARTY NOMINEES (175)
Nominated through direct primaries Includes: • nominees for statewide office • nominees for Congress • nominees for Legislature

NATIONAL DELEGATION
Duties: Represent state in national nominating convention, in writing national platform & in selecting Presidential & V.P.

COUNTY CHAIRPERSONS (58)
Duties: Chair committee, Head local party activity

NATIONAL COMMITTEE MEMBERS
Duties: Represent California on the national committee of party

STATE CONVENTION (Republican only)
Elected by committee
Duties: Draft state platform. Select presidential elector candidates
Membership: All party nominees, National Committeeman & Committeewoman, Chair and Vice Chair of State Central Committee.
Bonus for counties that voted Republican

STATE CENTRAL COMMITTEE
Duties: Elect statewide party officers. Coordinate party activities.
Membership: Republicans — state convention members, delegates appointed by party nominees, national committee members, chairs of county committees.
Democrats — similar but fewer appointed delegates by party nominees, election of delegates from county committees and by Assembly district caucuses, also presidents of Young Democrats and C.D.C.

EXECUTIVE COMMITTEE OF THE STATE CENTRAL COMMITTEE (164)
Duties: On-going business of party between meetings of convention & state central committee
Membership: central committee Heads of 58 county central committees Congressional district co-chairpersons 16 office holders

Elections

A person may register to vote in California who is 18, a citizen of the United States and a resident of the county of registration for at least 30 days prior to the election (and who is otherwise not disqualified, such as in the case of certain felons). There are several types of elections in California:

• *State primaries.* These take place the first Tuesday after the first Monday in June of even-numbered years. At these elections, nominees for national, state and some local offices are selected. Usually, there are a number of propositions also on the ballot.

• *State general elections.* These take place on the first Tuesday after the first Monday in November of even-numbered years, and voters make their selections from among the nominees chosen in the primaries. The ballot usually contains more propositions.

• *Special elections.* These rarely take place on a statewide basis because of high cost, although there was one in November 1973 when Governor Ronald Reagan put his tax-limitation initiative to a vote (it lost). Special elections are more often held locally to fill vacancies in Congress and the state Legislature. These are different from most other elections in that the voters are given a list of candidates of all parties. If no one candidate receives a simple majority, a runoff is held four weeks later among the top vote-getters in each party. In some cases, this means that candidates far down the list make the runoff while the candidate who finished second in number of votes does not.

• *Local elections.* Often, elections for local city council and special district-director posts are not consolidated with the primary and general elections and are held at various times during the year.

Political History

During the early years of state history, there were rapid political swings based on economics. When things went well, the big-business interests were in control. During a depression period in the 1870s, the Workingmen's Party under Denis Kearney of San Francisco came to power and managed to get much of its program enacted. When prosperity returned, the party disappeared. Economic and political power went into the hands of the "Big Four" — railroad magnates Charles Crocker, Mark Hopkins, Collis P. Huntington and Leland Stanford. Southern Pacific dominated California politics from the 1880s until the advent of the Progressives more than 25 years later.

The Progressives

Republican newspaper editors started in the first decade of this century to drum up opposition to the railroads and the boss of San Francisco, Abe Ruef. Disgruntled Republicans started the Lincoln-Roosevelt league, and graft-fighter Hiram Johnson became the group's candidate for governor. He pledged to kick Southern Pacific out of the Republican Party and out of California government. He won easily and immediately started enacting reforms such as the initiative, referendum, recall, cross-filing, civil service, and a multitude of other programs. Johnson went to the United States Senate in 1916 and was succeeded by another progressive, William D. Stephens. The movement lost its force in the 1920s as postwar prosperity produced political apathy. Until the next depression, the regular Republicans maintained control of state government.

The Great Depression resulted in the 1934 gubernatorial candidacy of muckraking author Upton Sinclair (his slogan: "End Poverty in California") with his radical plan for reforming the economic system. Republican Frank Merriam defeated Sinclair by about a quarter of a million votes. With the Democrats riding high nationally under President Franklin D. Roosevelt, the Republicans finally lost the governorship in 1938 to state Senator Culbert Olson.

Four years later, a new progressive era began under Earl Warren. Aided by cross-filing, the former Alameda County district attorney and state attorney general portrayed himself as a non-partisan official — an image he embroidered later as an activist Chief Justice of the United States. Warren's personal popularity was unprecedented in California political history. He was able to push most of his programs through the Legislature (with a compulsory health-insurance plan the notable exception). Warren was the Republican vice-presidential nominee in 1948 (with Thomas Dewey) and perhaps could have remained governor indefinitely. After 10 years as the state's chief executive, he was named U.S. chief justice by President Eisenhower in 1953.

The new governor was Goodwin J. Knight, who was reelected in his own right in 1954 but was unable to establish himself as leader of the Republican Party because he had to contend with two other major figures, then-Vice-President Richard Nixon and U.S. Senator William Knowland. In 1958, Knowland decided that for political and personal reasons — he thought being governor was a better stepping stone to the presidency — he would leave his safe Senate seat to run for governor. Knight was pushed aside and virtually forced to run for Knowland's seat. Knowland embraced a right-to-work initiative, setting the stage for a massive Democratic victory led by the gubernatorial candidate, Edmund G. (Pat) Brown. Nixon, defeated in a 1960 run for president against John F. Kennedy, tried an unsuccessful comeback by running against Brown in 1962.

In his second term, Brown became embroiled in a bitter intra-party fight with the powerful speaker of the Assembly, Jesse M. Unruh, and elected to seek a third term rather than give his arch-rival a clear shot at his job. In the primary election, Brown's forces concentrated on shooting down the moderate Republican candidate, former San Francisco Mayor George Christopher, preferring to run against the conservative Ronald Reagan, a former actor. Somebody goofed: Reagan crushed Brown in the general by a million votes.

Democratic nominee Unruh tried to unseat Reagan four years later. Although plagued by limited financial resources, Unruh cut Reagan's victory margin in half. Reagan kept his 1966 pledge not to seek a third term in 1974, leaving the gates wide open. Twenty-nine candidates ran in the primary, with Brown's son, Jerry, and Houston I. Flournoy emerging from the pack to represent the Democratic and Republican parties in November. Brown won by only 179,000 votes, almost blowing his big early lead. Four years later, he rebounded with a 1.3-million-vote victory over the GOP attorney general, Evelle J. Younger.

In 1982 Jerry Brown continued the two-term limit tradition and ran for U.S. Senator (he lost to San Diego Mayor Pete Wilson, a Republican). Attorney General George Deukmejian won a tough primary against Lieutenant Governor Mike Curb for the Republican party nomination and squeaked past the Democratic candidate, Los Angeles Mayor Tom Bradley, in November.

In a repeat in 1986, Deukmejian trounced Bradley, winning by over a million and a half votes. Alan Cranston won re-election to a fourth term in the U.S. Senate, defeating Republican Rep. Ed Zschau.

Pete Wilson maintained Republican control of the state's chief executive position with his victory over Democrat Dianne Feinstein in November 1990. Wilson's non-ideological, pragmatic philosophy is more in the Warren, not Reagan, mold.

For the first time this century both U.S. Senate seats were up for election in 1992, the extra seat as a result of Pete Wilson's resignation from the Senate. 🏛

SURLY VOTERS STAY HOME

Few citizens make decisions for everyone

By Richard Zeiger

Reprinted from *California Journal*, November 1990

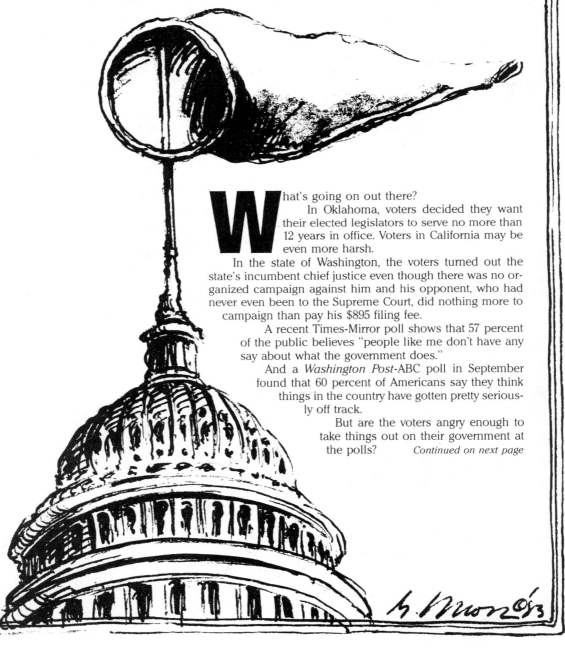

What's going on out there?

In Oklahoma, voters decided they want their elected legislators to serve no more than 12 years in office. Voters in California may be even more harsh.

In the state of Washington, the voters turned out the state's incumbent chief justice even though there was no organized campaign against him and his opponent, who had never even been to the Supreme Court, did nothing more to campaign than pay his $895 filing fee.

A recent Times-Mirror poll shows that 57 percent of the public believes "people like me don't have any say about what the government does."

And a *Washington Post*-ABC poll in September found that 60 percent of Americans say they think things in the country have gotten pretty seriously off track.

But are the voters angry enough to take things out on their government at the polls? *Continued on next page*

Party Identification

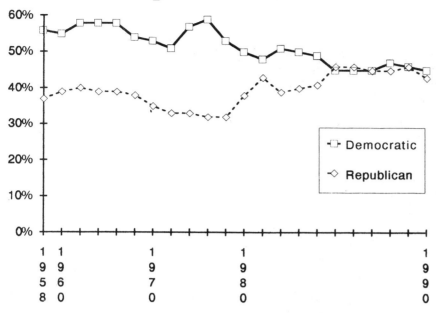

| | 1 9 5 8 | 1 9 6 0 | | 1 9 7 0 | | 1 9 8 0 | | 1 9 9 0 |

- Democratic
- Republican

——— Source: Field Institute ———

Political Participation

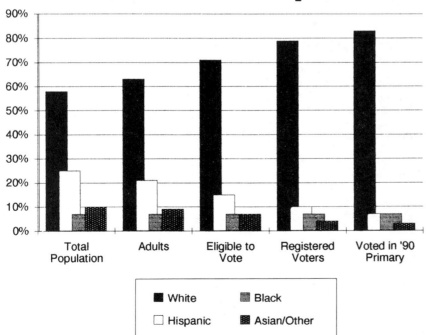

Total Population · Adults · Eligible to Vote · Registered Voters · Voted in '90 Primary

■ White ▨ Black □ Hispanic ▦ Asian/Other

By most accounts, they will not. With few exceptions, incumbents remain as safe as ever. Opinion polls, although showing a public increasingly disenchanted with government in general, still like their own elected officials.

If anything, voters are showing their unhappiness by just staying away on election day.

"We're throwing a national party, and nobody is showing up," notes University of California, Davis, political science professor Ed Constantini.

Things have reached such a state that the number of people voting in the 1986 primary and general elections was actually 140,000 *less* than the number that voted in the election held in 1966, 20 years earlier, despite the fact that the state had gained six million eligible voters in those 20 years.

And in all probability the percentage of voters actually going to the polls will continue to drop — even though in California there is an exciting race for governor and an array of important initiative measures to be considered.

"The ironic thing," notes pollster Mervin Field, "is that the voters are likely to approve [legislative term limits] with a record low turn-out vote. It's as if, as they are leaving, they're tossing a grenade back over their shoulders."

The California electorate is clearly changing. They are more suspicious of their government, question it's ability to accomplish anything of substance, and are more inclined to react by withdrawing completely.

And those left in the system are less and less like the state's population as a whole — a situation that some believe bodes ill for California's future.

In part the answer is one of demographics. The people voting now are the people who have always voted: They are Anglo, older, well-educated and more affluent than the population as a whole.

But in California, that group makes up a smaller and smaller portion of the population. The Field Institute, headed by Field, estimates that only about 59 percent of the state's 19 million eligible voters are actually registered. But the percentages change markedly as the population grows older. Of those between 18 and 24, only 33 percent are registered. Of those over 60, 72 percent are registered to vote. Field also finds 65 percent of the Anglo voters registered, but only 42 percent of the Latinos, 58 percent of the Blacks and

39 percent of the Asians.

Even when registered, Asians and Latinos are less likely to vote than Anglos or Blacks. This means is that in the June primary, where 43 percent of the eligible population actually voted, only 17 percent of the state's voters were Latino, Asian or Black, even though those three ethnic groups make up some 42 percent of the population.

Some of the reasons for this lack of voting are demographic. The minority population, particularly among Asians and Hispanics, is younger than the population as a whole, and many are not citizens.

In a speech delivered at UCLA earlier this year, Field said that he "would not be too disturbed if a 30 to 40 percent participation rate, or even lower, reflected a reasonably representative cross-section of the public. However, I am disturbed, if not alarmed, by what I see going on in California and in other parts of the country. Diminished turnouts mean that small numbers of elites are exercising more control. The agenda of the voting elites — whites, college-educated, older people, the unpoor — is obviously demonstrably different than those who do not vote. The more that non-voters become different than voters in color, in class, in attitudes toward life, we create and build threatening pressures which could easily explode and alter for the worse the future course of our precious democracy."

Field says these non-voters can be placed into four categories. The first, and probably the easiest to bring into the system, are the 10 percent of the non-voters who can't vote for technical reasons. Either they have recently moved and failed to re-register or they become interested in the election only to find that the registration deadline has passed. These problems can be eliminated by easing legal restrictions on registering to vote, Field believes.

Field believes that another 30 percent of the non-voters are what he called "contented apathetics." These are people who "believe their lives will go along in a generally tolerable state without their having to pay attention to what is going on politically." In the past, this group could be roused to vote on occasion by a neighbor, boss or union official. But now, many in this group have never been to the polls,

and it is becoming increasingly more difficult to entice them there.

"If you haven't ever voted, and you are in your 30s or older, there is little likelihood you will start voting," Field notes.

The biggest group, about 40 percent of the non-voters, are people who Field calls "politically passive or politically inert." Many have poor incomes and little education. "These people are devoting most of their daily energy just to keep up economically and to cope with life," he said.

The last group, about 20 percent of the non-voters, are the "politically alienated" who believe they can't have any effect on their government.

"They are cynical of candidate and campaign organization promises. They don't think voting will do much about the mounting and heavy problems facing our society. These people feel it doesn't matter whether a Democrat or a Republican wins ..."

The reduction in electoral participation has had substantial impacts on the political parties, with the Democrats, in most cases, hit hardest by the trend.

Certainly that is the case in California where Democrats have seen their registration edge diminish to only 2 percentage points, down from an 18-percentage point advantage 20 years ago and a 12-point advantage 10 years ago. Furthermore, Democrats generally believe that those who are not registered — particularly Latinos and Asians — are a natural Democratic constituency.

"The non-voting population has historically been on the left," notes UC Davis' Constantini.

That observation, however, may not be as true as in the past. The Field survey indicates that of those not registered, 45 percent consider themselves Democrats, but 44 percent say they would be Republicans — a 25-point change over the past 10 years.

Constantini noted that the big change came with Ronald Reagan, who was the candidate favored by the non-voting population.

As a result of this change, at least a few Republicans have been rethinking their traditional resistance to making it easy for citizens to register and to vote, perceiving that they may now have at least an even chance of signing up new voters. But the other side of that coin is that these new Republicans, should they be recruited to the ranks of voters, may turn out not to be

as loyal as traditional Republican registrants.

This historically different attitude between Democrats and Republicans has caused them to view the causes and effects of non-registration differently.

Earlier this year, Governor George Deukmejian expressed little concern that the number of voters is diminishing. Their lack of concern is merely an expression of passive approval of Republican policies — his and presidents Reagan and Bush — that have been successful.

Democrats, however, view the situation with alarm, saying that these disenchanted voters have been driven out of the system by Republican administrations that repeatedly ignored their needs. Some, indeed, see voter disenchantment as a temporary situation that will disappear when government becomes more responsive.

Walter Zelman, former California director of Common Cause, and an unsuccessful candidate for the Democratic nomination as state insurance commissioner, believes Democrats have been seduced by Reagan economics, and that, if the country enters a recession as expected, Democrats can bring back the disenchanted with their traditional economic appeals.

The state's non-voters are "people not well-off economically, without a great deal of education or interest, get cross-pressured. They worry about economic issues — a strength of Democrats — but they don't buy into a lot of the social issues, like crime, drugs, abortion or pornography," says Zelman.

Zelman argues that, in the Reagan years, even Democrats became conservative economically, favoring tax cuts that primarily benefited those who were already better off financially.

"Without the economic argument, why would they stay with the Democrats?" he asks.

But with a change of economic times, Zelman believes that Democrats will return to "their traditional soak-the-rich" politics and that these disenchanted voters will return to their ranks. Field, however, isn't as sanguine about the prospects for getting more Americans to vote.

"This is a trend that has been going on for 20 years. I don't see any signs that it's changing," he said. 🏛

ABSENTEE BALLOTS

Mail-order voters tip the balance in close elections

By Gale Cook

Reprinted from *California Journal*, February 1991

"The liar's club," California election officials used to call it. Those few determined citizens who completed a daunting affidavit to qualify for an absentee ballot were considered nuisances — cranks who found excuses not to go to the polls like regular folks. That view prevailed through decades when less than 2 percent of the election vote was absentee.

That was then.

This is now: Almost one in five voters routinely uses the absentee ballot. More than 18 percent of the 7.9

Gale Cook, a retired Capitol correspondent for the San Francisco Examiner, *is a freelance writer from El Macero.*

million men and women who voted in the November 6th general election were absentees.

Everyone is doing it. They don't need a reason. They just ask for an absentee ballot — in person, by messenger, by mail, by fax. They do it for convenience, because they're too busy to go to the polling place, or very likely because a political party or election campaign organization sent them an application. It's the new wave.

A water engineer in Davis votes by mail as early as possible (29 days before election day) and thumbtacks on his door the tear-off stub of his ballot, which says: "I have voted. Have you?" This discourages pesky campaign workers and reduces election leaflets left on his porch. When a political campaigner starts a telephone pitch, he cuts in, "I already voted."

The absentee phenomenon reflects an on-the-go society of always-busy, two-worker families. Its members are pressed for time and prefer to make a reasoned decision at the kitchen table about interminable and complex ballots. Wait in line at the polling place? Say, what?

The Democratic-controlled Legislature took the shackles off absentee voting in 1978, reasoning that the party would benefit from eased restrictions. As it turned out, the Republicans were first to cash that blank check. The Democrats seemed to have forgotten that John Kennedy narrowly won California in the polling booths in 1960 but lost the state to Richard Nixon through the absentee ballot count. A fluke, some said.

But 1982 was no fluke. The Republicans quietly sent absentee ballot applications to every GOP household in the state. Los Angeles Mayor Tom Bradley led in the race for governor by 20,000 votes at the polling places but lost to George Deukmejian by the Duke's 113,000-vote victory among absentees.

Democrats have struck back. In 1983 San Francisco Mayor Dianne Feinstein fought off a recall attempt by persuading 38 percent of the voters to cast ballots absentee. In a Stanislaus County special congressional election in 1989, Democrat Gary Condit defeated Republican Clare Berryhill through an absentee drive. Forty percent of Condit's 50,000 votes were absentee. Democrat Sal Cannella then used the same technique to win the Assembly seat vacated by Condit. In San Diego, Democrat Lucy Killea defeated Republican Carol Bentley in a Senate race in which absentees settled the matter.

Impressed, Stanislaus County supervisors briefly considered asking Senator Dan McCorquodale, a San Jose Democrat, to carry a bill to authorize all-mail elections, but backed off in the face of strong conservative opposition.

Election officials point out that under the present system each absentee vote costs counties about $10 compared to $2 per vote at the polls. On the other hand, all-mail elections — with a few polling places kept open for last minute voters — could cut election costs in half.

"I think that would be real difficult to get that to go over with the public at this point," said Karen Matthews, Stanislaus' registrar of voters.

California's absentee ballot system, one of the most liberal in the nation, was twice challenged in court last year by losers. San Francisco District Attorney Arlo Smith, the Democratic candidate for attorney general, led Republican Dan Lungren by about 30,000 votes in the election night count. Absentee voters, chiefly in Orange County, eventually gave the race to Lungren by about the same figure.

Smith challenged all 1.4 million absentee ballots on the grounds that, while election officials checked signatures on ballot envelopes, 37 counties didn't do so on ballot applications. The judge turned Smith down, saying that even if technical violations occurred, Section 1001 of the elections code required that the law "shall be liberally construed in favor of the absent voter."

In Berkeley, where Mayor Loni Hancock had a 77-vote lead in a runoff, her challenger asked the court to order counting of 386 mail ballots not received by the close of election day. The judge declined, pointing out that the law does not make an exception for delays in the mail, postmark notwithstanding.

Absentee voting is not new in the United States. In 1656 the Massachusetts Colony proclaimed that voters — in other words, male citizens — "shall have liberty ... to send their voices by proxy." The New Plymouth Colony ordained in 1672 that proxy votes would be permitted for reasons of "age, disability of body, urgent occupation and other inconveniences that do accrue sundry of the freemen." Proxy voting was a necessity in those days because in-person balloting would require the virtual evacuation of able-bodied men from the farmlands and frontiers.

The California Legislature first tried to permit absentee voting during the Civil War. In 1863 it passed two acts that would have allowed Union soldiers to vote away from home. A court held these statutes unconstitutional because the soldiers were not residing in their home counties.

In 1914, with the Great War beginning, a constitutional amendment was placed on the California ballot to allow absent voting by citizens who were 10 miles or more from home on election day. It was defeated 390,330 to 244,855.

Further attempts failed at the polls in 1918 and 1920, but in 1922, with opposition dwindling, voters narrowly approved absentee balloting, 352,822 to 340,257. Its use was rigidly defined, but the process was liberalized over the years.

The word "fraud" has been bandied about increasingly with the rise in absentee voting. Nobody can prove it, but the suspicion is there, bolstered by massive absentee-ballot drives in political campaigns. The state Republican Party mailed absentee-voter applications to four million GOP households last year.

Ernest Hawkins, Sacramento County registrar, cites the potential for creating a roll of "ghost voters." These ghostly intruders would be fake names enrolled by postcard registration, which is legal in California; the ghosts then would become undetectable absentee-ballot voters in future elections.

Privately, a Senate staffer said, "No [district attorney] in his right mind would waste his time on election violations with drug dealing and heavy crime around."

All this has caused harrumphing in newspaper editorial columns. Nobody comes right out against voting by mail, but the editorial board consensus is that the Legislature, which

> "We've found that it's an excellent way to mobilize the base and get votes in from people who for whatever reason might not make it to the polls on election day."
> — Dan Schnur

opened this tap, should — well — take a good hard look at it.

The *San Francisco Chronicle* declared recently: "It is important to encourage increased voter participation in a time of disappointing turnout, but the Legislature should explore the possibility of doing so without permitting the use of absentee voting as just another example of political guile."

Noting the potential for fraud, *The Sacramento Bee* warned that "there is a growing chance that public trust in the electoral process will be undermined," and called for "a top to bottom review of the absentee voter system."

While acknowledging that voting by mail one day may be the way to go, the *San Francisco Examiner* said: "But the Legislature needs to tighten the rules under which absentee ballots are distributed. Campaign workers should not be permitted to apply for ballots in behalf of voters. There is too much potential for abuse. Whether in person or by mail, voting needs to be honest." Most election officials say talk of fraud is blown out of proportion. One who makes no bones about it is Conny McCormack, San Diego county registrar and member of a task force created by Secretary of State March Fong Eu to study absentee issues.

"Most [fraud talk] is paranoia," she said. "I think it's totally not there. I think this is not a problem. We do not see fraud. I don't say we don't see mistakes. We just haven't seen fraud. I think it is just one of those red herrings for campaigns to talk about, especially losing campaigns."

Nevertheless, opponents raise a legitimate issue in charging that county registrars fail to check voter signatures on absentee-ballot applications as well as on the ballot envelopes when the vote comes in.

The language is murky indeed in Section 1007 of the Elections Code. It says the signature on an absentee-ballot envelope "must" be compared with that on the original voter registration. As for signatures and addresses on absentee-ballot applications, those merely "should" be checked.

It would be "hideously redundant and expensive ... to check the signature at the application stage," McCormack said.

Thirty-six other county registrars agree, and Melissa Warren, Secretary Eu's media director, said: "Our contention is that this is optional, that those counties [which skip the application screening do so] in the interest of getting the ballot to the voter."

Although Republicans traditionally oppose liberalizing the voting process, the party takes an understandably serene view of the absentee-ballot system in California.

"We're real supportive of an aggressive absentee program," said Dan Schnur, a former GOP spokesman who now serves as Governor Pete Wilson's deputy director for communications and public affairs. "We've found that it's an excellent way to mobilize the base and get votes in from people who, for whatever reason, might not make it to the polls on election day."

The opportunity for fraud does exist, Schnur said, and the party would view an all-mail ballot as extreme. The important thing is to give the voters an option, he said.

"Our concern is mobilizing the vote. Whatever the guidelines are, we'll follow to the nth degree. You set the rules and we'll play by them," said Schnur.

Senate Democratic leader David Roberti said he is worried that the proliferation of absentee voting may cause "an abridgement of privacy" through applications "filled out by persons other than the applicant."

Former Governor Jerry Brown, state chairman of the Democratic Party, said the absentee ballot increases

voter turnout but is hugely expensive as a campaign tool and tends to be used largely by upper-income and therefore more conservative voters. Most of the voters it rallies always vote anyway, he said, and new voters in that group may be only about 20 percent of the total.

"It's like a new high-tech weapon, which really doesn't give you any advantage because the other side has the same thing," he said. "I don't know about fraud, but it is an enormous expense, just another layer of campaign spending making politics more dependent on special interests money."

Brown said the increase in the use of absentee ballots obscures the fact that voter turn-out is declining. The 58.6 percent turnout of registered voters November 6th was the lowest of this century — and only 41 percent of the state's 19.2 million population. "Fewer people [175,183 fewer] voted in 1990 than voted in 1982 when I ran against Wilson," Brown said.

"The absentee ballot is good, but the state must [go to] automatic registration. With the absentee ballot should be state enrollment of all citizens over 18 to vote. The registration thing was invented to depress turnout. Before 1900 most states didn't have registration," said the former governor. "And we have to get some public financing in the form of discounted mailings and free television time."

Ever the visionary, Brown added: "I am in favor of voting by computer or by telephone ultimately. That's where we're going. We can't live in the horse-and-buggy age forever."

In any case, the absentee ballot is going to be reexamined in the Legislature this year and next. Hearings are being scheduled in the Assembly and Senate elections committees, and lawmakers are mulling over election-law bills to introduce.

"There will be a spate of legislation," one staffer predicted. Said another, "People just don't want to wait 40 days to find out the results of an election."

Caren Daniels-Meade, chief of the Secretary of State's elections division and chair of the absentee-ballot task force, said measures will be taken to standardize and clarify the handling, verifying and counting of absentee ballots.

All this might raise a smile from a one-time state senator and attorney general — the late Robert Kenny. In 1939 he introduced SB14 calling for all-mail elections. It was ignored. ▲

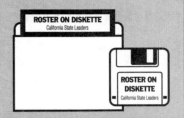

Candidates among the corn flakes

Buying television time for campaigns

Reprinted from *California Journal*, October 1991

By Chris Ziegler and A.G. Block

Ah, politics. The people's business. The wheeling and dealing of public policy-making. Speeches, balloons, bumper stickers, televised debate. But that's the visible part of politics, the tip of the iceberg. Below the surface lurks the business of politics. And lately, that business has become mighty lucrative for an increasing number of specialists who regard politics as something of a gold mine.

Politics is a large, profitable industry. And like any industry, it has its accompanying mini-industries of middlemen. For instance, no modern candidate would consider running for office without a campaign consultant, and probably a pollster as well. And few consultants enter a campaign without a sub-specialist — an expert who buys air time or space for the candidate's political advertisements.

These latter firms — called media management or time buyers, and long active in the advertising business — have become important because political campaign teams increasingly sell candidates like Kellogg sells corn flakes. Media-management firms are familiar with media business practices, buy time for them and know how to avoid being gouged by unscrupulous stations.

Most media-management firms serve both businesses and politicians, and the language of the industry is wholly that of television marketing. Buyers use the same demographic research television advertisers use, such as the Nielsen ratings and Arbitron, and speak in terms of ratings points, "spots," "the creative," and "lowest unit rate." Most firms are non-partisan, although some take positions on a few large issues. Media Plus in Seattle, Washington, for instance, is "a pro-choice shop," president Kathy Neukirchen says.

When a candidate wants to make a television commercial, his or her campaign consultant hires an advertising agency to design and produce the ad, called "the creative." Some consultants, like Republican-oriented Ray McNally, believe the time buyer should be included in planning campaign strategy, even helping decide what type of commercial should be made, based on the audience to be targeted and the stations that will broadcast the commercial.

Others, like Democratic consultant David Townsend, believe time buyers are "basically a brokerage."

The consultant generally hires the media buyer, although "we try to play as much of a role as the campaign will let us," Neukirchen says. She prefers to have contact with the campaign since it controls the money, and broadcasters require payment up front because political campaigns are often in debt. Time buyers receive between 3 and 7 percent of the cost of the buy, depending on the size of the purchase, and are paid by the consultant, McNally says.

continued on next page

Chris Ziegler was a California Journal *summer intern. A.G. Block is managing editor of the* Journal.

Once the advertisement has been designed and the particular audience targeted, the media-management company simply buys the broadcast time or ad space. While broadcasters have lists of rates for certain time spots, these prices fluctuate between $10 to $10,000 for a 30-second commercial, depending on the time slot, says Byron Elton, sales manager at KXTV in Sacramento. Time buyers hinge their reputations on their ability to get good rates for their clients.

"**A** good media service knows how to lock up the right spots for a candidate," says Milton Beckman, president of National Media Consultant.

There are several types of rates: the fixed rate, the charging of which is frowned upon by the FCC; and the lowest unit rate, which is the rate required by the commission to be offered to candidates, says Bill Maguire, salesman for Los Angeles television station KABC.

The fixed rate is a special category of charges for candidates, and the FCC disapproves of this because the cost is often higher than what other advertisers pay for their commercials to appear in the same time period. As its name suggests, the lowest unit rate is the lowest price paid by a corporate advertiser whose commercial is to be aired during the same time period as the candidate's ad, Maguire explains. The lowest unit rate must be offered to campaigns for 45 days before a primary and 65 days before the general election.

The FCC mandates that stations offer the lowest unit rate, but many consultants believe, and time buyers claim, that candidates would be overcharged for advertising without the guidance and expertise of media-management firms. Townsend charges that broadcasters raise their rates at the end of summer, just in time for the political season, and that "they usually just rape you if you're an issue," since the lowest unit rate rule applies only to candidates and not to proposition campaigns.

Stations hotly deny this assertion. "We try to treat everyone equitably." says Dave Ulrickson, business manager at Sacramento television station KOVR.

"I don't believe that when you're dealing with politicians that buying services represent an edge," Maguire says, adding that he considers media-management firms unnecessary if stations follow FCC rules and treat candidates like other advertising customers.

Not all broadcasters follow the rules, however. In September 1990 the FCC audited 30 stations across the country, including six radio and television broadcasters in the San Francisco Bay Area, and found overcharging of candidates, largely by offering fixed rates. According to Maguire, the FCC audit "was very effective" in that "it made stations pay more attention to what they were doing" in following FCC regulations on political advertising. And it prompted the FCC to clarify its rules, which stations and time buyers alike call very confusing and often changing.

Meanwhile, candidates themselves are becoming more and more grumpy about what they perceive as gouging. To this end, Governor Pete Wilson and his 1988 U.S. Senate opponent, Lieutenant Governor Leo McCarthy, recently filed suit against 22 California television stations, alleging that their respective campaigns were overcharged for advertising.

It is such incidents of gouging and consultants' insecurity about dealing with the broadcasting industry that cause them to turn to media-management firms for help with their advertising campaigns. "They help you make smart buys," McNally says. Time buying is "a speciality science, it's complex and it moves very quickly. It's rough and tumble." McNally has purchased air time for his candidates but he prefers to use a time buyer as a matter of efficiency and convenience. "A campaign must move a very large number of people from point A to point B" and anything that helps do this will be used, McNally says, adding, "We need to hit voters hard and we need to hit them often."

"They know the lingo; they know the game," says Townsend on why he uses buying services for many of his races. He adds, however, that he will buy the time himself if it is a local race, so he can maintain contacts with local media.

Media-management firms also see themselves as a tool to be used in winning a political race. "Our objective is to get the candidate elected," Neukirchen says. "The object is to win."

Neukirchen emphasizes the belief that the electoral process is vital and that candidates should have every resource available to them to disseminate their campaign messages. "If you have a bad sale, you can have another sale ... but you only have one day to win in a political campaign," Neukirchen says. "The stakes are so high ... it all comes down to one day."

Jean Brooks, senior vice president of Western International Media, compared candidates to corporations seeking to sell a product. "They must market themselves based on a specific message," she says. Politics has become so complex that "it does require that all sorts of tools are used to communicate to people."

"I'm very idealistic and the reason I'm involved in this is that I am idealistic," Brooks says. "I feel that what we're doing is providing a public service by providing access" for candidates to the electorate.

Brooks rejects the idea that the use of time buyers helps give politics a corporate image, which could alienate voters, and has raised the cost of running for office. "Debates still occur; there are still town hall meetings," she says.

Use of time buyers is extensive in campaigning, but not all consultants use them. Leo McElroy consults mainly for initiative campaigns, usually for the underdog side, and so does not often have a lot of money to spend on advertising. He uses a time buyer if a lot of money is involved or it is in the last days of a campaign when he has little time to haggle with stations. He also uses a time buyer if the advertisement is to be done by direct mail or in newspapers or magazines, because he is not familiar with those areas of the mass media, McElroy says. McElroy cites his 31 years work in broadcasting as the reason why he does not need to use media management firms, and says that stations call him when they are unclear on FCC rules.

McElroy appears to be an exception. Most consultants consider media-management firms a necessary tool when managing a campaign. Time buyers, of course, see themselves as indispensible to the political process. For the station salespeople, "It's pretty much business as usual," says Sacramento KRCA-TV advertising manager Ron Longinotti.

And the bottom line?

"The good thing about political advertising is that they spend a lot of money," Elton said. ▥

The Woman candidate

A different kind of politician

By Richard Zeiger

Reprinted from *California Journal*,
February 1992

Conventional wisdom says that reapportionment years are good for political outsiders. New districts shake things up, creating open seats that can be won by the traditionally disenfranchised.

So under any circumstances, this might turn out to be a good year for women politicians. Many women serve on city councils or boards of supervisors and are in position to take advantage of openings in the state Legislature or in Congress. But beyond that, there are many politicians who believe — with the electorate seemingly disenchanted with politicians — that this may be an exceptionally good time for women to win elective office.

Furthermore, there is an increasing body of evidence to show that the voters would be right when they think electing women will give them a different kind of politician. Recent studies completed by the Center for the American Woman and Politics at Rutgers University show not only that women politicians worry about a different set of issues than men, but

Christopher Elliot, a journalism graduate student at the University of California, Berkeley, contributed to this story. Richard Zeiger is editor of the California Journal.

that they actually operate in a different way than their male colleagues, trying harder to listen and bring in the opinions of groups that have been left out of the process.

The stereotypes about women, and particularly about women politicians, that have long functioned as a way of keeping them out of the political limelight, may now turn into an asset. Women were perceived as not tough enough to play on political ball fields; they didn't have the crass characteristics necessary to make it in the rough-and-tumble of politics. But now, polls say, the voters don't care much for the rough-and-tumble. They feel politicians care too much about the game, and not enough about the voters they are supposed to serve. The very "caring" nature — once viewed as a liability for women thought of as "too soft" for the political arena — is now perceived as an asset. And if voters are angry enough, it may be a very big asset to *not* be "one of the boys."

"It may be enough that we are viewed as part of the solution, and not part of the problem," noted Nevada Lieutenant Governor Sue Wagner.

"Women are more conscientious about their work and are less controlled by the process of politics," noted Republican state Senator Marian Bergeson of Newport Beach. "They are interested in finding solutions, and the public recognizes that."

Continued on next page

The number of women in public office, both in California and across the country has been steadily growing. In 1969 women comprised only 4 percent of elected representatives in state legislatures, compared with 18.3 percent in 1991. In California, 21 of the 120 legislative seats, or 17.5 percent, are held by women.

A study by the secretary of state's office indicates that, at least in recent years, women are winning office at about the same rate as men, an indication that, at least, there is no longer an electoral disadvantage to being a women. In the 1990 elections, 106 of 615 candidates were women, about 17.4 percent. This is roughly the same percentage that have sought office in each of the past five election cycles, according to the study.

But in that first year, 1982, only 14 women were elected to the state Legislature, or under 12 percent.

Gains at the higher levels of politics have been slower in coming. The Congress, for example, remains a male bastion. As of last year, women held only 6.4 percent of the seats in the House of Representatives and only two seats, or 2 percent, in the Senate.

Indeed, it was the lack of representation in the Senate, graphically on display during hearings on Clarence Thomas' confirmation for the U. S. Supreme Court, that has become something of a rallying point for female politicians across the country. Groups promoting women candidates in both parties reported a surge in donations following the hearings. The money will provide an early boost for women candidates at all levels during the coming election season.

Deborah Hicks, communications director for Emily's List, a national group whose members promote women candidates, said the group's membership increased by 70 percent in the months following the Thomas hearings.

The situation in California has not escaped the attention of women's groups. After all, it is possible, with former San Francisco Mayor Dianne Feinstein running for one U.S. Senate seat and Democratic Congresswoman Barbara Boxer running for another, that California by itself could double the number of women in the U.S. Senate. Emily's List, for example, has already sent out a mailer to its members urging them to support both Boxer and Feinstein.

But if gains have been slow at the top, they have been nothing short of spectacular at lower levels. For example, the number of women on city councils or as mayors in California has increased by 111 percent, from 220 to 465, during the 10 years before 1985, according to a study by the Rutgers center.

And it is these lower-level political offices, on city councils or school boards, that have traditionally been the point of entry for women politicians. Their male colleagues might jump to the Legislature from private industry, or, more likely, from the staff of an incumbent, but women win their stripes the hard way.

But even if they have labored for years at lower governmental levels, women still are perceived by the voters as outsiders. And in this election year, that might prove to be an enormous advantage. Furthermore, the new study by the Center for the American Woman and Politics shows that women really do behave differently than most male politicians.

For one thing, the study shows that women have a significantly different policy agenda than men. They are more

likely to make issues involving health care or children — and, of course, women's rights — their top legislative priorities than are men. Even Republican women legislators were more likely to have one of these issues as a top priority than their male colleagues, even when party differences were taken into consideration. Not only that, but women legislators apparently have a significantly different style of lawmaking than do their male colleagues. The study shows that women are more likely to reach out to citizen groups or to the economically disadvantaged for legislative support than are men. And they are more adamant that government be conducted in public than their male colleagues.

The study also showed that these policy differences and differences in approach to government hold up even when women move into leadership positions within a legislature.

The differences don't exist for all women or all men, but the study shows that, more likely than not, when voters select a woman, they really *will* be getting a different kind of politician.

Still, there are major hurdles to be overcome before women can expand their numbers, and impact, substantially.

Although the amount of seed money for women candidates is growing, they still fall short when it comes to collecting the early money necessary to get a campaign started.

And although many women believe that Proposition 140, the initiative measure limiting terms in the state Legislature to six or eight years, will, at least in the short run, be good for women, others think that, ultimately, professional women politicians will find the limits just as discouraging as do their male colleagues.

Indeed, there are those who believe that women, who now hold a higher proportion of local offices, may be unwilling to give them up for the relative insecurity of life in the state Legislature.

"It could be that women don't want to run for a few short terms in office," noted Nettie Becker, co-chair of the Los Angeles Women's Campaign Fund, "They'd be putting all that time and money into a campaign and then be out there afterwards looking for a job."

And while disenchantment with the political system and "politics as usual" may work to the advantage of women candidates, it is not clear what effect a sagging economy will have on their fortunes. After all, economics, money, has traditionally been the province of men.

State Treasurer Kathleen Brown, for one, believes that women candidates have a harder time than men proving they understand money and the economy.

"At every stop in my campaign I'd have to go over the size of the budgets I'd administered and how many bonds I'd sold. I'd have to prove myself each time. It became my mantra," said Brown.

If a woman can overcome this initial skepticism, though, Brown, too, believes women will have an advantage in this election year.

"Women have an extremely good opportunity to move in this environment. We're positioned; we're moving up," she said.

Bergeson, among others, argues that even questions of the economy will work for women this time around. "In tough times," she said, "it comes down to setting priorities. And the issues that concern women, health and the family, are right at the top of most people's priority lists."

Who are they?

Check out their political agenda: public financing of campaigns; pro-choice on abortion; universal health care; radical cuts in military spending; bans on clear-cutting forests, pesticides, animal-growth hormones and offshore oil drilling; basic rights for housing, child care, education and employment for all — regardless of race or sexual orientation.

The Democratic Party, you say?

Try again — Democrats hate them.

Surely not the Republican Party?

No, but Republicans — including some of the more conservative — like them and wish them well.

Confused?

They're — ta da — the Green Party. And as of January 1, 1992, they'd registered 96,354 Californians under their banner — substantially more than the 80,000 signatures needed to qualify us for a spot on the 1992 ballot. Come June, they'll be right in there with Democrats and Republicans and Libertarians and American Independents and Peace and Freedomites.

The Green Party is the first new party to qualify for the California ballot since the Libertarians appeared in 1980. Two other so-called "third parties" were founded in 1968: the American Independent Party and the Peace and Freedom Party.

The decision to launch the Greens' voter-registration effort in California grew out of a dream by activist Kent Smith, a Sacramentan who has since become state party chairman. According to Smith, he dreamed about a lush soccer field where two teams held sway. Smith and his fellow activists were relegated to the bleachers. "I saw us sitting on our hands while Republicans and Democrats dominated the field of public policy," Smith said. Motivated by that dream, Smith helped organize a meeting of 60 like-minded activists from around the state. And from that meeting, held in Sacramento in February 1990, came the decision to launch a statewide voter-registration drive meant to put Greens on the 1992 ballot.

The California Green Party is part of an national environmental movement known as the Green Committees of Correspondence, a nationwide organization formed in 1984 and made up of more than 200 local groups across the United States. About 40 of these groups are in California. It is modeled after European Green parties, which were successful in gaining significant political influence in the 1980s, especially in Germany and in Sweden. In the United States, the Greens already have made it on the ballot in Alaska and expect to make it soon in Hawaii, Arizona and Pennsylvania.

To qualify in California, the Green Party mounted a volunteer-driven voter-registration drive that featured tables at supermarkets, college campuses and civic and shopping centers across the state. According to Smith, the Green Party drive was unique because it was a statewide effort that was localized, featuring separate drives in what Smith called "10 autonomous regions."

"It was truly a grass-roots effort," said Smith. "We are not a centralized party. We are decentralized, and we think our success proved that you can succeed statewide using autonomous regions." As to be expected, the party was most

---

Christian Ettinger is a California Journal *intern. A.G. Block is managing editor of the* Journal.

New party has Democrats seeing ... Green

By Christian Ettinger and A.G. Block

Reprinted from *California Journal*, February 1992

suc-cessful recruiting members from the nine-county San Francisco Bay area, which supplied more than 51,000 signatures.

The Greens' recruiting drive snared a cross section of Californians. According to Hank Chapot, a Bay Area Green activist, 20 to 30 percent of those who signed up for the Green Party were previously unregistered, 50 percent were former Democrats and 20 to 30 percent were former Republicans. There were even a few Peace and Freedom converts.

The Greens registration drive may have come along at just the right time because of widespread dissatisfaction with business-as-usual politics. "You just have to spend one weekend registering voters to realize how great a demand exists for an alternative party," said Shelley Martin, director of the San Francisco registration drive.

The state Democratic Party is less than enthusiastic about the Greens' presence on the ballot because it sees it as a threat to the Democratic voter base. Bob Mulholland, the Democrats' political director, warned that the Greens actually could harm the environmental movement by weakening Democrats and giving Republicans and their business allies more room to exploit the environment. According to the *San Francisco Bay Guardian*, Mulholland was so concerned about the Green threat that he tried to squelch the Greens' voter-registration effort by offering jobs to Green organizers Joe Louis Hoffman and Hank Chapot and by sending out a mailing to Green Party members urging them to abandon the party before the December 31st deadline.

"All other parties are enemies. The Greens are no different than the Republicans," Mulholland told the *Guardian.* "If the Greens became a party in California, Republicans will be the happiest party in the state."

Mulholland denied the charges levelled at him in the *Guardian.* "The story ... was one of the most inaccurate stories I've ever read. I never made an offer to Hank Chapot, but he did come up and visit me here in Sacramento and jokingly said to me, 'Make me an offer.' As for Joe Louis Hoffman, he had previously worked in a Democratic voter-registration drive. I called to rehire him and had no idea he worked for the Greens. Finally, I am considering a mailing to Green voters in retaliation for a Green mailing to 18,000 registered Democratic voters signed by David Brower with a voter registration card enclosed."

Mulholland also responded in a letter to the *Bay Guardian.* "While the Democrats backed crucial state initiatives like Big Green and Prop 65, the toxics initiative, where were the Greens?" he asked. "The Republicans opposed us, and the Greens were meeting in a mountain retreat, I guess."

The *Guardian* article also inferred that California Republicans offered to fund the Green Party's ballot drive — a charge hotly denied by the Greens. "We have no money," said Chapot. "This is a volunteer effort."

Party chairman Kent Smith, however, did acknowledge that an anonymous "angel" stepped forward with a $20,000 donation to fund a last-minute paid, signature-gathering drive that added 10,000 members to the Greens' roll. Smith said the extra signatures turned out not to be necessary.

Not all Democratic Party officials agreed with Mulholland's gloom-and-doom assessment. Said one party spokesperson: "A Green Party could strengthen the hand of our progressive wing. We'll be able to say, 'Look, if we don't address environmental issues, we'll lose people to the Greens.'"

According to Smith, party activists are split on how best to proceed with involvement in the upcoming election. Some want no Green candidates because they feel the party isn't ready to compete and could emerge from the elections with the image of a loser. Others feel the party ought to gain electoral experience by running candidates everywhere. Still others want the party to run candidates in selected legislative and congressional races where Green candidates could help decide an election by playing the role of spoiler. Ultimately, Smith said, the decision on whom to run, and where to run, will be left to local Green regions.

Chapot indicated that if the Greens plunge into the 1992 elections with slates of candidates, the bulk of the party's focus will be on city council and supervisorial races.

Party officials want it understood that the Greens are not just an environmental party but are concerned with linking environmental issues with economic, peace and social-justice issues. Many of the party's leaders are veteran activists from single-issue causes like pro-choice, disarmament and toxics.

The Greens have a nine-point platform that goes beyond caring for the environment. Among other things, it stresses electoral reform and campaign funding limits, public financing of campaigns, term limits and more statewide initiatives. It also calls for universal health care; rights to housing, child care, education and employment to all regardless of race or sexual orientation; steep cuts in military spending; and a multi-cultural curriculum in education. The Greens also are pro-choice on abortion. And, of course, they are staunch for laws that protect the environment: elimination of unnecessary packaging and a recyling model that provides a market for recycled products; bans on pesticides, animal growth hormones, clear-cutting of forest lands and offshore oil drilling.

The Green platform is similar to that of the Peace and Freedom Party, but P&F officials do not feel threatened. Maureen Smith, a representative from the Peace and Freedom Party, does not feel as though the Greens invaded their electoral territory. "The Greens will be a positive addition to the ballot," she said, adding that there is a large enough pool of dissatisfied and unregistered voters to keep both parties on the ballot. "There is room enough for both parties to thrive," Smith said. "What we need is an ambitious voter registration to bring all these non-voters into the political process."

Next on their agenda, according to Hank Chapot, is the goal of a half-million registered voters statewide. "We're nowhere near our saturation level," he said. "Even in the Bay Area, where we've gotten most of our voters, there remain many more potential Greens."

"We're determined to do things differently," said party chairman Smith, referring to the Greens' emphasis on local autonomy and grass-roots organizing. "That's more important that winning elections."

Even if a Green candidate never wins an election in California, Smith considers the party successful because California is a bellweather state. He predicts that, because of his party's success in California, Greens will be on the ballot in a majority of states by 1994. The Greens' success in California has, in Smith's words, "galvanized voter registration efforts all over the country. They tell us, 'If you can do it in California, we can do it anywhere.'" 🏛

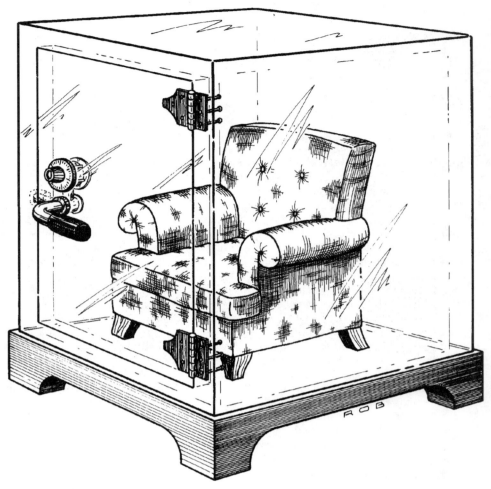

W hen Governor Pete Wilson threatened to veto the Legislature's redistricting scheme because it failed to create genuinely competitive districts, political insiders reacted with understandable cynicism. Not that Wilson's threat lacked credibility; Wilson vetoed the plans on September 23rd, then watched as lawmakers failed to override his action.

No, insider cynicism came from the knowledge that "electoral competitiveness" does not drive the reapportionment game. Incumbent safety drives it. Reapportionment is a contest where the main players are preoccupied with creating districts that one political party or the other can claim as its "own." It is, as *Sacramento Bee* political columnist Martin Smith observed, aimed at "minimizing the number of competitive districts." It is a game that, according to Alan Heslop of the Rose Institute at the Claremont Colleges, has led to "the death of competition in California politics."

It may well be that a few noncompetitive, or "safe," seats assure a measure of legislative stability and are therefore important for a legislative body to operate effectively. No matter how strong the winds of political change

Ed Costantini is a professor of political science and Charles Dannehl is a PhD candidate at the University of California, Davis.

SAFESEAT

What is a competitive district?

By Ed Costantini and Charles Dannehl

Reprinted from *California Journal*, November 1991

Party Registration and Election Competitiveness 1972-1990

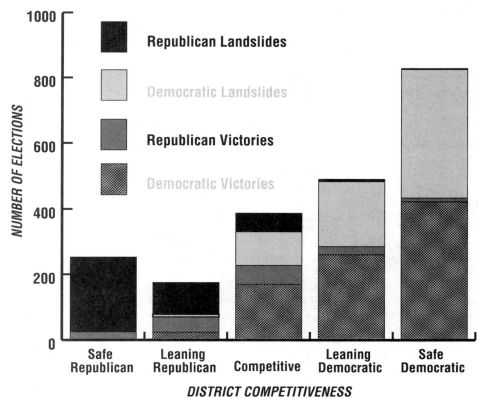

sweep across the electorate, safe seats guarantee a cadre of legislators who know the process, understand the issues and recognize the competence and trustworthiness of other relevant political players like legislative staff, lobbyists and bureaucrats. And congressional studies have suggested that members from non-competitive districts are more likely to produce legislation, develop specialized policy expertise that is often key to legislative success, do less public posturing, and devote more energy and staff to legislative matters than to constituency services than are their less-secure colleagues. Safe seats also tend to produce more openly partisan legislators, which some view as a drawback, but which gives solace to those believe American political parties lack sufficient ideology.

But too many safe seats are at odds with a common-sense understanding of how democracy works and with well-established democratic theories of representation. Thus in evaluating any given reapportionment scheme from the standpoint of democratic values, electoral competitiveness is an appro-

priate criterion, albeit one that is generally ignored.

Democracy does not flourish just because a society holds elections. Otherwise, the pre-glasnost Soviet system and even Nazi Germany would be included in the pantheon of democracies. Citizens must have genuine choices at election time. In a two-party system, major party candidates should have a reasonable chance of capturing legislative districts. If they do not, legislator accountability becomes a sham and elections become meaningless. The party destined for defeat may find it difficult to recruit effective candidates, thus enhancing the safety factor in many districts. Nor is there much incentive in a safe district for the minority party to engage in voter registration or other activities aimed at broadening the scope of citizen participation. According to veteran Democratic political organizer Marshall Ganz, a party "customarily confines its voter registration efforts to adding voters in the few genuinely competitive legislative districts." When safe seats are common rather than aberrations, the cumulative effect is voter apathy and a

sense of political futility. If there is no real choice, why play the election game at all?

Not every district can be competitive, however, and there are practical circumstances that may make the creation of safe seats during reapportionment unavoidable. For example, Republicans dominate areas where voters tend to be more conservative, such as the suburbs of Los Angeles, San Diego and the San Francisco Bay Area. Democrats dominate urban areas where residents tend to rely more on government services supported by Democrats. So, where one party has won the hearts and minds of the vast majority of a particular area's electorate, creating competitive legislative districts may be difficult or impossible. But pockets of one-party solidarity aside, the general parity of California's major parties hardly makes the safe-seat phenomenon as pervasive and as convincing in California as it was during the 1930s in the once "Solid South."

Of course, other "public interest" values also militate against the achievement of competitiveness in specific districts. For example, the "one person-one vote" requirement, the recognition of topographical and political boundaries, and an interest in district compactness and contiguity may all contribute to the creation of an occasional safe seat. The same may be true of the federal Voting Rights Act requirement that legislative district lines be drawn to "maximize the opportunity" for under-represented minority groups. To the extent that the act leads to "packing" African-Americans, Asians or Hispanics into districts, the likely result will be non-competitive, Democratic urban districts and correspondingly non-competitive Republican suburban districts.

These sorts of practical considerations have a place in the reapportionment process. Like legislative effectiveness, they must carry some weight; in some cases, the law does not permit otherwise. But electoral competitiveness is so important to a democratic society that political cartographers should bear the burden of demonstrating in any given instance that creating a safe district was unavoidable.

There are several ways to assure competitiveness.

• Term limits. When safe districts are commonplace, frustrated voters may resort to forcing incumbents out of office by imposing term limits, which assure the turnover that safe seats work to preclude. Term limits have drawbacks, however. First, they do nothing to make a district more competitive between the parties. Thus, they treat the symptom of safe seats — impregnable incumbents — but not the disease itself. Second, they eliminate candidates who have already served as legislators, thus limiting voter choice. Term limits also may undermine the effectiveness of the legislative branch vis-a-vis other political actors — bureaucrats, staff and lobbyists.

• Proportionality. Some observers believe that a fair system of competitive legislative elections is one where the proportion of legislative seats held by each party reflects the proportion of votes received by that party's legislative candidates statewide. This may be an attractive, post-election method to evaluate a given reapportionment scheme, but it offers no guidance for drawing district lines. Nor does it address the issue of district competitiveness or the genuineness of voter choice. For example, all 80 Assembly districts could be safe for one party or the other, while the Assembly as a whole proportionally represented the support each party's candidates received statewide. In any event, California has single-member districts with plurality vote victories, and not proportional representation.

• The formula approach. Buried in the fine print of the failed Proposition 119 (June 1990) was a proviso meant to assure that "the greatest number of [California legislative] districts should be competitive." A district was considered "competitive" if the registration within the district of the state's two largest political parties was "no greater than two percentage points above or below that party's registration in the state as a whole." Thus, a precise indicator of competitiveness — party registration in districts — may be used as a decision-making guide for reapportioners rather than just a post-reapportionment tool for critics.

But Proposition 119's formula settled on a single "magic" number — statewide Democratic registration — and permitted very little deviance (up to 2 percent) from that number. A formula for achieving district competitiveness that gives reapportioners no maneuvering room is neither practical nor consistent with the goal of legislative effectiveness. If it succeeds in producing districts that are all magnificently and perfectly competitive, the makeup of the Legislature could lurch from total domination by one party to total domination by the other; the Legislature would become overly sensitive to every election-year breeze, and small shifts in the public's partisan predispositions would produce massive shifts in the Legislature's partisan makeup.

Also, Proposition 119's formula worked only as long as Republicans and Democrats stayed within hailing distance of each other in voter registration. If one party achieved statewide registration dominance, all districts could become safe for the dominant party, and the Legislature could conceivably be comprised entirely of its members.

But there may be a way to overcome the weaknesses of the above approaches; for example, a method that builds on Proposition 119's reliance on party registration but seeks to avoid the negative aspects of searching for a magic number.

To illustrate the method, take data from Reports of Registration and Statements of Vote published periodically from 1972 through 1990 by California's secretary of state. That time span included 10 general elections and 1435 races for legislative office (U.S. House of Representatives, state Senate and Assembly). The focus is on the relationship between Democratic Party share of two-party district registration and Democratic candidate share of two-candidate vote for the 1435 races. The two variables prove to be strongly correlated.

When those districts are arrayed along a line from least Democratic registration (the 70th Assembly district in 1984 where Democrats has only 29 percent of the two-party registration and Republican Gil Ferguson received 73 percent of the two-candidate vote) to the 53rd Assembly District in 1976 where Democrats had 92 percent of the two-party registration (and Republicans gave Bill Greene a free ride), a clean pattern can be discerned.

Using this scale, "safeness" or competitiveness is determined by the likelihood that a given level of Democratic registration resulted, over those 1435 races, in the election of Democratic legislative candidates, and in the candidate of the predominant party receiving at least 60 percent of the votes cast in the election. These two criteria lead to cutting points along the registration-based array of cases. Shown in the accompanying table, these cutting points permit distinguishing between "safe," "leaning," and "competitive" seats. In this study, only two-party (Democratic and Republican) registration was considered. For example, in the 18th Senate District race in 1986, Democrats had 47 percent of district registration; Republicans had 41 percent. While Democrats had less than 50 percent of the total district registration, they had more than 50 percent of the two-party registration.

Seven observations may be made based on this study:

(1) A district is considered "safe Republican" when the Democratic share of two-party registration falls under 50 percent. That occurred in 18 percent of the 1435 races, or 253 elections. Only once in those 253 elections did the Democrat win — Deirdre Alpert's upset of incumbent Sunny Mojonnier in the 75th District in 1990. GOP victories in 90 percent of the 253 races were of landslide proportions, or better than 60 percent.

On the other hand, a "safe Democratic" seat occurs when Democrats enjoy a 67 percent share of two-party registration. That took place in 438 races, or 30 percent of the 1435. In only 3 percent of these 438 cases did the Republican candidate win, and in 89 percent of them the Republican was buried in an election landslide.

Not that districts that do not fall within these boundaries provide water hazards for the party with the highest percent of registration. Over the course of the study, districts regarded as "leaning" produced a victory rate of over 85 percent for the dominant party. One could make the argument that these seats, too, are safe for one party or the other.

(2) The data suggests the magnitude of Democratic fall-off. Democratic legislative candidates generally have failed to do as well as their district's Democratic registration. Presumably, a disproportionate number of registered Democrats have been "deadwood," non-voters or defectors. On the average, Democratic candidates in contested races between 1972 and 1990 (1134 of 1435) ran 6 to 7 percent behind party registration. Thus, it is not surprising that races we categorize as "competitive" occurred where Democratic registration was in the 54-61 percent range,

rather than being evenly matched with that of the Republicans (the 48-52 percent range).

(3) Nearly half (48 percent) of legislative races in California between 1972 and 1990 were held in "safe" districts. Thus, these election outcomes were essentially forgone conclusions where voters were denied a genuine choice at election time. Another one-third were held in "leaning" districts. In a competitive two-party state, it seems impossible to explain away this phenomenon on the grounds of "practical necessities" or to justify as necessary for legislative effectiveness.

(4) In the 1990 election, 52 percent of the 145 legislative races were in "safe" districts. Only one registrationally advantaged candidate in those races lost, and 86 percent won by a margin of 20 percent or more. In other words, the most recent election presented no marked departure from the pattern evident from the larger, 10-election time frame.

(5) Approximately 60 percent of the safe races since 1972 have been safe for the Democratic candidate — almost precisely the percentage of races that Democratic candidates won overall and a reflection of Democratic predominance among the voters and in the Legislature during the period.

(6) Safe districts are associated with uncontested races. Such races are the ultimate affront to the value of electoral choice and can be the most extreme manifestation of how the reapportionment process in even a highly competitive two-party state can produce districts so "safe" that challenging the advantaged party's candidate is hopeless. One hundred and one one-candidate races (7.5 percent of the total) took place between 1972 and 1990, and 60 percent of them involved registrationally safe seats. Another 30 percent occurred in seats categorized as "leaning" to one party or the other.

(7) There are exceptions to the general pattern, cases where candidates of the dominant party in safe districts somehow defied the odds and blew an election. The last incumbent to perform this trick was Mojonnier in 1990. Plagued by ethics problems, she lost to Democrat Alpert in a district with only 39 percent Democratic registration.

Three Republican legislators account for 10 of the 14 races where GOP candidates have won in so-called "safe"

Democratic districts. Paul Bannai and then-Assemblyman Ken Maddy each overcame the odds three times during the early-to-mid 1970s. San Francisco's Milton Marks was elected and re-elected to the Senate on four occasions in an overwhelming Democratic district (once without contest). He eventually switched to the Democratic Party. The most recent Republican upset occurred in 1986 when Democrat Ed Waters (Congresswoman Maxine's son) lost to Republican Paul Zeltner in a district where the Democrats enjoyed 71 percent of the registration. Zeltner lost two years later to Democrat Willard Murray.

But these exceptions are few and far-between. They should not detract from the main focus: that district party registration may be used to indicate whether elections will be competitive. So armed, any citizen may determine if the latest reapportionment left him or her without an effective choice in legislative and congressional elections.

In addition, relying on party registration data allows prospective thinking and the use of quantitative evidence as guide for reapportionment decision-making. It means turning to data that politicians routinely consider when deciding to run for office, to invest resources, and to draw district lines during reapportionment. Unfortunately, they are not typically used to assure electoral competitiveness but to assure precisely the opposite.

It is not a matter of finding some magic registration percentage that will maximize competitiveness in all districts — an endeavor that may undermine legislative effectiveness and run afoul of the legal and political considerations that should enter into the reapportionment process. It is not a matter of requiring legislators engaged in reapportionment to commit acts of political self-immolation, forgo the use of political bargaining skills, or suit up in some decision-making straitjacket.

Rather, it is a matter of accepting the value of competitiveness as central to democratic elections, and of identifying a registration range that will produce a preponderance of districts where both parties' candidates have a reasonable chance of electoral success. If election results over the last two decades provide the basis for estimating future election outcomes, then a Democratic registration between 50 percent and 66 percent produces such a district (although a

stricter understanding of competitiveness might suggest a 56-61 percent range). No district should fall outside that range unless it can be demonstrated that other values associated with or mandated in the reapportionment process cannot be otherwise met.

Given all the other considerations, competitiveness is a tough objective for reapportioners to agree upon, let alone to achieve. It deserves a try nonetheless. At stake is a central component of the democratic creed. 🏛

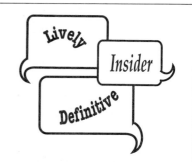

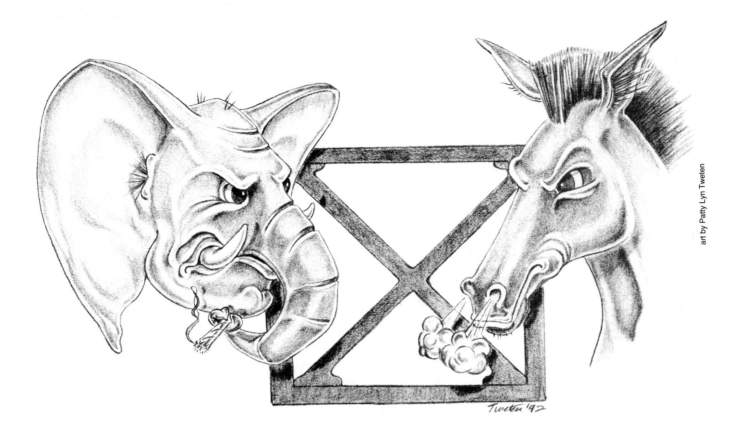

art by Patty Lyn Tweten

Years of legal wrangling over whether California can prohibit political parties from endorsing candidates before primaries have not produced definitive answers. The issue still is clear as mud.

The most recent attempt to produce a pre-primary endorsement occurred earlier this year by President George Bush's California Republican operatives (including state Chairman James Dignan). Despite a rule adopted by the party not to give pre-primary endorsements, Bush's inner circle thought that a California GOP endorsement would give the president's campaign a critical lift after the New Hampshire primary and before Super Tuesday (the southern regional primary). Momentum was needed in the Bush campaign because of the surprisingly strong showing of Patrick Buchanan, a former TV talk host and former Nixon staffer, in New Hampshire (he received

Charles Price is a professor of political science at California State University, Chico, and a frequent contributor to California Journal.

Political parties back away from pre-primary endorsements

By Charles Price

Reprinted from *California Journal*, April 1992

37 percent of the vote to Bush's 53 percent).

But when the Bush campaign sought an endorsement at the state party convention, held in Burlingame in late February, it encountered embarrassing opposition. Changing the party rule required a two-thirds vote of the convention, and Buchanan supporters and GOP opponents of endorsing were strong enough to get Bush supporters to back down. Although a meaningless "straw vote" of delegates gave Bush an overwhelming margin, the president had been handed a setback.

While Republicans have decided they don't want to give pre-primary endorsements, Democrats, after giving pre-primary endorsements in 1988 and 1990, decided to forgo this practice in state legislative and congressional races in 1992. What's going on here?

Californians have been struggling with the issue since the turn of the century, when Progressive reformers swept into political power here and in other, mainly western states. In California, they were concerned about the domination of California government by special interests (in particular, Southern Pacific Railroad) and were appalled by the power wielded by party bosses and political machines. To cleanse California politics, Progressives promoted a host of political reforms which soon became part of the Elections Code and the Constitution. These included strict regulation of parties, the Australian secret ballot, the office block ballot, civil service (to discourage patronage appointments), non-partisan local elections, direct democracy (the initiative referendum and recall), cross-filing, and the direct primary. Smarting from these reforms, the California Republican and Democratic parties have never been as powerful as their counterpart organizations in the eastern half of the country.

Progressives promoted the direct primary election so that rank-and-file voters, via the ballot box, could elect the party's nominee for a particular office rather than having politicians hand-pick their choices at party caucuses. Progressives also championed cross-filing to allow candidates of one party to run in the other party's primary to provide voters the widest latitude in voting choice. (This feature was eliminated in 1959).

Yet to this day, scores of party leaders, a growing number of political scientists and some media pundits believe that party leaders and not the voters should pick party nominees, particularly presidential candidates. In a recent article, NBC commentator John Chancellor wrote, "Primary elections and party caucuses should be abolished. ... The best reform would be to let party professionals and elected officials choose the party's standard-bearer for the fall campaign."

While the primary today is a feature in the nominating process of all 50 states, in many states party organizations designate their choices in the primary. Indeed, in Colorado, candidates running for office must receive at least 20 percent of the vote of local endorsing caucuses, or they may not file. Officially endorsed candidates not only are guaranteed a slot on the party slate-mailer, they also receive available campaign money and the grunt-work help of party, grass-roots activists. Moreover, given the importance of this endorsement, in some states unendorsed party candidates decide not to file or to withdraw from the race. Of course, efforts of party leaders to discourage primary competition undercuts the Progressive notion of a free and unfettered primary.

Because pre-primary endorsing was of dubious legal status, for most of this century statewide party organizations and county central committees seldom attempted to designate their choices in a contested primary in the state. Instead, endorsing was left to unofficial party groups such as the CRA (California Republican Assembly) or the CDC (California Democratic Council). Occasionally, a Democratic or Republican activist county central committee might decide to endorse, but there were no formal rules or regulations on the subject, nor was it done systematically in the various races. To clarify matters, in 1963 the Legislature approved and the governor signed a bill prohibiting parties from endorsing in primaries. And, as legislative party leaders built power in the 1970s and 1980s through amassing immense campaign war chests which could be divvied out to their anointed choices, they were not enthusiastic about sharing this endorsing role with the party rank-and-file. After all, locals might choose the "wrong" person.

For years, volunteer activists (particularly in the California Democratic Party) have argued that if party organizations were to be effective and taken seriously, they had to be allowed to designate their choices in the primary. Endorsing, they believed, would minimize the opportunites for extremists in party ranks — say, a Ku Klux Klan-Republican or La Rouche-Democrat — from capturing the nomination and embarrassing the party. Candidates who had "paid their dues," been involved in local party activities and had developed friendships with local activists would be in the best position to be endorsed. Moreover, endorsing, it was argued, would provide grass-roots, party volunteers a more meaningful role to play than simply doing campaign drudgery work, such as walking precincts or stuffing envelopes. Endorsing, it was believed, would contribute to more vibrant, influential party organizations.

Not surprisingly, political parties in California historically have been less inclined to endorse in non-partisan races. In fact, the California Constitution stipulates that local elections are to be non-partisan, and many interpreted this to mean no party involvement. In addition, the state Election Code stipulates that nomination papers of those running for non-partisan office shall not "contain the name of any political party, or any signer thereto, nor shall the candidate be referred to as a candidate for the nomination of any party." However, on a few occasions over the last several decades, because of the legal confusion, a Democratic or Republican county central committee has endorsed in a local race. And, as the state Supreme Court became more politicized in the 1980s, California's Democratic and Republican parties became more entangled in supporting or opposing (unofficially) the 1986 confirmation elections of a liberal bloc of judges (justices Rose Bird, Cruz Reynoso and Joseph Grodin). Interestingly, while several other states bar parties from making judicial endorsements, California is unique in prohibiting endorsing in local, non-partisan contests.

Some authorities argue that local issues — dog-leash laws, for example — tend to be non-partisan. Consequently, there is no need for parties to be mucking about backing local candidates. Others contend that local issues can frequently have a partisan overlay, such as a policy regarding the homeless. In any case, since many local officials move up the political ladder to run for the state Legislature or for Congress, some activists believe that endorsing for these offices is critical, too.

In 1979 Samuel Unger, a private citizen, filed a lawsuit against the Marin County Democratic Central Committee because it had endorsed a local school board candidate. Unger won. In 1984, however, the state Supreme Court rejected Unger's claims in a second suit (dubbed in the press Unger II), which he brought this time against California Republicans for their involvement in a recall campaign against Chief Justice Rose Bird. The California Supreme Court noted that a federal court had already ruled that parties could not be barred from giving partisan endorsements because that restricted their First Amendment rights of free speech. In addition, the Court argued, there was nothing in the state Constitution prohibiting parties from endorsing in non-partisan contests.

In response, in June 1986 the California Legislature passed and voters adopted Proposition 49, a constitutional amendment barring parties from endorsing candidates running for any non-partisan office — judicial, school board, city council or county supervisor. This amendment, in turn, was struck down in *Renne v. Geary* in the Ninth Federal Circuit Court in 1990. It subsequently was appealed to the U.S. Supreme Court. In June 1991 a majority of the U.S. Supreme Court decided the case was not justiciable because it was not a live case, which in effect overturned, at least temporarily, the Ninth Circuit Court ruling. But it left the issue up in the air.

Because the U.S. Supreme Court has not ruled definitively whether states have the right to bar parties from endorsing in non-partisan races, the legal controversy continues. In October 1991 the Santa Clara County Democratic Central Committee ignored the state ban and voted to support two city council candidates, one in Sunnyvale and the other in Palo Alto. Local Democratic officials contended that the ban on their endorsing in local races was unconstitutional. However, both Democratic Party-endorsed candidates lost in their city council bids. Local Republicans were incensed over the Democrats' intrusion into the race. Don Minutillo, a Santa Clara Republican activist commented, "Boy, that's unbelievable. It's distressing. If it were [legally] possible for the Republicans to

endorse in non-partisan races, we would do it." No legal action has yet been taken against Santa Clara Democrats.

In the fall of 1991 the San Francisco Peace and Freedom Party endorsed Gloria LaRiva, a mayoral candidate in the 1991 election, and the city attorney filed a lawsuit against the party for its violation of election law. In February 1992 oral arguments were heard in this case. There is a reasonable chance that *LaRiva v. Wong* will be appealed eventually to the U.S. Supreme Court.

The Committee for Party Renewal (composed of Democratic activists, academics and several Republican and Libertarian officials), which brought a 1984 suit to challenge the state's endorsing ban, did so for three reasons: it was a free-speech violation in that all other political groups could endorse; it would provide parties more control over who runs under their banner (extremists could be dealt with more effectively); as a way of restoring party vitality by giving party activists a more significant role to play.

After their 1984 court victory, the Democratic Party's rules pommittee drafted a set of endorsing procedures and regulations which were incorporated into Party by-laws. To handle the endorsing, regional conferences composed of various Assembly district caucuses were established. Quorums were required at endorsing meetings, and proxy voting was not allowed. To be endorsed, a Democratic incumbent has to receive 50 percent plus one of the votes, while non-incumbents need 60 percent. Caucus participants also have the right to vote for no endorsement. And, unendorsed Democratic candidates are encouraged to withdraw from the race to encourage a unified effort on behalf of the endorsed candidate. Endorsement recommendations from local units are then submitted to the State Central Committee for final approval; thus far, no local unit recommendation has been rejected by the State Central Committee. The SCC also handles endorsements in statewide contests.

In 1988 all Democratic incumbents running for re-election were endorsed with one exception: state Senator Dan Boatwright lost the party endorsement to his Democratic challenger, Supervisor Sunne McPeak. (Boatwright had long been at odds with local Democratic leaders). Nevertheless, Boatwright

went on to win the primary and later to defeat his Republican opponent in the general election.

In 1990 all Democratic legislative incumbents were endorsed by local endorsing caucuses. Perhaps the two most controversial endorsements of this election were in only two open statewide contests: the governor's and the newly established elected insurance commissioner's races. John Van de Kamp was the Democratic Party's endorsee for governor, but Dianne Feinstein beat him in the Democratic primary. So, too, in the insurance commissioner's race: the endorsed candidate, Bill Press, lost to his Democratic opponent, John Garamendi, in the primary.

Obviously, if party endorsees lose regularly in the primary, the endorsement becomes meaningless if not counterproductive. As Olive Lewis, former executive director of the state Democratic Party, noted, "If you're going to endorse, you've got to be able to deliver something beyond just a stamp of approval. You have to be able to deliver campaign funds and party workers to those who are endorsed."

Thus far, 1988-1990 Democratic endorsements have had little impact on elected party officeholders since nearly all were endorsed. And in open statewide races, the party failed to elect its anointed in the primary. Moreover, no unendorsed Democratic candidates withdrew from the race when they failed to receive the nomination. Indeed, when asked whether non-endorsed Democratic candidates should withdraw, Bob Mulholland, political director of the Democratic Party, said, "Is that what our by-laws say? That's ridiculous!" Executive member and legislative staffer Teri Burns said that greater efforts will probably be made in future years to get unendorsed Democratic candidates to withdraw.

Since attaining the legal right to endorse, California Republicans have opted not to endorse GOP candidates. Republican leaders fear that endorsing might be divisive and could lead to rigged meetings and "smoke-filled room" decision-making. Moreover, if party endorsing were to be adopted, there could be conflict between Republican legislative leaders (who have at times given endorsements) and local GOP activists over which Republican candidate in a primary should be supported. While some GOP activists are disgruntled by the endorsing ban, for the most part, party stalwarts seem content with it.

The executive committee of the Democratic Party felt that given all of the logistical problems with the drastically revised, incumbent-neutral districts the state Supreme Court drew for the 1992 reapportionment, attempting to hastily organize for endorsing would have been chaotic. In addition, there were seven new House seats to be factored in. Moreover, the term limits mandated by Proposition 140 have encouraged many legislators to retire. Thus, because of all of these complicating factors, the Democratic executive committee decided endorsing should be deferred for this year. As state Democratic Chairman Phil Angelides put it, "We have decided to concentrate all of our time and energy on the general election rather than endorsing in the primary."

Kathy Lynch, a long-time party activist and member of the rules committee which drafted the endorsing provisions, commented, "If all the [district] lines had been determined by September 1991, endorsing would have been possible." But since district lines weren't finalized until late January 1992, candidates had to delay filing decisions. "It would have taken a monumental effort of party staff to get the regional caucuses established; the window of opportunity was too short."

Those who drafted the endorsing provisions never envisioned the massive problems that could accompany reapportionment, according to Lynch. "When the court ruled in favor of pre-primary endorsing, [it] stipulated the process must be orderly," Lynch said. A substantial majority of the party's executive committee concluded this would be impossible with the 1991 reapportionment. Lynch noted there was another concern among committee members. "Endorsing might have violated the spirit of the Voting Rights Act," she said. "Some white male incumbent Democrats had been reapportioned into new districts with sizable minority populations. Endorsing caucuses would probably have favored incumbents to the disadvantage of aspiring minority candidates."

Proponents of endorsing on the executive committee argued endorsing would discourage entrepreneurial slate makers from profiting in the vacuum. Burns commented that some board members favored endorsing because of all the new Democratic candidates running in the redesigned districts. Party registrants needed the help. However, the predominant mood among executive committee members was: this isn't the year.

Sacramento Bee political columnist Dan Walters viewed the decision by state Democrats to forgo endorsing as a "retreat from democracy," and speculated that the "temporary" ban might well become permanent. "One experience with participatory democracy apparently was more than enough for the grandees of the California Democratic Party," wrote Walters.

Angelides, however, stated unequivocally, "The party declared its intention to return to pre-primary endorsements in 1994, and may still choose to endorse for the two U.S. Senate seats that are also up for election this year."

Walters hypothesized that Democrats decided not to endorse in 1992 because some of their incumbents might face stiff opposition from Democratic challengers in the new districts and didn't want to risk local party groups endorsing their opponent. Lynch disagreed. She stated that many of those favoring deferring endorsing in 1992 were *not* professional politicians. "Many Democratic legislators wanted to have endorsements [in 1992] so that local party groups could give them their stamp of approval."

In future years, the main impact of Democratic endorsing probably will not be at the state level where money and media are the critical factors. Rather, the endorsing impact will be felt most profoundly in House, state Senate and Assembly contests in *open* districts with sufficient Democratic registration to make them potentially able to be won or in districts where particular Republican incumbents are vulnerable. In these districts local party activists can provide legislative candidates important help. For example, in 1990 in the 4th Senate District, two Democrats — Mike Thompson and Charlie Cochran — sensing state Senator Jim Nielsen's political vulnerability, filed for the Democratic nomination. Both went before the local endorsing caucus seeking its support. Realizing he had few votes in the endorsing caucus, Cochran urged members to make *no* endorsement and remain neutral. Instead, the caucus overwhelmingly endorsed Thompson. Mike Thompson said that local party people were very helpful in his race, assisting in the myriad activities of the campaign. With Proposition 140's term limits looming, the likelihood is that in future years there will be dozens of open districts. For new Democratic legislative candidates, having the support of the local party organization could be a real plus. 🏛

DIRECT DEMOCRACY

In California government the people have three tools that make them very powerful participants in the decision-making process. The initiative, referendum and recall were instituted by Governor Hiram Johnson and the progressives in part to break the hold of the railroad interests on state government in the early 1900's. With all three of the direct democracy devices, a simple majority of those voting determines whether the proposal passes.

- *Initiative.* The initiative gives the people the right to place local or state measures on the ballot if they obtain the required number of signatures. It has also been used by governors, legislators and special-interest groups to get what they want after the Legislature has rejected or been unable to meet their demands. To qualify for the ballot, a statewide constitutional initiative requires signatures equal to eight percent of the vote cast in the last gubernatorial election; initiative statutes require five percent.

After the 1990 gubernatorial election the number of signatures required is:

Constitutional initiative - 615,957
Statutory initiative - 384,973

Today, a powerful and sophisticated initiative industry has developed: signature-gathering firms, pollsters, political lawyers, and campaign management firms specializing in the qualifying and passing of ballot measures.

- *Referendum.* This is a procedure that can be used by the public, if they can gather sufficient signatures, to block a state statute or local ordinance pending a popular vote on the issue. It is not used often, but the threat of a referendum occasionally has the effect of blocking enactment of legislation. This procedure cannot be used to stop urgency bills, and for this reason emergency measures require a two-thirds vote rather than a simple majority in the Legislature. The referen-dum procedure was used successfully at the statewide level to place four measures — the Peripheral Canal and three reapportionment plans — on the ballot in June 1982.

The number of signatures required is the same as for a statutory initiative.

- *Recall.* The third of the Johnson direct-government reforms establishes a petition procedure for placing on the ballot the question of removing any elected official or officials from office. Recall elections are common in local government but have never been employed successfully at the state level in California.

California's system of direct democracy does not stop here. The Constitution and local-government charters can be amended only by a vote of the electorate. Neither the state nor any local governmental agency may incur a general-obligation debt without prior approval of the electorate (although revenue bonds can be sold without such approval). At the state level, a simple majority vote is sufficient to approve bond measures for such purposes as higher-education construction, park acquisition and development, the Cal-Vet farm and home program, and water-pollution plants. But at the local level, all bond proposals — even school bonds — require a two-thirds majority.

In recent years, the potency of direct democracy in California has grown. This power was demonstrated by the far-reaching tax revolt, which started with Proposition 13, the Jarvis-Gann property-tax initiative in 1978. This was followed with the "Spirit of 13" spending-limitation measure enacted in 1979, a successful Jarvis-sponsored income-tax indexing proposal in June of 1982, the successful Gann Legislative Reform Initiative of June 1984 and a number of other Proposition 13 follow-up measures thereafter. The number of measures qualifying for the ballot shows no sign of abating in the near future.

With these tools, there is hardly any aspect of state government that cannot be controlled by the people. 🏛

LAWMAKERS AND INITIATIVES

Are ballot measures the magic ride to success?

Reprinted from *California Journal*, September 1988

By Charles Bell and Charles Price

Early this century, California Progressives, led by their fiery governor, Hiram Johnson, put into state codes and the state Constitution a monumental package of critically important political reforms. More than 75 years later, these reforms continue to shape and influence contemporary political life in this state. Among the many reforms promoted by California Progressives, none, perhaps, has had more significance and long- lasting impact than the initiative. The initiative grants the public the right to propose and enact laws and constitutional amendments through a petition and election process. Progressives wanted the public to have the last word in case legislators were corrupt, overly partisan, or dominated by special interests.

Since its adoption in 1911, hundreds of initiatives have

Charles G. Bell is professor emeritus, California State University, Fullerton, and visiting professor, UC Davis. Charles M. Price is a professor at California State University, Chico.

been filed by private citizens or interest-group leaders seeking change from outside the governmental system. Elected officials, on the other hand, have invariably pursued change from within the system in the Legislature and executive. As Kelly Kimball, president of the signature-gathering firm of Kimball Management, noted, "Prior to the 1970s most California legislators were only vaguely aware of the initiative process and how it worked. They rarely thought about it as a potential option for them to use in pursuing their legislative objectives." Indeed, many state legislators would have viewed initiative authoring by members as a breech of legislative protocol.

Over the last two decades, however, this attitude has changed dramatically. Today, state officeholders and ex-officeholders are major participants in initiative authoring. Since 1970, approximately 15 percent of all initiatives filed have been by officeholder-proponents. Indeed, over the last several years (since 1983) about 22 percent of initiatives introduced yearly have been authored by current or ex-officeholders.

Moreover, elected officials are more successful at getting their measures on the ballot and have been proponents of more than one-third of all the initiatives qualifying for the ballot over the last two decades. As Mike Arno of American Petition Consultants (another professional petition company operating in California) states, "Officeholders are more realistic [than private citizens] about the difficulties of qualifying initiatives. They understand the need to raise money, and they know how to raise it. Also they don't wait too late before planning their signature drive."

However, once initiatives have qualified for the ballot, private citizens' initiatives win voter approval (39 percent) at about the same rate as do officeholders' initiatives (41 percent).

The trend toward officeholder initiative lawmaking, coupled with private-citizen proponents hiring specialized petition attorneys skilled in formulating law (see "The petition business," *CJ*, July 1985) to draft their measures, means that a substantial number of direct-democracy propositions qualifying for the ballot lately have been written by the "experts." Thus, the criticism by some Democratic legislative leaders that initiatives are largely the product of cranks, crackpots and curmudgeons — people abysmally ignorant of the complexities of lawmaking — does not accurately reflect a substantial portion of recent initiatives qualifying for the ballot.

Why are so many state elected officials mounting initiative drives these days? First, the increase in initiatives written by officeholders began at about the same time as the overall resurgence in initiative filing. Thus, only 17 initiatives were filed in the 1950s, only 44 in the 1960s, but 180 were filed in the 1970s and some 204 thus far have been filed in the 1980s. Many of the same reasons cited by direct-democracy experts to explain the increase in initiative filing generally are also factors encouraging elected officals to try to bypass their colleagues as well. Factors such as lack of confidence or trust in state governmental institutions, popularity of particular initiatives (such as the Jarvis-Gann Proposition 13 of June 1978), and the ease in hiring experts from professional-petition firms to secure at least some, if not all, of the signatures needed might presumably encourage officeholders to try the initiative process.

Second, for conservative Republicans in the Legislature, the initiative (and referendum as well) has provided a tantalyzing way to tweak Democratic leadership noses while at the same time achieving policy objectives.

"We've seen increased partisanship and bitterness in the Legislature, which has led to deadlock and frustration with the process," noted Republican Assemblyman Ross Johnson of Fullerton, author of several ballot measures, including the successful June 1988 campaign-reform initiative, Proposition 73.

Tony Quinn, a Republican reapportionment expert, argues that prior to Proposition 13 of 1978, Republican officeholders tended to shy away from authoring initiatives because the process was viewed as an anti-establishment device. "Proposition 13 suggested the initiative could be used to make policy from the right," Quinn stated.

The success of that initiative wasn't lost on conservative Republicans. "Jarvis and Gann became folk heroes," noted Johnson, "Now, politically ambitious people see the initiative as a [public relations] vehicle."

Since 1978 Republican incumbents have proposed twice as many initiatives as have Democrats. Republican Johnson, author of five separate initiatives in the 1980s (two were on the same ballot), has become the Legislature's equivalent of Paul Gann. Other conservatives in Republican legislative ranks, such as H.L. Richardson, former state Senator John Briggs, John Doolittle, Richard Mountjoy, Don Rogers, Doris Allen, Tom McClintock and Congressman William Dannemeyer, also have been active authoring initiatives.

Indeed, one recently filed criminal-law initiative has no less than nine co-proponents, including three Republican state legislators — Ed Davis, Ed Royce and Johnson — plus six other Republican local activists. While most of these conservative Republican initiatives deal with substantive policy issues, a number have been directed against the Democratic legislative leadership. Former Sonoma GOP Assemblyman Don Sebastiani's reapportionment initiative, Governor George Deukmejian's initiative to have retired appellate judges do reapportioning, and Assembly Minority Leader Pat Nolan's sponsorship of the Gann legislative-reform initiative are examples.

Third, on the Democratic side, a few moderate or liberal legislators have also on occasion proposed initiatives, such as Assemblyman Lloyd Connelly of Sacramento, Senator Joseph Montoya of Whittier, Assemblyman Richard Polanco of Los Angeles and former Santa Clara County state Senator Arlen Gregorio. Some Democrats have turned to authoring initiatives because Republican Governor Deukmejian has vetoed or threatened to veto their bills. However, if Republicans should capture control of the Legislature in the 1990s, it is highly likely that many more Democratic legislators will begin to energetically exercise this option, while Republicans may prefer to work within the legislative arena.

Fourth, some of the Legislature's leading mavericks, such as Democratic Senator Alan Robbins from the San Fernando Valley, independent Senator Quentin Kopp of San Francisco, or former Republican Assemblyman Sebastiani are also found in the initiative-author ranks perhaps because they see themselves as outsiders in the legislative system. Indeed, one might also anticipate initiative salvos from the Assembly's "Gang of Five" in the months ahead.

Fifth, politicians anticipating runs for higher political office sometimes author initiatives to help generate publicity for their campaigns. For example, former Secretary of State Jerry Brown championed Proposition 9, the 1974 Political Reform initiative, in his quest to become governor, and Briggs authored death penalty and homosexual teacher initiatives in his bid to become governor. Clearly, it was the fame Paul Gann derived from authoring so many controversial initiatives that made him a formidable candidate when he sought the Republican nomination for U.S. Senate in 1980. There also appear to be definite political overtones to Superintendent of Public Instruction Bill Honig's full-page advertisements in several of the state's major newspapers endorsing the insurance industry's no-fault car insurance initiative.

Sometimes, however, a politician-sponsored initiative may actually hinder its sponsor's bid for higher office, or the bid for higher office may doom the initiative. According to Caren Daniels-Meade, press secretary to Secretary of State March Fong Eu, Eu's "Dimes Against Crimes" initiative was hurt by her U.S. Senate candidacy. "On occasion people were reluctant to support Eu's initiative because it might be viewed as if they were endorsing her candidacy in the U.S. Senate race."

Even though Eu eventually suspended her U.S. Senate campaign in order to get potential financial supporters off the hook, it was too late. And, without financing, Eu could not afford to hire a professional petition company to collect the necessary signatures.

Finally, a prime advantage of initiative-passed law over legislative-passed law is that the former locks in change. Laws passed by the Legislature are constantly being amended; initiatives once approved are far more difficult and cumbersome to amend, and this asset is well understood by elected officeholders.

Ever since the initiative was incorporated into the California Constitution, there has been substantial overlap between the legislative and initiative lawmaking processes. Over the years, legislators have sometimes been threatened by potential proponents that if they didn't pass a particular bill, an initiative would be filed which would be far more extreme than the legislative measure.

In turn, legislators have sometimes passed constitutional amendments to go on the ballot as alternatives to previously qualfied initiatives. Currently, for example, the Senate Insurance, Claims and Corporations Committee reluctantly approved a constitutional amendment by Democratic State Senator Herschel Rosenthal to establish an insurance commission which would be charged with approving or disapproving insurance-rate hikes. Though several committee members felt Rosenthal's constitutional amendment was flawed, they voted for it to head off eight separate insurance-reform initiatives seeking qualification on the November 1988 ballot (five eventually qualified). Ross Johnson, for one, believes the initiative process gives him added clout. "The initiative does work as a lever on pending legislation. I have demonstrated that I can get an initiative on the ballot," Johnson said.

On some initiative efforts, officeholders are heavily involved in the drafting and also are publicly identified as sponsors of the measure. But for a variety of strategic or political reasons, they are not listed as proponents. For example, Governor Ronald Reagan (tax-reform initiative of 1973), Governor Jerry Brown (Political Reform Act of 1974), or conservative Republican Assembly Minority Leader Pat Nolan (Legislative Reform Initiative of 1983), while prominently involved with sponsoring these measures, were not technically their proponents.

Also, because of their political prominence, office-holders are frequently asked to write the pro or con arguments in the secretary of state's official *Voters' Handbook*. In addition, incumbents sometimes tape television or radio spots to extol or attack a proposed initiative. For example, Governor George Deukmejian urged voters to support his initiative to establish an independent reapportionment commission, and Attorney General John Van de Kamp said voters should vote "no" on the "deep pocket" insurance-reform initiative (Proposition 51, June 1986).

What are the implications in having officeholders author so many initiatives? In theory, the initiative was supposed to be a sort of last-resort option for private citizens to propose new laws or constitutional change, thus bypassing a recalcitrant Legislature. In reality, the problems such as heightened partisanship, special-interest influence, political opportunism, public distrust and friction between the governor and the Legislature have contributed to a shift to initiative lawmaking and away from legislative lawmaking. Until these problems are resolved, it is likely that there will continue to be a significant number of incumbent initiatives. And, the more officeholder initiatives on the ballot, the likelier the frustration in an increasingly irrelevant Legislature. Indeed, one of the initiative's sharpest critics, Assembly Speaker Willie Brown, commented recently that he wished a particular initiative had been launched in the Legislature.

"I'd prefer to see it debated, the dialogue elevated, in the halls of the Legislature," he said, admitting, "Politicians are usually not risk-takers and that even if similar legislation were introduced, it would be a slow, ponderous procedure."

There were six initiatives on the June 1988 ballot, an unprecedented number for a primary election. There are 12 on the ballot in November. And the state may be fast approaching (if it hasn't already) the point of no return in terms of voter overload. Extensive initiative lawmaking by politicians clearly indicates a troubled state Legislature. 🏛

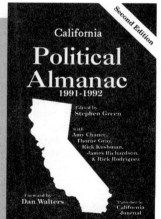

Initiatives: too much of a good thing?

By Charles Price and Robert Waste

Reprinted from *California Journal*, March 1991

The old bromide about the weather — "Everybody talks about it, but nobody can do anything about it " — has also been true of California's initiative process. For years, critics of this direct-democracy technique have complained about the problems and abuses inherent in the process. But thus far, efforts to substantially reform the initiative have failed.

Politicians have usually been wary of proposing major changes because the initiative has always been popular with the public. As a result, initiative procedures today are approximately the same as in 1911 when the process was first adopted, even though the state's population-growth now mandates the collection of hundreds of thousands of signatures (5 percent of the vote cast for governor in the most recent election for statute initiatives; 8 percent for constitutional amendments) before a measure can qualify for the ballot.

Despite the hurdle, the initiative process is more popular than ever. Modern campaign methods, including computerized mailing of petitions and paid circulators, have encouraged those who can raise the necessary $1 million or so to bypass the Legislature and go directly to the public.

However, there are indications that the public, deluged by ballot measures in the past few years and faced with an increasingly complex array of issues to discern, now may be willing to accept some changes in the initiative procedure. Some legislators have quickly stepped in and are proposing major alterations in the state's process of direct democracy.

The initiative was promoted by reformist Progressives early this century as a last resort technique for the public. If the Legislature were corrupt or controlled by special interests or party bosses, voters using the initiative process could adopt laws and constitutional amendments without the Legislature or governor. During the early decades of this century the initiative was employed frequently. But by the 1940s, during World War II and in the years immediately afterwards, initiative activity declined sharply. However, in the 1970s-80s and in 1990, there has been a tremendous resurgence of initiative activity.

The number of initiatives filed has nearly doubled each decade from the 1950s to the 1990s. More initiatives have been filed in a single year, 1990, than in entire decades from the 1910s through the 1960s. Intriguingly, while only about one-third of initiatives were approved by voters up to 1979, in the 1980s nearly one-half were approved.

There are a number of reasons for this surge in initiative activity, including the development of a professional petition industry — petition companies, initiative attorneys

Charles Price and Robert Waste are political science professors at California State University, Chico.

and campaign consultants whose livelihood depends on a continual fresh flow of initiatives; a public angered by legislative inaction and political scandals; the success of some efforts, such as property tax-slashing Proposition 13; the growth of single-issue politics; increasing use of counter-initiatives (groups threatened by an initiative place an alternative initiative on the ballot); and a growing trend towards elected officials authoring initiatives as part of their campaign strategy in running for statewide office.

When only a few initiatives qualified for each ballot, the process was grudgingly accepted by state officeholders. However, adoption by voters of the Political Reform Act (Proposition 9, 1974), the Gann state spending limitation initiative (Proposition 4, 1979) and, perhaps most important, the term-limit initiative (Proposition 140, 1990) which may cut legislative careers to a maximum of six or eight years, angered a great many public officials. Through the mid-1980s, however, polls showed the public overwhelmingly supported the initiative process. Mervin Field reported in 1979 that 83 percent of the California public thought the initiative was a "good thing," while only 5 percent thought it was a "bad thing." The public seemed to agree with the theme of the "yes on Proposition 13" campaign — the initiative was a good way to "teach the politicians a lesson." Therefore, attempts by various, mainly Democratic California legislators to reform the initiative (usually proposals to make it harder to qualify initiatives — e.g., raising the filing fee or requiring that petitions be signed in a certain number of counties) were regularly defeated. In addition, in *Meyer v. Grant* (1988), a federal court ruled that states could not prohibit paid signature soliciting — a favorite target of initiative critics.

However, the convergence of a number of factors indicates that for the first time this century the time may be ripe for significant initiative reform. Why is this so?

• First, clearly, the public was very unhappy with the number of voting decisions facing them in the 1988 and 1990 elections, caused mostly by the number of initiatives on those ballots. An all-time record number of initiatives, 18, qualified in 1988; two years later, this figure was equaled when another 18 initiatives appeared on the primary and general election ballots. However, ballot length was not simply a result of too many initiatives. As Bill Arno of American Petition Consultants noted, "Actually, there were more legislatively referred measures than initiatives on the 1990 ballot, and if the Legislature had been doing its job there wouldn't have been so many initiatives."

• Second, the public was upset with the length, complexity and confusing nature of many of the 1988-90 initiatives. The 1990 Ballot "Pamphlet" and supplement came to 221 pages of complicated legal argument. In this vein, pollster Mervin Field reports that public support for the initia-

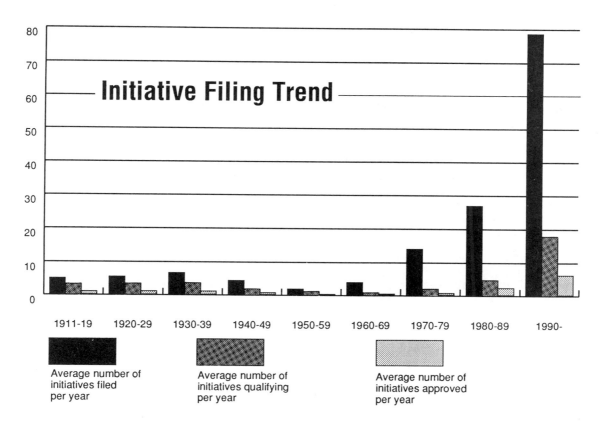

Initiative Filing Trend

| | 1911-19 | 1920-29 | 1930-39 | 1940-49 | 1950-59 | 1960-69 | 1970-79 | 1980-89 | 1990- |

Average number of
initiatives filed
per year

Average number of
initiatives qualifying
per year

Average number of
initiatives approved
per year

tive process has declined 16 percent since 1979. Currently, "only" 66 percent of Californians view the initiative as a "good thing."

• Third, initiatives have not been faring well in the courts lately, and this adds to public frustration over the process. Thus, just a few weeks prior to the November 1990 general election, Propositions 73 and 68 — two campaign-finance initiatives approved by voters in June 1988 — were declared unconstitutional. In addition, Proposition 103 — the auto-insurance rate-reduction initiative from November 1988 — has been so enmeshed in legal challenge that public hopes for quick insurance-rate reductions went unrealized. However, two years after the adoption of Proposition 103, State Farm Mutual in December 1990 under a plan approved by the Department of Insurance will substantially lower its rates for "good" drivers. The courts even stepped in and voided Proposition 105, an omnibus "consumer protection" measure that required disclosure of everything from insurance policies to household toxics on the previously uninvoked restriction in the state constitution requiring initiatives to deal only with a "single subject."

• Fourth, there is growing public resentment over the devious, deceptive and expensive media campaigns by initiative sponsors and opponents. In addition, the new trend evidenced in 1988 and 1990 revolves around electoral competition between environmental or political reform groups and their corporate opponents. If the former gets its initiative on the ballot, the latter will hire a petition firm to put forward its own counter-initiative on the same topic. There were four sets of counter-initiatives on the November 1990 ballot, while in the November 1988 election, five separate initiatives focused on auto insurance. Counter-initiatives have one main objective: confuse voters. As Kelly Kimball of Kimball Petition Management stated, "I'm disgusted with groups that put measures on the ballot to confuse and deceive voters, and who prefer that their counter-measures don't pass. Enough's enough."

• Fifth, many officeholders were bitter that a majority of the electorate would support the term-limits initiative, which not only cut short legislative careers but imposed a nearly 40 percent reduction in the Legislature's own budget, causing widespread layoffs among legislative staff and did away with legislators' retirement benefits.

• Sixth, there was a massive "no" vote registered against most of the initiatives (10 of 13) and most of the other propositions and bond measures on the 1990 general-election ballot. As Democratic Senator Milton Marks of San Francisco noted, "The outcome of the November [1990] election was a clear indictment of the initiative process."

• Seventh, many of the major players in the state's initiative industry — for example, Ted Costa, executive director of the Paul Gann People's Advocate, and petition circulators Kelly Kimball and Bill Arno — now believe the process needs to be reformed.

• Eighth, rejection by voters of Proposition 137 (November 1990), an initiative designed to make it more difficult to reform the initiative process (it would have required a majority vote of the public before any change could be made in the initiative process) and recent Mervin Field polls indicate growing public support for initiative reform. Joel Fox, executive director of the Howard Jarvis Taxpayers Association, said, "The public's rejection of Proposition 137 caught me by complete surprise."

Thus, there is at least some support among officeholders from both parties and the public that special interests have tended to monopolize and control the initiative process and that reforms are needed. What is not clear is the shape reforms should take. Should reform aim at discouraging use of the initiative, as some legislators want? Or, should reform aim at restoring the process to the people? And, as both Kelly Kimball and Bill Arno noted, if the Legislature adopts measures to make it more difficult to qualify initiatives, this will benefit their petition-for-hire companies because they will be the only ones around who have the expertise to collect the hundreds of thousands of signatures needed.

Among the various reforms being proposed by elected officials, Senate Republican leader Ken Maddy of Fresno has proposed a constitutional amendment to more clearly express the single-subject initiative requirement — "An initiative measure embracing more than one subject may not be submitted to the electors or have any effect."

Should Maddy's bill pass, initiative provisions would have to be reasonably germane and interdependent with other provisions of the measure. Of course, what is "reasonably germane" is subjective and subject to court interpretation. Ironically, the Maddy bill passed the Senate but failed in the Assembly last year when it was *joined* to a proposal to move the presidential primary ahead.

Opponents of "Big Green" (Proposition 128, November 1990) argued that it failed to meet the single-subject requirement, but since it was not approved the question is moot. Proposition 105, the court-voided consumer-information initiative approved by voters in November 1988, had five separate sub-categories — toxic substances, fraudulent health insurance, nursing homes, initiative campaign funds and stock-selling corporations conducting business in South Africa. Although the court acted in this case, it historically has been loathe to do so. The last time the court struck down an initiative for violation of this principle was 1948. Unquestionably, lengthy propositions with many subsections complicate decision making for voters but agreeing on what is "reasonably germane" is not easy.

Among other legislators who favor reform of the initiative, Assembly Speaker Willie Brown of San Francisco favors having initiatives voted upon only during general elections, not during primaries, because of the poor turnout in these June contests. (Of course, the percentage voting in the general election these days is not very high either). If this were implemented, it would mean the general-election ballot would be substantially longer and might further voter frustration.

Senate President pro Tempore David Roberti has suggested that initiative petitions should have to obtain signatures in a certain number of counties. Democratic Senator Gary Hart of Santa Barbara is contemplating legislation to prohibit bond issue initiatives. Independent Senator Quentin Kopp unsuccessfully authored a bill in the last legislative session aimed at discouraging initiative proponents from building support for their measures by offering groups who joined the coalition funding from the measure for their pet projects. Of course, log-rolling is a long-time practice in the Legislature. Proponents raise money for their initiatives, then pay themselves substantial consulting fees from the campaign treasury. Marks stated, "We need to somehow take away the profit involved with initiatives."

Republican Assemblyman Stan Statham is the author of AB 3148 which was signed into law by former Governor George Deukmejian. This law requires a notice that the petition may be circulated by either a volunteer or by a paid signature gatherer, and the public has the right to inquire as to the circulator's status.

Statham noted that, "Not a soul at the Capitol doesn't know that the initiative process is warped and out of control." Democratic Assemblywoman Jackie Speier of South San Francisco proposed in a bill last session that the Secretary of State do a legal analysis of a proposed initiative to ensure the proposal was in proper legal form. At present, initiative proponents can seek aid from the Legislative Counsel in drafting their proposals. But, according to Ted Costa, when he asked the Counsel's office for help in drafting an initiative, he was told that because of the passage of Proposition 13 and state spending limits, the counsel's office did not have sufficient staff to help him. Not surprisingly, initiative advocates worry that if the secretary of state's office or attorney general's office did a precirculation legal review of the initiative it could be partisanly-inspired because these are elected partisan officeholders.

UC Berkeley Professor Eugene Lee argues that "consideration be given to a minimum threshold in turnout, say, 50 percent of registered voters, as a condition of passage to ensure the 'people's voice' is heard." However, initiative advocates might well ask, why should this only affect initiatives? Shouldn't candidates be under the same proviso? And, since turnout in primaries is usually below 50 percent of those registered, how would we nominate our candidates? Lee also proposes that the Legislature and governor be allowed to amend and repeal statutory initiatives after a specified time and that the constitutional amendment initiative signature threshold percentage be raised from 8 percent to 10 percent.

Yet, while the time may be ripe for reform, there may be good reason to proceed slowly. There are always unanticipated consequences of any reform. In one sense, the abuse of the initiative process in 1990 was dealt with by the voters. They massively voted "no" — not a bad strategy considering all of the confusing proposals on that ballot. And, because they voted down so many measures, won't those who buy their way onto the ballot be less enthused about trying this tactic in 1992? Also, the election of Governor Pete Wilson may encourage environmentalists to pursue the legislative path once again. As Gerry Meral, executive director of the Planning and Conservation League, said, "The PCL had to go the initiative route because of Governor Deukmejian's obstinance. We may not have to do this with Wilson."

It should be emphasized: An overwhelming majority of the public (66 percent according to Field) still supports the initiative. Efforts to discourage initiative use according to Ted Costa might lead to a coalescence of interest groups ranging from Tom Hayden's Campaign California, Harvey Rosenfield's Voter Revolt, Ralph Nader's Public Interest Research Group, environmental groups such as the Planning and Conservation League and Sierra Club on the left of the political spectrum to Ted Costa's People's Advocate, Richard Gann, Ralph Morrell, and Joel Fox of the Howard Jarvis Taxpayers Association on the right. These disparate groups might be willing to pull together to thwart legislative attempts to discourage initiative use.

Finally, are initiatives the central problem facing California government? Democratic Assemblyman Ted Lempert of San Mateo, a member of the Assembly Elections and Reapportionment Committee, doesn't think so. "Initiatives are usually a yes or no on a basic idea. That's good and has its place but the Legislature is where the real work is done. That's where we have the hearings and make detailed policy. That's the level at which we have to get the people interested again. That's the real reform of all of this."

And echoing these sentiments, Martin Smith, political editor of *The Sacramento Bee* observes, "The problem is not so much initiative procedure as an underlying problem of government not working. Maybe something can be done at the margins with initiatives but the real disease is government that doesn't work and hasn't worked in at least 16 years of not very dynamic leadership."

DERAILING INITIATIVES

(before they reach the ballot)

By Bill Ainsworth

Reprinted from *California Journal*, January 1992

n the past, there have been campaigns against candidates. And campaigns against initiatives and other assorted ballot measures. And campaigns against reapportionment plans, city-county mergers, sales-tax increases, *ad nauseum.*

And now comes the latest wrinkle — the campaign against a campaign.

As far as voters are concerned, this new kind of campaign differs from its nearest cousin — the campaign against an initiative, which is noisy and fought out in full view of the public. The campaign against a campaign, on the other hand, is like aerial dogfights between the Royal Air Force and the German Lutwaffe during the Battle of Britain: The bulk of the combat takes place above the clouds and beyond the reach of those on the ground.

The campaign against a campaign is a new and more sophisticated strategy in the ever-escalating war between well-heeled interest groups, a campaign meant to convince one group or another to abort an initiative before it can even get it on the ballot.

Does it work? Just ask an alliance of health insurers and small business groups. Last summer, their pre-emptive efforts — their campaign against a campaign — helped convince the influential and wealthy California Medical Association to abandon plans to put a universal health-

Bill Ainsworth covers the Capitol for The Recorder, *a San Francisco-based legal daily.*

insurance initiative on the November 1992 ballot. The alliance, known as the Consumer Health Insurance Coalition and funded by health insurers, engaged in a $300,000 lobbying effort whose sole purpose was to intimidate the CMA and scare away its potential allies.

The coalition took polls, conducted focus groups, sponsored letter-writing campaigns and hired a public-relations firm to convey the message that any health-care solution requiring tax increases would be defeated at the polls. In addition, it warned trade associations that joining a doctor-sponsored plan would be costly and futile.

"We worked very hard to isolate the CMA," said Richard Claussen of Goodard/Claussen Campaigns, which ran the campaign. "That was a significant factor in their decision. ... There's never been a campaign like this before."

CMA officials denied that the unusual lobbying effort had any effect on their decision. "We knew all along that there would be strong opposition," said Dr. Howard Lang, president of the CMA.

The medical association dropped its plan, Lang said, because it failed to find more allies and because the economy had gone sour. His announcement came three days after the state said it was facing a $3 billion deficit due to the recession.

The CMA's decision leaves only one possible health-care initiative proposal for the November 1992 ballot — a measure calling on the Legislature to extend health insurance to all the state's uninsured residents. The measure is backed

"They limit legislative debate and constrain possible solutions because no one is willing to oppose these PACs and risk the loss of their campaign contributions."

The major players — doctors, health insurers, small business, and union and consumer groups — have all been able to block bills they oppose in the Legislature. At the same time, no group has been able to get major changes approved.

Each of the major interest groups has a different agenda. Physicians, for example, want to broaden the existing system, with more money for Medi-Cal and mandatory health insurance for everyone. They say they have been forced to bear the burden of treating the poor.

"There's been a major cost shift in health care," said Ralph Thomas, a spokesman for the CMA. "The private sector pays what the government is not paying."

The doctors' initiative would have set up a $125 basic health insurance policy. Employers would have paid 75 per-cent of the costs, with workers paying the remaining 25 per-cent. That policy would have cost $8 billion in additional state spending on health, including a $2 billion increase in taxes. Some of the money would go towards subsidies for low-income workers and small firms. Over six years, the plan would have extended health care to all of the uninsured, said Carol Lee, associate director of governmental affairs for the medical association.

To fund its proposal, the CMA had sought a sales-tax increase. But when the Legislature raised sales taxes to close the 1991-92 budget deficit, the CMA dropped the idea of a sales-tax increase and began searching for a new source of funding, Lee said. By the time it dropped the plan, the medical association had not yet found that source.

The CMA had begun planning for its ambitious initiative almost two years in advance. Last year, its conference of delegates voted to spend $1.5 million on a signature-gathering campaign if the political atmosphere was judged favorable and if the CMA could line up allies, said Eugene Ogrod, vice chairman of the association.

Doctors also might have been hoping that the mere threat of an initiative would put pressure on the Legislature to pass its proposal. But the legislation failed.

Meanwhile, the early warning gave industry leaders extra time to plan an opposition strategy.

In the past, when dealing with initiative proposals it opposed, business has waited to begin its campaign until the measure qualified for the ballot. Only 31 percent of the proposals turned in to the secretary of state's office succeed in gathering the signatures needed to qualify.

But most groups lack the power and the money of the CMA. With its 40,000 affluent members, the CMA has long been a giant political force. Its political action committee is usually the single largest campaign donor in the state. This clout made opponents of the medical association's initiative take notice.

In April, Goodard/Claussen proposed the unusual early lobbying strategy to its health-insurer clients. Four important clients — the Health Insurance Association of America, the Association of California Life Insurance Companies, Aetna and Travelers Insurance — gave it the go-ahead, determining that they had nothing to lose.

"We wanted to avoid a costly ballot fight," said Martyn Hopper, state director of the National Federation of Small Business, which later joined the anti-CMA campaign. Since the strategy worked, industry avoided a bruising ballot fight in

by Michael Weinstein, who raises money for Los Angeles-based AIDS treatment centers. Political observers, however, believe his effort has little chance for success.

That leaves virtually no hope of ballot relief for a health-care system on the verge of crisis. Chronic underfunding of public health care has forced hospitals and trauma centers around the state to close, while the spiraling cost of health insurance has made it more difficult for people to obtain coverage. More than 20 percent of the state's residents do not have health insurance.

It would seem, therefore, that the CMA's attempt would fill some need — if nothing more than to put the entire issue of health care before voters. But it was not to be, and not everyone is happy about CMA's default.

Maryann O'Sullivan, director of Health Access, a labor and consumer coalition, called the campaign against the CMA's initiative "scandalous."

"The group that organized this campaign of opposition is opposing everything," she said. "They aren't doing anything for the six million people without health insurance."

So far the Legislature hasn't done anything, either. The CMA turned to the initiative process out of frustration with state lawmakers. For the past six years, the health interest groups have fought to a stalemate at the Capitol. California Common Cause says the reason is simple: money. Last month, it released a study showing that medical industry political-action committees have donated $23.1 million to state candidates over the past 10 years.

"The medical industry PACs create policy paralysis on health-care issues," said Lisa Foster, executive director.

November for a fraction of the estimated $7 million to $8 million it would have cost to run a full-scale opposition campaign.

Even if the strategy had failed, CMA opponents would have gained a head start in organizing their coalition.

This task of organizing proved difficult at times. Mistrust between small business and the insurance industry prompted a rivalry within the opposition camp. Several important small business associations decided against joining with the insurance industry because they feared that insurers might eventually agree to mandatory insurance. With the economy in a recession, owners of small businesses worried that any mandated insurance would put many of them out of business.

"This issue represents an absolute threat to our members," said Jo-Linda Thompson, lobbyist for the California Restaurant Association.

In July, the restaurant association, along with retailers and hotel and motel owners, formed an opposition group separate from the insurers' coalition. Called Health Coalition '92, it hired the public-relations firm of PBN at $5000 to $7000 a month to begin organizing potential opponents to the CMA's initiative.

Despite this split, however, the employers' campaign and the much larger campaign by the insurance industry complemented each other. And had the CMA actually gone full bore for its initiative, the two opposition groups probably would have combined forces for the November campaign.

As the opposition gathered its forces, the CMA announced in August that its initiative was a *fait accompli,* causing the insurance industry's coalition to swing into action. Its members visited editorial boards, produced campaign brochures, disseminated press releases and set up a phone bank to gather opposition. The coalition also hired an attorney to write up a possible counter initiative.

As part of the campaign, the insurers sent mailgrams to the CMA and other trade associations. One mailgram warned the California Association of Hospitals and Health Systems against joining the doctors.

"The public will be extremely skeptical of such a measure, particularly given the broad and aggressive opposition it will generate," the mailgram cautioned. "Millions will be spent on a battle that will almost certainly result in the measure being defeated."

Undaunted, the CMA continued trying to enlist allies in its cause. In September, the association began talks with a coalition of 170 consumer, union and church groups called Health Access. Health Access favors a Canadian-style system that would extend coverage to all, while reducing administrative costs by eliminating most private insurance. This plan would make most doctors state employees. Not surprisingly, it has generated fierce opposition from both physicians and insurance companies.

In the end, the doctors could not overcome their differences with the consumer/labor coalition. Health Access opposed pouring more money into what it considered a bankrupt system, while the doctors could not agree to a state-run health system.

Left with only three allies — Kaiser Permanente, the California Association of County Supervisors and the California Association of Hospitals and Health Systems — the CMA executive committee voted on October 22nd to drop its initiative.

"The lack of a consensus coupled with a recession and the state's gloomy economic picture convinced us not to go forward," Lang told reporters at a news conference.

Although the CMA proposal is dead, the early lobbying strategy is likely to live on as a result of this success, insurance lobbyists said. Clayton Jackson, whose firm was involved in the lobbying effort, said he believes the campaign was most successful at keeping allies away from the CMA.

"The CMA's an experienced, wealthy, tough operation. It's hard to influence them directly," Jackson said. "What you're doing here is influencing the environment of a decision-maker as opposed to influencing the decision-maker directly."

Jackson and other lobbyists believe the strategy will be used again, though they caution that it will not be appropriate for every initiative battle. "We're going to see more and more efforts to shape the political environment," Jackson said.

O'Sullivan of Health Access agreed. If Health Access decides to go ahead with its universal health care initiative, the group expects to face a similar lobbying campaign. "We're talking about moving billions of dollars around. There are huge vested interests that are doing quite well under the current system," O'Sullivan said. "I don't think they will hesitate to spend money up front against an initiative they don't like."

In the meantime, the problems in the health-care system are expected to get worse.

"This problem isn't going to go away," said the CMA's Lee. "There are still six million Californians suffering." 🏛

LOCAL GOVERNMENT

One reason why Californians have so many elections and frequently such long ballots is that the state has a complex system of local government. Every citizen in the state probably is a resident of a dozen or more units of local government, among them:

Counties. The state has 58 counties (counting San Francisco), some of which are governed by general state law and others by charters (similar to constitutions) voted by the people.

Cities. Most Californians live in one of the state's 468 cities, but many live in unincorporated areas in which municipal services are provided by the county and special districts. General law cities (384) operate through a structure established by state law. Charter cities have more flexibility in their structure and procedures.

City-county. San Francisco is a combined city and county operating under a charter.

School districts. Public schools from kindergarten through 12th grade are operated by independent districts with directly elected governing boards. There are about 1200 school districts in the state.

Community college districts. Directly elected trustees also run community colleges, which provide freshman and sophomore courses.

Special districts. These can vary from large regional districts such as the Metropolitan Water District in Los Angeles to a local mosquito-abatement district. There are more than 3,000 special districts formed to provide specific services for a defined area. Most directors are elected by the public.

Local Agency Formation Commissions. Each county has a commission that serves as clearinghouse for annexation of territory by a local agency and for formation of new cities.

Regional governments. There are no all-powerful regional governments in California, but there are numerous limited-purpose regional agencies such as the Bay Area Air Pollution Control District, Rapid Transit District and Sewer Service Agency. Efforts have been underway for years to enact a powerful regional government for the San Francisco area. There are several voluntary associations of local governmental agencies designed to help resolve regional problems; these include the Association of Bay Area Governments and the Southern California Association of Governments.

City and county government

Counties are run by boards of supervisors elected by the public, usually by district. In most counties, the board appoints an administrative officer to supervise the details of county government. Counties also have other directly elected officials, such as the district attorney, the sheriff and the assessor.

Cities are operated under a variety of systems. Under one basic arrangement not widely used, the strong-mayor system, the mayor is the chief-administrative officer of the city, and policy is set by the council. The more common system establishes the mayor, who may be elected either by the people or by the council, as the ceremonial chief of the city and puts the administration of municipal affairs under the control of a powerful city manager or administrator. The council has the power to appoint and remove the manager. Under this council-manager form of government, the council is supposed to be limited to the setting of policy, but there have been a few cases in which a mayor, by virtue of a strong personality, had been able to run the city government, relegating the manager to the role of errand boy.

More frequently, however, the manager, by virtue of the fact that he is a full-time employee with a large staff, plays a role as large as or even greater than the council in establishing policy.

Special districts are usually administered by a superintendent, general manager or other executive selected by the governing board. 🏛

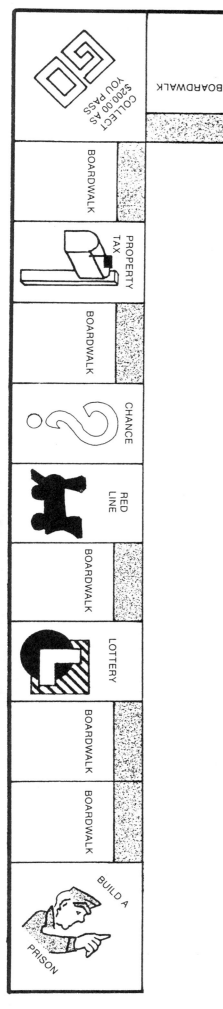

COLLECT $200.00 AS YOU PASS

BOARDWALK

PROPERTY TAX

BOARDWALK

CHANCE

RED LINE

BOARDWALK

LOTTERY

BOARDWALK

BOARDWALK

BUILD A PRISON

BOARDWALK

LOTTERY

BOARDWALK

INCOME TAX PAY 10% OR $200

BART

BOARDWALK

CHANCE

BOARDWALK

Regional government: Everyone wants to land on Boardwalk

By Craig Hamley and A.G. Block

Reprinted from *California Journal*, November 1990

A behind-the-scenes political battle is being fought in California. As battles go, this one is small; it's not nearly as attention-grabbing as political showdowns over water allocations and offshore oil drilling. Yet the future importance of this fight should not be underestimated, for it involves control over land-use authority and its outcome could reshape the political landscape of California.

The protagonists are city and county government officials, who want to retain current authority over land-use decisions, arrayed against members of the state Legislature, who seek to create a new system of regional government which may cut into that authority.

Growth management is the central issue around which the contest over land-use control has arisen. According to proponents of regional government, the current system of cities and counties has failed to adequately or comprehensively manage land use during California's intensive population growth. Without consistent area-wide land-use planning that only a regional government can offer, proponents argue, growth-related problems

Craig Hamley was a California Journal *intern. A.G. Block is managing editor of the* Journal.

like smog and gridlocked freeways may never be solved, for those problems cross city and county boundaries.

Regional-government advocates base their argument on the fact that California's current system of local government is outdated, having been designed in the 1850s when California's original 27 counties were created. That system is unable to cope with a state that is no longer largely rural but dominated by urban sprawl. Proponents of regionalism claim that problems occurring over entire regions encompassing many cities and counties cannot be adequately dealt with by separate entities acting alone.

On the other hand, groups such as the League of California Cities and the County Supervisors Association of California don't deny that land-use planning has been poor. Instead, they blame growth-management problems on fiscal constraints imposed by outside influences such as the property tax-slashing Proposition 13 of 1978.

According to the League and to CSAC, local authorities have been forced into what is commonly called "cashbox zoning" — making land-use decisions based on how much tax revenue a development will bring in rather than on its need. As a result, too many shopping malls and large corporate developments have been built without adequate freeway or parking support or enough affordable housing within easy commuting distance.

"To talk about setting up a new form of government without taking into consideration the financial aspects would merely be setting up another straw-man doomed for failure," says CSAC's executive director, Larry Naake.

Indeed, in its report entitled "Action for the '90s," the League of Cities found that "... when adjusted for inflation and population growth, city general-purpose revenues have declined by more than 15 percent per capita" since pre-Proposition 13 days.

Despite this shrinkage in local tax bases, not everyone agrees that shrinkage alone is completely responsible for all the current planning problems.

"I think you can trace some of the problems to revenue difficulties, but not all of them," said former Assemblyman John Knox, a strong proponent of regional government during a nearly identical battle during the 1960s when he chaired the Assembly Local Government Committee. "You've got all the cities trying to sneak some pork out of the barrel, and the counties doing the same thing, and nothing's approached on a regional basis."

Knox believes a coordinated regional government would strengthen rather than weaken existing local authorities.

"Cities and counties would have a better definition of what their jobs were, and they would have a better place to go to seek redress of their grievances on a regional basis," Knox stated.

Knox's support of regional government goes back to his days as a legislator, from 1960 to 1980, when he saw his own regional-government bill die on the Senate floor because supporters refused to allow the plan to go to a referendum of the people — the price asked by several conservative senators who wanted to preserve local control.

"I felt strongly that it was something the people should not have had to vote on. It's very complicated, and it would have just been demagogic," Knox said. He added that hardline conservatives will probably oppose any regional-government plan this time around as well but probably don't have the votes to kill it.

The basic idea of coordination among regional authorities is one that both CSAC and the League of Cities are in agreement with because they feel it would eliminate confusing and many times clashing signals received from the various regional entities that already exist.

This is the general thrust of AB 4242, carried last session by Assembly Speaker Willie Brown of San Francisco, the strongest piece of legislation in a series of bills dealing with growth management. The speaker's involvement has also helped push the issue into the limelight. "The seriousness of the speaker in carrying this bill certainly raises the profile of this issue," said Todd Kaufman, a principal consultant with the Assembly Office of Research.

Brown's bill died in the Assembly Local Government Committee during the waning days of the 1989-90 legislative session, but the speaker has promised to revive a similar piece of legislation in 1991. Had it survived, however, AB 4242 would have created regional agencies with the authority to mandate local change through land-use planning. These new regional agencies would have been put together by consolidating already existing single-purpose agencies into single units. No fewer than five other bills dealing with institutional change were also introduced during the last session, with a common thread to deal with growth management. None of the bills survived.

The focal point for these legislative battles was the Assembly Committee on Local Government. With so many different ideas on growth management, a special group within the committee was formed to resolve potential conflicts between the bills. The Local Government Committee also held a hearing on regional governance and a joint Senate and Assembly hearing, entitled "Managing California's Growth: Striking the Balance," in an effort to reach a consensus on the issue.

Besides the work of the Local Government Committee, the Assembly Office of Research is currently working with CSAC, the League of Cities and a number of other interested parties to overcome what proved to be fatal problems associated with AB 4242's version of regional government. Chief among the concerns was the measure's failure to address fiscal problems facing local government.

According to Democratic Assemblyman Sam Farr of Carmel, chairman of the Assembly Local Government Committee, it was the fiscal issue rather than partisan conflict that slowed immediate progress on the growth issue. Farr, who unsuccessfully carried a bill that would have created a state planning agency, also underscored the need for the state to take a much stronger role in stating its policy concerning growth management. "Part of the problem is that the state's got to get its act in order, because you can't ask local government to fall into a parade when there's no clear direction in which the parade is going," he said.

Currently there appears to be a great deal of cooperation between the Legislature and concerned parties like CSAC and the League of Cities. "We don't want to be obstructionist to this process ... we would like to ideally view this as a kind of cooperative partnership approach on solving problems that face our mutual citizens," said Naake.

Despite this apparent cooperation, however, it is clear that local entities wish to forfeit as little land-use authority as possible, no matter what new governmental structure the Legislature might create, if any. Local agencies say they have already been forced to give up a portion of their land-use authority to existing single-purpose regional agencies such as air-quality management districts and transportation-planning agencies. Now they are fighting to keep their remaining authority. Whether or not local agencies can hold their own remains to be seen.

The problem, claim local officials, lies in trying to decide what regional land use falls under the authority of whatever regional agency might be formed, and what local land use falls under the authority of the city or county.

"I think local government is very interested in a better way of looking at those truly regional land-use decisions, but at the same time interested in retaining authority over local decisions," said Donald Benninghoven, the League of Cities' executive director. "And when there's a difference of opinion on that basic issue, which there will be, then there needs to be a mechanism for resolving those disputes."

The problems created by poor planning and heavy growth stare everyone in the face. Once quaint and peaceful, many Northern California cities now resemble the mess of smog, water shortages, gridlocked freeways and overpriced housing that has been the status quo for much of Southern California for years. Resolution of the problem will involve complex negotiations, and some recognition by everyone involved that the old way of parceling out authority no longer solves problems. 🏛

In case of earthquake, call your accountant

By Elizabeth Schilling

Reprinted from *California Journal*, August 1991

Recovery continues to be a rocky road for many of the communities shaken during the October 1989 Loma Prieta Earthquake. Immediately following that 7.1 earthquake, the Central Coast cities of Santa Cruz, Watsonville, San Francisco and others looked to state and federal agencies for relief.

Aid from various agencies has proven vital. Still, many communities say they have had a rude awakening to learn the extent to which they are on their own in dealing with a major disaster. If others will listen, those who have been through the state's most recent disaster have some practical words of advice: Be patient, prepare your accounting systems and be ready to dig deep in local pockets for recovery funds.

While totals of public and private damage from the quake reaches to the billions of dollars, only a portion will be covered in reimbursements from the Governor's Office of Emergency Services or the Federal Emergency Management Agency. As of May, FEMA had paid out $270 million for repairs related to the 1989 quake. Officials say at least another $400 million will likely be paid to local governments as more complicated cases of reimbursement are resolved during the next few years.

While FEMA officials say they must pinch pennies to ensure that things balance out across the nation, many local governments feel they are being dragged through bureaucratic battles

Elizabeth Schilling is a writer living in Santa Cruz.

to get what is rightfully theirs. Lawsuits occasionally result, as in the recent case in which the Oakland area won $24 million dollars to replace some housing for homeless and low-income tenants.

"I can't emphasize how extremely cumbersome all this has been," says Mary Ortendahl, an administrative analyst with Alameda County who is charged with coordinating earthquake recovery funds. Her county estimates it is eligible for $8.7 million from FEMA, but so far has received less than half that amount.

"Things get a little muddy about what will be reimbursed," says Ortendahl. She says she has found FEMA repre-sentatives cooperative, but very nit-picky. "Along with our county, they are hoping it's just a matter of paper work, but the further you get from the disaster the harder it is to document."

Ortendahl, like officials in other effected areas, continues to meet regularly with FEMA representatives to resolve claims. For example, still unresolved is reimbursement for hours put in by workers in the Alameda County sheriff's and coroner's departments during the days they served on emergency response at the collapsed Cypress Freeway structure.

Differences of opinion in Watsonville

Watsonville

Watsonville was quick to begin rebuilding its damaged downtown since the Loma Prieta Earthquake.

"From the start we took the position that it's up to us if we want to make a comeback," said Watsonville Finance Director Terry Stigall. "We pushed from the beginning, regardless of knowing if we would be reimbursed."

Watsonville has been paid back almost three-quarters of the $6.4 million of damage it claimed. The sticking points that remain don't have easy solutions.

Disputes in many cases with FEMA center around figures used in damage statement reports (DSRs). Agencies consider FEMA notorious for low-balling repair work. For example, the federal estimate for the Watsonville City Hall was $27,000. The city disputed that figure, hired their own inspector and got an estimate of $116,000 to do the job, Stigall says.

"FEMA sent inspectors from Colorado, North Dakota and Florida who had no understanding of California's labor costs, permit procedures or building code requirements," says Stigall. "We had expected they would have at least been trained in a day class about things to consider in California."

Another landmark site key to Watsonville's recovery is the Porter building. Built in 1880, the 5500-square-foot building of office and retail space remains red-tagged and empty. A fence around the building keeps cars and people away from the danger of crumbling walls that teeter overhead. For nearly two years now Stigall has actively pursued applications with state and federal agencies to attempt to deal with the Porter building.

The first application for funds was to FEMA, but the city was told they were not the proper since the building was under a 25-year lease. Then the lessee applied for funds from the Small Business Administration. This rejected application also brought scrutiny from state historic preservation officials who prohibited the option of demolition. At this point Stigall said FEMA reversed its position, recognized the city as owner and asked for another application. Now Watsonville is stuck between policies of two agencies: The state won't allow demolition, but FEMA won't give money for repair because it believes the building is more than 50 percent damaged.

"After all this time we're told to go back to square one," says Stigall. Although it may not have been the right solution for the Porter building, Stigall says such frustrations make him reflect differently on those cities that moved decisively with wrecking balls within days of a disaster.

—Elizabeth Schilling

"Even FEMA agrees these costs were directly related to the earthquake, but because our employees didn't put the right code on their time sheets it is not considered properly documented. It's very expensive for the county to go back and find the necessary figures," says Ortendahl. "With the next disaster we'll have what we should have had —a separate accounting system that can be activated by pushing a button."

On the matter of accounting, Santa Cruz had in place

Watsonville

what Alameda wishes it had. Fire and flood disasters during the '80s gave Santa Cruz the experience in dealing with FEMA, according to Santa Cruz Finance Director Jack Ness. A detailed emergency accounting system has allowed Santa Cruz to recoup $8.5 million in earthquake-related expenses on everything from fire department overtime to meals for visiting building inspectors. Santa Cruz and FEMA are still negotiating on several major items, Ness says.

"We were lucky to know the system," he admits. "When FEMA came to us after the earthquake we knew where to send them and how to assist their engineers and inspectors. I saw other local agencies who weren't prepared or who hadn't identified their problems. They had trouble. If FEMA comes and you don't know what you're doing, then they do things their way, not the way the city wants it done."

Overall, Ness reports that Santa Cruz is satisfied with the money it is getting from both FEMA and the state Office of Emergency Services. Ness and other local representatives hail efforts by the state, which for the first time came to the financial aid of localities. Usually damage reimbursement is covered 75 percent by FEMA with a 25 percent match by local governments, but due to the scale of damage from the Loma Prieta Earthquake the state covered the local share.

"The state has been a great help," says Ness. "But in light of the budget problems before the state, they can't be depended upon for relief in future disasters."

Even with this unprecedented help from the state, Santa Cruz needs much more money to rebuild its downtown that was destroyed in the quake. A major cost is replacing infrastructure — construction that is beyond what FEMA is willing to support. While FEMA will cover the cost of *repairs* to the antiquated underground sewer and water lines, the city believes such work would be senseless on 100-year old pipes. Instead the city opted for a completely new system at a cost of $4 million.

To pay for this, and other infrastructure projects, county voters approved a ballot measure that adds a half cent sales tax for one year. Projections estimate that $18 million will be raised for county-wide recovery projects.

Additional local taxes must now be expected in other communities should an earthquake, flood or other natural disaster strike their home, according to Eileen Baumgartener, assistant director of Plans and Preparedness with OES.

"People have rising expectations for relief with each disaster," Baumgartener observes. "The reality is you can expect some financial assistance, but it won't make you whole. After a disaster most localities are surprised with how costly recovery is."

A frequent controversy in recovery is repair of historic buildings, several of which were damaged in many cities in the earthquake. While landmark buildings may be invaluable to the local community, FEMA may view the old building as too costly to save.

"The federal programs will choose the cheaper option — probably demolition," says Baumgartener. "If local governments want to save something, they will usually have to come up with the money."

Issues such as this, and others related to the Loma Prieta Earthquake, have broadened the discussion about what full recovery means, according to Baumgartener.

"A good thing that came out of Loma Prieta is that people can see there is more to an earthquake than just 'response.' The disaster isn't over when you put out the last fire or close the last temporary shelter," says Baumgartener. "After the initial response comes a lengthy recovery and then an even longer-term reconstruction period."

The expense and trauma associated with the last two phases are areas where localities need to do additional

emergency planning, according to those who have been through a disaster. How to do so is the subject of many recent and upcoming conferences and publications, such as "Earthquake Recovery and Reconstruction Planning Guidelines for Local Governments," recently published by the Southern California Earthquake Preparedness Project.

Agreeing with the distinctions among response, recovery and rebuilding is Roy Gorup, chief of FEMA's Public Assistance Branch. Local governments are right to expect quick response, but after that, "Our agency is not meant to take care of the full bore of the problems," says Gorup. "Local governments often have expectations that shouldn't be there. They have to recognize they are going to have to supplement."

Whether a local government feels helped or hindered by FEMA is up to each city's administration, Gorup contends. He has seen localities deal with one disaster after another and some, he says, never seem to learn from the experience.

"Dealing with a federal agency is no picnic," says Gorup, "but it's one of those things a city has got to be prepared to do."

While one city may be super-prepared for a disaster that may never come, another, he says, won't even go to the trouble of spending the relief funds approved for them.

"It depends on the administrators of the city and what level of importance they place on preparedness," says Gorup. "When we run seminars we often just get the management types. When they go back I think there is often a failure to pass on what is learned."

Training and organization must be department wide if success is to be ensured, Gorup advises, otherwise preparedness may be as fleeting as job turnover.

In connection with the October 1989 earthquake, Gorup's Region 9 office has processed more than 9,500 claims from about 650 agencies.

Some who weathered the quake advise establishing a personal relationship with someone in FEMA. An excellent idea, says Gorup, but that might be difficult since his staff of 22 is often on the go. In the months since the earthquake his office has also handled major natural disasters,, including typhoons, hurricanes, lava flows and fires, in a region that includes Arizona, Nevada, Hawaii, California, American Samoa, Guam and the Trust Territories.

With all the talk recently about earthquakes, Gorup thinks potential flood disasters are being overlooked. New laws require flood insurance for all structures built in identified flood hazard areas. The federal agency will no longer come to the aid of local governments who have not followed up on private insurance.

"More surprising than what people learned after the earthquake will be what might happen after major flooding," warns Gorup. "Local governments may face a tremendous shock."

Be it flooding, or the inevitable "Big One," much can, and should be done by local governments to prepare, says Gorup.

"There is a lot of strange thinking around disasters," he says. "We talk about preparedness, lots of people even get started. But there's something about human nature that seems to make us forget. After a while people even fail to recognize that destruction ever occurred." 🏛

Creative mutual aid goes beyond fire and police

If local governments are disappointed in help from state and federal agencies, they may have better luck turning to each other in times of need.

In the days following the Loma Prieta Earthquake, assistance flowed to the struck area from sympathetic communities around the nation. Charleston, South Carolina, sent police. Orange County sent drivers with backhoes, while San Diego sent structural engineers.

"One of the greatest things that happened to Watsonville was that the City of Long Beach sent us a senior accountant and a grant accountant," says Finance Director Terry Stigall. The telephone call that offered help came out of the blue from someone Stigall had never met. "In the confusion following the quake the last thing we could do was think of a new accounting system. I didn't even know what I needed."

The visiting accountants stayed 10 days and developed a supplemental system that was put into operation immediately. Stigall estimates Watsonville spent about $2000 on the care and feeding of the visitors, and reaped more than $500,000 in returns from FEMA because of the new tracking system.

Mutual aid has become routine between neighboring police and fire departments, often with great cost savings. Stigall thinks the concept should be expanded among other professionals — both for preparedness planning and at the time of emergency.

—*Elizabeth Schilling*

Community colleges back on track

Reprinted from *California Journal*, February 1989

By Judy Tachibana

YOU ARE HERE

OR MAYBE HERE

ROB '89

California's community college system, even with a new state chancellor and a recently passed reform bill, faces major challenges before the system can be restored to the national stature it once held.

Much ground was lost during the late 1960s and 1970s when the two-year colleges were unsure of their mission and were struggling to keep up enrollments at any cost to secure attendance-based financing from the state. As a result, many two-year colleges, the traditional entry point for the state's

Judy Tachibana is a reporter for the Sacramento Bee.

poor and minority populations, took a detour into programs that were popular but of dubious value to those who were on either a four-year college program or those seeking vocational education.

California's two-year college system had been considered a national model before fiscal difficulties began in 1978 with the passage of Proposition 13. Because the property-tax limit shifted the system's funding base from local districts to the state, some schools began to offer some less-academic courses to keep their enrollment — and thus, funding — from dropping. (Under the reform bill, funding based on enrollment is to be phased out and, by 1991, replaced with program-based funding.)

A controversial $50 tuition fee imposed in 1984 ended California's traditional no-fee community college education. Enrollment in the early 1980s began slipping and is just now showing signs of recovery.

The schools underwent microscopic examination for several years, resulting finally in a reform bill authored last year by San Jose Assemblyman John Vasconcellos, Democratic chairman of the Assembly Ways and Means Committee. The bill reaffirmed the traditional mission of community colleges — to provide vocational education and to prepare students for transfer to universities — and restricted them from attempting to be all things to all people.

Now, the colleges feel they are back on track. Proposition 98, approved by voters last year, has provided them with additional money for regular operating expenses, but Governor George Deukmejian cited passage of the measure as one reason for cutting back discretionary programs, and his initial budget provided little of the $70 million sought by the system to implement the first year of its reform program.

Still, the perception of the need
Continued on next page

for change is widespread and some of the local districts began reform measures before they were formally adopted by the Legislature last year.

These efforts have increased overall rates of transfer to four-year colleges and are in part a result of programs to identify prospective transfer students and help them plan their curricula, often through transfer centers, according to a report by the California Postsecondary Education Commission.

In the Fall of 1987 transfers from community colleges to University of California campuses increased by 12.5 percent above the Fall of 1986, and transfers to California State University campuses increased 1.8 percent over the same period.

Sacramento's Los Rios Community College District, for example, has worked with nearby universities to arrange agreements wherein if a student fulfills certain requirements, he or she is guaranteed a place in a particular program at the university. However, transfer rates vary widely throughout the state. More than a mandate will be needed to overcome low transfer rates at some colleges where less than a half-dozen students transfer to UC campuses each year. For instance, Los Angeles Southwest College sent one student to UC during the 1987-88 school year. And while enrollment is increasing, the number of students Southwest sends to CSU has dropped to 51 students — less than half the number sent in 1981-82.

In the area of vocational education, years of underfunding has left much of the training equipment out-of-date or in need of repair, despite a recent infusion of funds for instructional equipment.

Another major challenge faced by community colleges is the lack of minorities in the faculty and administrative ranks of California's community colleges. More than half of the 71 local districts would have to at least double their minority faculty members to achieve adequate minority representation, according to a report by the state chancellor's office earlier this year.

Over the next decade California community colleges will be replacing about half of their faculty due to retirements and an anticipated 16 percent student enrollment increase. More than 18,000 new faculty members will be needed by 1995, according to the report.

The reform bill creates a Faculty and Staff Diversity Fund to pursue two goals: that by 2005 the system's workforce will reflect proportionately the adult population of the state; and that by 1992-93, 30 percent of all new hires in the system will be ethnic minorities. In the last budget and in the governor's proposed budget, money has been allocated for these goals.

Since the "window of opportunity" to diversify the staff will be opening not only for community colleges, but for UC, CSU and for colleges across the nation, the system of two-year colleges will be competing with many schools for the same limited pool of minority instructors and administrators.

"We all recognize that the pool is not real large. There are qualified people, that's not the question. But the pool is not very large," said James Kellerman. Kellerman is chancellor of the North Orange County Community College District and past president of the California Community College Chief Executive Officers Association. "We have to find ways ... to get young ethnic minority men and women into graduate school."

Growth is also an issue. In some districts, enrollment is growing at an explosive rate. College of the Canyons in Southern California cannot serve all of those who would like to attend and has had to turn some students away. Enrollment at the college grew by more than nineteen percent in 1987, but the school was funded for only about four percent of them. This Fall about 5200 students registered, compared with 4600 last Fall. The additional students will cost the district about

$2 million — an amount that will not be reimbursed by the state. (The state spends about $3500 a year on each community college student compared to $12,000 a year on each UC student.)

Under present finance law, community college districts may not increase their funded enrollment faster than the increase in adult population, which has averaged about two percent statewide.

In the Foothill-De Anza Community College District in the South Bay area, some students are being taught university style — in large lecture halls seating 350 to 400 per class. The district, which has stopped recruiting students, served more than 900 full-time students above the number for which the state paid.

Legislative action is needed to remove or adjust the cap. David Mertes, new chancellor of the community college system, suggested using a three-year average in the change in adult population rather than just the previous year's change. But the governor's proposed budget did not come close to fully funding reforms contained in the Vasconcellos reform bill, which went through years of discussion and revision before educators and legislators agreed on necessary changes. It called for $70 million to trigger the implementation of the major reforms. Deukmejian instead budgeted $6.5 million for the reforms. He proposed $5 million for staff development, $1.3 million for affirmative-action programs and $200,000 for instructional-improvement programs.

The governor overall proposed $2.45 billion for California's 107 community colleges, an increase of 7.2 percent above last year's budget. Educators were pleased with the general increase and with $111 million for capital outlay construction and $6.4 million for a sorely needed management-information system.

"We are disappointed because we don't have $70 million right away, but it's his [Deukmejian's] first move," said Larry Toy, president of the Faculty Association of California Community Colleges and chairman of Californians for Community Colleges — a group of major statewide community college organizations.

"Proposition 98 threw in a last-minute glitch," said Karen Sue Grosz, president of the state academic faculty senate. Some reforms can take place without additional funds, Grosz said, like the development of the transfer core curriculum. But the major reforms won't take place until the colleges get the money.

Reforms that will have to wait include the hiring of more full-time teachers, evaluation and tenure reforms and the repeal of teaching credentials and replacing credentials with minimum qualifications.

The state chancellor remained optimistic that money would come through for reforms. "I am confident that the Legislature and governor will see to it that colleges are funded to carry out the mission that has been assigned to them." he said.

David Brown, president of the California Community College Trustees Association and a Los Rios trustee, agreed. "We didn't expect $70 million after the passage of Proposition 98," Brown said. "But we are hoping the reforms will be funded in the future."

Robert Gabriner, president of the Community College Council of the California Federation of Teachers said: "I am fairly confident that the $70 million will be authorized by the governor and the Legislature. I remain steadfastly optimistic. I don't believe this is the last and final word on the issue. Within a $47-billion budget, I think they can find $70 million for reforms."🏛

D
r. Barry Munitz, the new chancellor of the California State University system, has a long list of academic credentials. His resumé, on paper, is impressive. Munitz was chancellor of the main campus at the University of Houston from 1977-82. He served in several administrative positions at the University of Illinois from 1970-76. In addition, he taught for two years at the University of California, Berkeley, has doctorate and master's degrees in comparative literature from Princeton University, and a bachelor's degree in the classics and comparative literature from Brooklyn College.

But Munitz' academic credentials were amassed in another life. After leaving the University of Houston, he stepped away from academia and into the speculative and often-controversial world of corporate finance. For the past nine years, he has served as an executive with a bevy of Houston-based corporations owned by Charles Hurwitz, a modern tycoon whose empire was fueled in part by the machinations of junk-bond wizards Michael Milken and Ivan Boesky.

And it was the 49-year-old Munitz' corporate credentials as an administrator with negotiating experience — perhaps more than his academic background — that caused the CSU Board of Trustees to appoint him to head up the nation's largest university system. Munitz will be on

Tricia Reader is a California Journal *intern. A.G. Block is managing editor of the* Journal.

**Chancellor-designate
Dr. Barry Munitz of CSU**

Is there a boardroom takeover of academia?

By Tricia Reader and A.G. Block

Reprinted from *California Journal*, July 1991

board at CSU August 1st after completing his job as a top executive of several of Hurwitz' aluminum, lumber and real estate corporations.

Not everyone is enamored of Munitz' appointment, however. Although legislators have expressed a desire to work with the new chancellor, CSU faculty, staff and students have come forward with serious reservations about his corporate ties. They are concerned that for the past nine years Munitz has been a decision-maker for a business conglomerate responsible for, among other things, clear-cutting old-growth forests in Northern California and attempting to build a hotel in the desert on Bighorn sheep land. They are also concerned with Munitz' relationship to a failed savings-and-loan that had to be rescued by the federal government at a $1.4 billion potential cost to taxpayers. At his one public campus visit to date, Munitz was pelted with hostile questions and confronted by demonstrators who expressed doubt about his choice as chancellor.

"A colleague of mine told me, 'Don't be so hurried to get rid of [former Chancellor W. Ann] Reynolds; you don't know who you'll get,'" recalled Thaddeus Shoemaker, a professor of government at CSU, Sacramento. The Sacramento campus, the most politically active with regard to Munitz' appointment, has been the scene of petition drives asking trustees to reconsider their decision. Those petitions question Munitz' ethics as evidenced by his work for Hurwitz.

The top administrator at CSUS, however, President Donald Gerth, disagrees with the petitions. "I do not think the petitions are a good idea. We're at a point in the CSU when we need to pull together," said Gerth. "We need to get behind and give support."

Humboldt State University in Arcata is another CSU campus where Munitz' appointment was received less than enthusiastically. HSU is located near the Humboldt County forests logged by Pacific Lumber Company, taken over in 1985 leveraged buyout by the Hurwitz-owned Maxxam Incorporated. Munitz was vice-president of Maxxam, which expanded Pacific's clear-cutting of old-growth forests from 40 to more than 500 acres. Maxxam-controlled Pacific also borrowed from employee pensions to pay off a $795 million corporate debt amassed due to the financial manipulations employed by Maxxam to gain control of Pacific (see "Epic struggle over redwoods," *CJ*, March 1990).

Munitz acknowledges that as a Maxxam board member he voted to approve the Pacific Lumber takeover, but he said he reminded company officials to be cautious because environmental concerns were involved. And for that, he has been described as Maxxam's "voice of moderation" and the company's "closet environmentalist."

But corporate takeovers, a Hurwitz specialty, also helped build Munitz' reputation as a mediator. "Where there's been a takeover, a change in peoples' lives, there's nervousness. He's really good at calming the nervousness and getting people to work together," said Maxxam's president, John Seidl, during an interview with the *Los Angeles Times*.

While Munitz' connection with Hurwitz has CSU faculty and students concerned, legislators seem willing to give the new chancellor the benefit of the doubt. Even so public an environmentalist as Democratic Assemblyman Tom Hayden of Santa Monica, chairman of the Committee on Higher Education, seems ready to work with Munitz. "He has good educational values and is highly qualified," said Hayden. "I can't say more because he hasn't taken a stand on CSU." Hayden's primary concern is not Munitz' background but the fact that he won't be on board until August 1st and thus will have little participation in a state budget process where CSU faces a 10 to 20 percent cut. "Right now we don't have a permanent chancellor on the job. There are a lot of concerns and questions," said Hayden, citing problems with CSU's uncertain direction and overenrollment.

Hayden said he was curious why CSU trustees rushed the appointment of Munitz with little review from the Legislature, media or CSU faculty and students, but then won't have him on the job until after budget deliberations are completed.

Board chairman William Campbell explained that Munitz has been involved in all substantive decisions and has been kept informed of all important issues. But, added Campbell, "It's impossible to bring someone in who hasn't worked with the budget and ask him to work with it and make cuts." Campbell also said that the trustees wanted to give both acting-chancellor Ellis McCune and Munitz time to finish up their respective jobs.

Other lawmakers also have expressed a willingness to work with Munitz, and to accept the trustees' decision. For one, Assembly Speaker Willie Brown, an ex-officio member of the board of trustees, believes the CSU system has been in trouble for some time and it is therefore important for him to work with Munitz.

"The speaker's job right now is to support the leadership," said Brown spokesman Michael Reese.

Assemblyman John Vasconcellos, a San Jose Democrat who sits on the Assembly Higher Education Committee, also is ready to work with Munitz. Vasconcellos was impressed with Munitz after the new chancellor made a one-hour visit to the assemblyman, asking his opinion of issues facing CSU.

Vasconcellos said he has "no knowledge and no interest" in Munitz' background and only is concerned that Munitz use his leadership, among other things, to help CSU build its own identity and emerge from the shadow cast by the University of California. In addition, Vasconcellos said that Munitz and he talked about strengthening multicultural education, improving rapport with faculty and working relationships with constituency groups, as well as improving credibility with the Legislature.

Those who have met Munitz characterize him as bright and ambitious. He and his wife, Anne, who worked for the Houston Grand Opera, are popular Houston socialites, successfully entertaining in their duplex condominium. He's been described as a good listener, with good concentration and diverse knowledge. When Munitz interviewed for the position of chancellor, he impressed the selection committee with his articulate speech and down-to-earth demeanor. He spoke on a first name basis with committee members, insisting he be called "Barry."

"It's unusual to have that kind of informal interaction," said Aristide Collins Jr., a Hayward State University student who was selected by the CSU trustees to sit on the selection committee. "He lets people know their ideas are important."

"He has a firm education," said Collins. "He's worked with so many people in higher education; they are too numerous to name. He's like a prodigy in academia."

Says Campbell: "He has an openness without taking offense. There is no ego blocking it. He is not a person who will be in conflict with the presidents of the universities or other systems. They will follow him."

Munitz was selected to replace Ellis McCune, who has served as acting-chancellor since May 1990 when former Chancellor W. Ann Reynolds resigned because of public opposition to a 43 percent salary increase. Reynolds and other top administrators were given pay boosts after a closed-door session by trustees. Reynold's salary was bumped to $195,000. Munitz will receive $175,000 to lead the 20-campus, 369,000-student system. He will move into a million-dollar home close to CSU headquarters in Long Beach, receiving an automobile from the trustees' fleet and an entertainment budget. He will take a large pay cut from his previous $400,000 corporate salary. Munitz, who said he knew he would always return to higher education, was a candidate for the CSU job in 1982, when trustees named Reynolds. Munitz dropped out of the competition to work for Hurwitz. "I wanted to see how the other side worked," he said.

While Munitz' appointment is bathed in controversy, supporters say it comes at a time when the CSU system needs a strong leader who will have good ties with to universities as well as to the Legislature.

"I think he was a very good choice given what I think are important needs of the system," said Ray Geigle, former chairman of the system-wide Academic Senate and member of the chancellor's selection committee. Geigle is also a political science professor at CSU, Bakersfield.

Characterizing Reynolds' approach to the CSU system as autocratic, Geigle said that individual campuses need more automon, and should be saddled with "far less policy coming from Long Beach." Observers say Reynolds, who was dubbed "Queen Ann" for her imperious management styles, also damaged relations with the Legislature after the salary increase controversy.

Geigle believes that because Munitz is known nationwide in both academic and business circles, he will be able to strengthen the system during times of severe budget crises.

Munitz' critics, however, fail to see the positive side of his corporate experience.

"It's a 'get-all-you-can-get (and get it now no matter who is hurt)' phi-

losophy. The message is loud and clear," said Wade.

Thaddeus Shoemaker said the CSUS faculty involved in research is "fearful that the chancellor will have no sensitivity to scholarship." Shoemaker said the faculty is concerned that if Munitz pursues a stated goal of arranging for corporate backing for various university projects, professors will be obligated to perform corporate research and that results of such research will belong to the corporations.

"We don't mind money from an outside source," Shoemaker said. "But when you get a guy like this, there are all kinds of strings attached."

Citing Munitz' involvement as the "right-hand man" of Charles Hurwitz, Shoemaker said, "Hurwitz may have decided he wanted to own his own university."

Angus Wright, an environmental-studies professor and member of the CSUS Academic Senate, is concerned with Munitz' involvement in United Savings Association of Texas — a company which failed under his leadership and had to be bailed out by the federal government.

"There are very complicated questions. It is hard to see Munitz' role. But it is clear to see that he held positions of responsibility," said Wright. "I don't think we should be reaching for someone who's involved with questionable financial dealings to take as the leader of the institution."

Munitz was chairman and chief executive officer of United Financial Group, the parent company of United Savings. Because of the thrift's decline, UFG also fell into trouble. Munitz told *The Sacramento Bee* that the company faces bankruptcy because of a $534 million Federal Deposit Insurance Corporation claim against it which is currently not being pursued.

But Munitz' corporate experience has endowed him with assets as well as with liabilities. For instance, his reputation as a negotiator was solidified during a fight between another Hurwitz entity and officials in the city of Rancho Mirage over a luxury hotel and housing development. Lawsuits against the city council brought on by Hurwitz left Rancho Mirage Mayor Jeffrey Bleaman angry with Hurwitz. Although Munitz' job was to oversee the project, Hurwitz is said to have handled the finances and negotiations. Munitz reportedly worked out a deal with the city to allow the

hotel construction to continue but to keep 1000 acres of land for a Bighorn sheep preserve. Bleaman was so pleased with the compromise, he recommended Munitz in a letter to the CSU trustees a day before his selection.

Pushing for Munitz' appointment was selection committee chairman J. Gary Shansby, a CSU trustee and well-known San Francisco corporate executive. Reportedly, the committee performed an extensive search of Munitz and found that Hurwitz — and not Munitz — was responsible for the failure of United Savings and for the takeover of Pacific Lumber.

"He has a superb balance of education and finance. Despite his association with Hurwitz ... Barry Munitz is very clean. [He] was not out sawing lumber trees ... he does not know Michael Milken or Ivan Boesky," Shansby told the *Hornet,* a CSU, Sacramento, campus newspaper.

Munitz said during a late April telephone interview that his first priority as chancellor will be to work through the system's budget crisis. His strategy is to incorporate private industry into the funding of CSU through research support, successful alumni support, and also by using corporate strength to back programs and projects of interest. He said his top priorities are promoting undergraduate teaching, improving the racial mix of students, linking CSU with the kindergarten through 12th grade system through teacher training and introducing the children to the idea of higher education and, finally, having an influential voice in the Legislature.

Responding to criticism from University of Houston faculty, who felt Munitz did not work well with faculty and did not spend enough time teaching classes, Munitz told the *Los Angeles Times,* "Obviously there are some faculty who can look at my background and say, 'Well this is a problem. This is not a person who has spent 20 years as a distinguished member of the faculty, of any faculty.' That's clearly true." 🏛

Higher education for all

That "automatic" degree may be a thing of the past

By William Trombley

Reprinted from *California Journal*, December 1991

Crowded classes, canceled classes, higher student fees, faculty layoffs, students who can't get the courses they need to graduate on time, students who can't get classes, period. These stories have rolled in from across the state throughout the fall term on California's public college and university campuses.

While the immediate cause is the state budget crisis that led to spending cuts in both the University of California and California State University systems — and only a small increase for the community colleges — this year, the larger question is whether the state's 31-year-old Master Plan for Higher Education, with its promise of "higher education for all," is still viable.

Many believe it is not.

"There is a fundamental mismatch between resources and enrollments," said William Storey, an assistant director of the California Postsecondary Education Commission (CPEC). "Unless the budget situation improves, those [enrollment] numbers are going to have to come down."

William Trombley is a Capitol reporter for the Los Angeles Times.

Storey referred to recent CPEC projections that enrollment in the University of California will increase from 160,000 to 226,000 by the year 2005, that the California State University will grow from 375,000 to at least 495,000 and that community college enrollment will make an astonishing leap from 1.5 million to 2 million. David Mertes, chancellor of the statewide community college system, said even those numbers are conservative and that he expects enrollment in the two-year colleges to reach 2 million before the end of this decade.

While enrollments soar, state financial support for higher education is declining.

Warren Fox, new director of the Postsecondary Education Commission, which advises the governor and the Legislature on higher-education policy, noted that the percentage of state general fund revenues going to higher education (community colleges, CSU and UC) has dropped from 15.9 percent in 1984-85 to 13.5 percent this year.

That is why many believe a day of reckoning is coming soon for the Master Plan, especially for its promise of a place in a public college or university for every student who could benefit from higher education.

"The structure of the Master Plan will stay," former UC

President Clark Kerr, one of the plan's architects, said, "but the question is whether the state will be able to fulfill the promise of higher education for all who want it."

To Barry Munitz, the new chancellor of the California State University system, the answer clearly is "no," not unless state financial support is increased.

A $60 million reduction in state funding for CSU this year has resulted in laying off or not re-hiring 3000 instructors, eliminating 868 non-faculty positions and wiping out more than 3800 class sections this fall.

If there are more actions like this, Munitz has been telling audiences around the state recently, CSU will not be able to accept the top one-third of California high school graduates — its assignment under the Master Plan.

"We cannot continue to bear a greater and greater burden without fundamentally affecting the quality of the education we deliver," he said.

Although the University of California is not as dependent as CSU on state funding — only about 30 percent of the total UC budget comes from the state, with federal research grants and contracts, student fees and private gifts accounting for most of the rest — the nine-campus UC system still was hit hard by this year's budget cuts. Only by raising student fees a whopping 40 percent and persuading some 4000 faculty and staff members to take early retirement was UC able to avoid canceling class sections this fall.

But outgoing UC President David Gardner said drastic measures such as these cannot be repeated. He warned that UC would begin to deny admission to eligible freshmen (the top 12.5 percent of the high school graduates) if budget cuts continue and if the state is unwilling to pay for a new campus in the San Joaquin Valley.

Some education specialists in Sacramento argue that there is room for UC to expand on several existing campuses, especially at Irvine and Riverside. But Gardner insisted that most UC campuses already are at full capacity or face strong community opposition to expansion.

"We can't build up existing campuses," the UC president said. "Berkeley [current enrollment: 30,500] can't grow to 45,000; Santa Cruz [currently 10,300] can't go to 30,000. Even at levels we think are reasonable, we've had trouble with our communities."

Gardner said he will ask Governor Pete Wilson and the Legislature "if they want to build the tenth campus or not; and, if the answer is 'no,' then I will say, 'All right, under those circumstances, we will not be able to offer a place to all the eligible students seeking admission.'

"'Now you tell us what you are willing to pay for. Should we take just the top 10 percent of high school graduates? Or 8 percent or 7 percent, or what? This is a public policy question that the state of California must answer."

The state's community colleges, which have been the entry point to higher education, as well as to occupational training, for vast numbers of California young people (and some not so young) face even more serious problems than either UC or CSU. If enrollment jumps by half-a-million students over the next decade or so, as is predicted, almost all of the existing 107 two-year colleges will be filled to capacity and 25 to 30 new campuses must be built.

Where will the money come from to build them? Or to operate them, once built? No one knows.

Mertes, the statewide community college chancellor,

said there already are about 100,000 "unfunded" students in the system — students whose educations must be financed by local community college districts because state funds have run out. Typically, districts dip into their reserves to pay for unfunded students, which means that a single unexpected problem — a corroded gas line or an air conditioning system that fails — could drive a district into the red.

Mertes also complained of another Master Plan violation. He said many qualified community college graduates are unable to transfer to a four-year campus because there is no room for them.

Although UC and CSU still are able to offer a place on one of their campuses to every qualified transfer student, that place may be so far from the student's home and job as to make attendance impractical. Mertes called on each four-year campus to announce in advance how many transfer spaces would be available each year "so we don't waste our time and our students' time."

Even if problems like a shortage of transfer places could be solved, there is a growing feeling that the Master Plan cannot be patched and stitched together much longer and probably must be abandoned.

State revenues are running below estimates and another multi billion-dollar state deficit in 1992-93 seems probable. Even if the revenue picture were brighter, higher education still would be forced to compete with increasing demands for other state services, like Medi-Cal and elementary and secondary education.

"The future looks bleak," said Carl Rogers, education specialist in the state Department of Finance., "We don't know how we can afford it [i.e., the Master Plan]."

Maureen DiMarco, secretary for child development and education in the Wilson administration, said, "We may not be able to fulfill the Master Plan guarantees, and we ought to confront that very quickly."

Said Harry Wugalter, a member of the Postsecondary Education Commission, "The 'higher education for everybody' idea was developed under a completely different set of circumstances ... it was a great idea but we can't afford it anymore."

Some believe the plan's promise of a college education for all who could benefit from one already has been broken.

"Universal access is shot," said Patrick Callan, former director of the Postsecondary Education Commission and now a higher education consultant. "We're squeezing admissions requirements at UC, pushing more students into CSU, where they can't find classes, so they go to community colleges, where they can't find classes, either."

"In effect," Callan added, "the state is doing away with the Master Plan in a way that leaves no fingerprints."

Kerr said a basic assumption of the Master Plan was that state economic productivity would increase by at least an average 2 percent a year, but it has not done so. Nor, Kerr added, did those who drew up the plan foresee the huge increases that have come about in state spending for health, welfare, elementary and secondary education and prisons.

Between 1988 and 1998, state spending for debt service on state bonds will increase by 16.3 percent, prisons 11.1 percent and Medi-Cal 8.2 percent, but support for UC and Cal State will increase by just 5.6 percent, according to estimates prepared by the Postsecondary Education Commission.

With budgets tightening and the Master Plan in jeopardy, new approaches are being suggested.

"The Master Plan captured the imagination of the country and the world in the 1960s," Callan said, "but now it has become a straightjacket. There's room for a lot of creative thinking about how to move forward."

One of the questions that Callan and others have raised is whether the University of California needs to offer a complete range of graduate and professional programs on all eight general campuses (and on the new San Joaquin Valley campus as well). These critics suggest it would be more cost-effective for the university to concentrate many of its graduate and professional specialties on one or two or three campuses. They also believe the state cannot afford the $1 billion or more that a new, full-blown research campus in the San Joaquin Valley eventually would cost. They suggest that an under-graduate campus, with a few graduate programs, would make more sense.

But Gardner insisted that UC already limits the number of new doctoral and professional programs it initiates, and he suggested that in some fields, the university should be training more professionals, not fewer. For instance, he noted that less than 20 percent of the state's physicians have been trained at the five UC medical schools.

Gardner also defended the plan for the tenth campus, with the same full range of undergraduate, graduate and professional programs found elsewhere in the UC system.

"To assure access and quality, we cannot have what one might call one, two and three-tier institutions in the university," he said. "We know what our institution is and how it works and what it can do. Therefore, when we propose to add a tenth campus, we're not proposing a campus with a different mission."

"This is institutional hubris," Callan responded. "These people are saying, 'We're going to do things the same way we've been doing them for 45 years and, if anybody doesn't like it, that's just too bad.'"

Some have suggested the state could save money by requiring University of California faculty members to do more teaching. Typically, a UC professor teaches one or two classes each quarter or semester, while his counterpart in the California State University system teaches three or four. The rationale for the difference is that UC faculty members are expected to do "cutting edge" research as well. However, many UC officials acknowledge that some professors do little research at all, whether at the cutting edge or not, and don't teach much, either.

Former UC President Kerr said that when he served as chancellor of the Berkeley campus in the 1950s, he sought to determine the average faculty teaching load but soon found that "at the University of California, like other research universities, all of that happens at the level of the academic departments, where there are few policies and nobody keeps records." Kerr concluded that "it would be insanity for any chancellor, or president of the university, to try to do anything about this."

CSU faculty members also will be teaching less as the result of a new agreement between the faculty and the CSU administration requiring efforts to reduce the average teaching load from 12 units per semester to nine over the next three of four years.

Other changes that have been proposed in the state's higher-education arrangements include:

• Increasing the number, and the amount, of "Cal Grants," so that high school graduates may afford to attend one of the state's private colleges or universities instead of a public campus.

• Changing the ratio of upper-division to lower-division students on UC and CSU campuses from 60-40 percent to 75-25 percent so that more freshmen and sophomores could be educated at the less-expensive community colleges.

• Changing state financial incentives so that UC and CSU are rewarded for graduating students, not just for enrolling them. Only 30.5 percent of freshmen who enrolled at a UC campus in the fall of 1982 earned a degree in four years. At CSU, only 27.7 percent of first-time freshmen enrolling in fall 1983 earned a degree in five years.

• Establishing an expansion policy for all three segments — UC, CSU and community colleges — instead of allowing the three segments to lobby the governor and the Legislature for new campuses.

• Using some of the now-sizable pot of UC and CSU student-fee revenue to pay for educational programs, instead of limiting its use to non-academic programs and financial aid.

Mertes startled a meeting of community college chief campus officers a few weeks ago by proposing that the two-year schools dramatize their financial plight by limiting enrollment to students in pre-college or vocational training classes. This would eliminate thousands who come to community colleges to learn English and other basic skills. It would also mean that thousands of disadvantaged students in the state's major cities would be deprived of a chance to prepare for a four-year college or for a vocational career.

"That would be a disaster" in a district like Los Angeles, said Donald Phelps, chancellor of the nine-campus, 122,000-student system. "About 70 percent of our students are minority and many of them lack the basic skills needed for success in four-year colleges. That's why they come to us."

Phelps, who went to college after leaving the Army and began his teaching career at the age of 30, said, "I would have been one of the students eliminated by such a policy." He also warned that limiting access to public higher education just when minorities are beginning to attend in significant numbers would be unwise and dangerous for the state.

State Senator Gary Hart, a Santa Barbara Democrat and chairman of the Senate Education Committee, sounded the same warning. "If we cut back on the 12.5 percent [the UC admissions pool] or the 33 percent [the CSU pool], then all of these issues of affirmative action and ethnic diversity, which are so sensitive, will become even more so," Hart said.

Whatever is done to change the Master Plan for Higher Education will face strong institutional and political opposition. However, unless there is a miraculous change not only in California's year-to-year budgets but also in the state's underlying economic and social conditions, change surely is coming.

Things have gotten so bad, said DiMarco, Governor Wilson's education adviser, that "I have even heard people ask if we can afford to improve K-12 education. If we do, they argue, we'll collapse the whole higher education system because we'll produce more high school graduates and there won't be room on the campuses for them." 🏛

Tapped out in California

Five-year drought exposes deficiencies in state's water system

By Nancy Vogel

Reprinted from *California Journal*, April 1991

For the people who control the labyrinth of dams and aqueducts that quench most of California's thirst, gambling is a career. Each year since 1986, when floods plagued the northern half of the state, dam operators bet on wet years.

They lost.

Now it is as clear as the skies that 1991 will be a fifth consecutive drought year.

Reservoirs that usually swell with winter rain are more dirt than water. The water project that serves two of every three Californians has almost shut down. Desperate cities are weighing the costs of desalinization plants, farmers are struggling to keep trees alive and fire threatens parched forests.

In a state where water, money and power are interchangeable, there has never been so little water and so many Californians. Early this year Governor

Nancy Vogel writes for the California News Service, a project of the University of California graduate school of journalism at Berkeley.

Pete Wilson, at no small political risk, stepped in to manage the drought, and many observers say that so far he is playing his hand well. But if it does not rain hard soon, the stakes will soar.

Even in wet years nothing splinters California as sharply or along so many lines as the subject of who gets how much water. So it is no surprise that this drought, which bares inequalities like an empty reservoir exposes boulders, has prompted calls for reform.

"Our water system is based on an article of faith that whether it rains or not we should allow anyone to use as much water as they want for whatever they want at a reasonable price," said Sacramento's Democratic Assemblyman Phillip Isenberg — one of the strongest advocates of shunting water from thirsty crops, such as rice and cotton, to cities.

Others say California's future wa-

ter policy lies in building more reservoirs, in conservation, or in water transfers — none of these new ideas, but all of them argued passionately now that Los Angeles is fining water wasters and dry fields are lying fallow.

Whether the state's water policy will be business-as-usual once the rains return is, like predicting *when* the rains will return, anyone's bet.

The source of California's water wrangling is simple.

Hydrologically speaking, California is lopsided. About three-quarters of the fresh water available in the state originates north of Sacramento, while 75 percent of the demand — most of the farms and people — lies to the south. To balance the supplies, two major water projects suck Sierra snowmelt south.

The Central Valley Project, completed in the mid-1940s, is run by the federal Bureau of Reclamation. It can deliver about seven million acre feet of water a year from reservoirs on the Sacramento, American and Trinity Rivers. (An acre foot — 326,000 gallons — is enough water to supply a family of five for a year, or to irrigate a third of an acre for one growing season.)

The main components of the second water provider, the State Water Project, were finished in the early 1970s. The state Department of Water Resources operates this 500-mile project, which begins with Oroville Dam on the Feather River and ends below Los Angeles. It supplies some two million acre-feet of water to San Joaquin Valley farmers and cities in the north and south. Metropolitan Water District, the project's largest urban contractor, serves 15 million people from Los Angeles to San Diego.

Because the Central Valley Project was built to help settle arid California under the federal Reclamation Act, its water is subsidized by taxpayers. Users do not pay the costs of maintaining and operating the $2.4 billion system, let alone the interest on building it.

For example, the Westlands Water District in Fresno County, the largest federal water contractor, gets subsidized water for $17 an acre-foot while the full cost rate is $42 an acre-foot, according to a 1989 General Accounting Office study.

Water from the state project is more expensive. Its 30 contracting agencies pay construction, interest and transportation costs. Kern County farmers pay about $50 an acre foot, for example, while the Metropolitan Water District pays $250 an acre foot because to reach Los Angeles, massive pumps must ship the water 2000 feet over the Tehachapi Mountains.

Besides bringing water to some of the richest land on earth and allowing semi-arid cities to spread, the projects stave off floods and drought. Proof lies in the fact that agriculture, which uses 80 percent of California's water, generated record high gross receipts of $17.8 billion in 1990, a fourth continuous year of drought.

But each year compounds the next, and the tenacious drought has struck hardest this year.

With each new sunny day, the state moves closer to matching the severity of the historic 1929-1934 drought. University of Arizona scientists who studied Sierra tree rings say that those years may have been the driest in California in the past 400 years.

In the four years between 1931 and 1934, for example, estimated runoff hit only 37 million acre feet, or about half of average. Runoff in the past four years averaged 42 million acre feet. But 1991 may well be dry enough to make the five years since 1987 as dry as, if not drier, than the six-year Dust Bowl drought.

Faced with an early February Sierra snowpack just 10 percent of normal, major reservoirs at half the average storage, and insufficient rain, water

project operators slashed deliveries. The State Water Project first cut all water to farmers. Two weeks later it asked cities to get by with only 10 percent of the usual amount.

The Central Valley Project followed suit, announcing that as of March 1st, most of its agricultural contractors would get only 25 percent of their entitlements. Water to the two million people in cities it serves would be slashed by 25 or 50 percent, officials said.

In the rush to ration after the announcement of the cutbacks, the most severe since the projects began pumping water, few people questioned whether better planning could have prevented such drastic action.

But Patrick Porgans, a Sacramento resource consultant, charges the state with mismanaging its reservoirs. The state project operators made full deliveries to farmers in the first three years of the drought, he says, which cut the supply available later for cities.

"This amounts to a bail out of agriculture at the expense of municipal and industrial users," says Porgans. In 1987 and 1988 testimony before state water officials, he predicted — correctly, it turns out — that the state project would run out of water if the drought dragged on and farmers got full deliveries.

Under the terms of state water contracts, farmers take the first cutbacks in dry years. Although 1987, 1988 and 1990 were all classified as critically dry years (1989 was "dry"), the projects made full agricultural deliveries until 1990. That year farmers' supplies were cut by 50 percent.

"They were playing Russian roulette and the public lost," said Porgans. He argues that operators made full deliveries to farmers in those drought years to secure the project's financing. If farmers got no water and could grow no crops, they might miss their water payments to the state. Contractors must pay for water whether they receive it or not.

Non-payment by farmers could put at risk the revenue bonds the project floated in 1960 to finance construction, says Porgans. If the project's bond rating slipped, the state would in turn have to pay higher interest rates on any new bonds floated to finance new construction, he says.

And project managers have long sought more reservoirs and aqueducts. At current capacity, the project can deliver a firm yield of only 2.4 million acre feet a year, not the 4.2 million acre

feet a year its long-term contracts call for by 1990.

The fact that the huge Metropolitan Water District contracts and pays for much more water than it now uses allows the project to meet the needs of all of its clients and to even sell surplus water to growers in most years.

But state project managers look anxiously to the day, probably in the next decade, when the MWD will demand its full entitlement. That day is hastened by non-stop growth in Southern California and court decisions that limit the amount of Colorado River and Mono Lake water that the MWD can take.

Robert Potter, deputy director of the Department of Water Resources, which runs the State Water Project, blamed nature for this year's water shortages. If managers had known 1991 would be so dry, he said, they "certainly would have run the operation differently."

The State Water Contractors agreed to the full agricultural deliveries, said George Baumli, executive director of the group that represents 28 of the 30 agencies buying state water. "It appeared to make the most sense at the time," said Baumli.

Theoretically, under the project's delivery rules, cities should have still gotten 50 percent of normal deliveries when agriculture was cut 100 percent in February. But there simply was not enough water.

The state project recently set up an internal borrowing program for five agricultural agencies in danger of missing their May payments. In five years the agencies must pay back the Department of Water Resources funds, with interest.

The Central Valley Project is not without its critics, either. Congressman George Miller, a Democrat from Martinez and acting chairman of the House Interior Committee, recently accused the federal project of squandering its meager supplies on farmers growing subsidized crops at the expense of thirsty cities. Miller urged Interior Secretary Manuel Lujan to suspend even the project's reduced deliveries to growers, which will draw the project's reserves to their lowest levels ever by October. The U.S. Bureau of Reclamation, which runs the project, says that to do so would violate contracts.

Others warn that the Central Valley Project must hold back its reserves so that if the drought continues, water is available to repel salt water in the Sacramento-San Joaquin Delta. Both projects pump the bulk of their water from the Delta.

"If we don't send less water to the farmers we'll face disaster," says Gerald Meral, executive director of the Planning and Conservation League. It could take years to cleanse reservoirs of salt-water, he says.

The Delta—where the Sacramento and San Joaquin River mingle and run into San Francisco Bay—is the heart of California's water system and its water battles. It drains 40 percent of the state's water and nurses the remnants of a once-thriving fishery. It also feeds the huge pumps of both projects.

Since 1964 the State Water Project has planned to build a peripheral canal to skirt the Delta, pulling clean Sacramento River water directly to the south Delta pumps. Water is degraded by agricultural runoff and salinity as it winds between peat levees in the Delta, and meandering sloughs inhibit the pumps.

But a 1982 referendum killed a bill to fulfill the State Water Project's canal plans. Environmentalists feared that more water diversions would harm the fragile estuary, and some powerful San Joaquin Valley growers felt the bill contained too many environmental protections. Southern Californians, too, opposed it because they felt that, at $3.1 billion, it cost too much.

A 1984 plan sponsored by former Governor George Deukmejian to build a shorter canal was also defeated by public opposition. Outrage over "Duke's ditch" soured Deukmejian on water policy for the rest of his years as governor.

Less grand additions to the State Water Project eventually met legislative approval, however, and work on a new south Delta reservoir and an underground water bank in Kern County are underway. These will help to capture high spring flows through the Delta to store for summer use. Taken together, with the widening of Delta channels, they are expected to increase the state project's capacity by up to 845,000 acre feet a year.

But visions of a peripheral canal to draw south more water never faded away. In this fifth year of drought, water planners are gauging the public's mood.

"There's heightened interest," says Arthur Littleworth, a lawyer for the State Water Contractors. "I think what people are finally going to understand is that we've got unstable water supplies."

Littleworth noted that 20 years have passed since a major water project

(the New Melones Dam on the Stanislaus River) was built in California. Since then the southern state has added about seven million people, he said. "Some additional facilities are needed," said Littleworth. "We can't meet our needs with reclamation or conservation or even water transfers."

The man who sponsored the peripheral canal bill also has his finger to the wind. State Senator Ruben Ayala, a Chico Democrat and legislative point man for Southern California water interests, says that he senses "a cohesive effort to protect what we have and get more at a later date."

But he says he's not the man to do it now.

In his peripheral canal campaign, Ayala says, water agency lobbyists abandoned him and Northern Californians nearly "tarred and lynched" him. He won't support another canal bill, he says, until the timing is right. And although Los Angeles City Councilman Nate Holden recently asked him to introduce a canal bill and threatened to gather enough signatures for an initiative if Ayala refused, Ayala says the momentum is still building.

"They can get someone else to lead the parade," says Ayala. "I'm not the only one who likes to have his head cut off once in a while."

Many people who support the idea of a canal through or around the Delta agree that strong salinity and freshwater flow standards should be solidly in place before discussions begin.

Southern Californians seek to protect the Delta from levee collapse and saltwater intrusion because it is their main source of drinking water. Northern California environmentalists argue that the Delta deserves protection because it is a priceless ecosystem, critical to salmon, striped bass and several endangered species.

"The state needs to come forward and say that above all it will protect the Delta," says Sunne McPeak, a Contra Costa County supervisor who also chairs the group Committee for Water Policy Consensus and who helped lead the fight against the peripheral canal in 1982. Such a guarantee would give everyone a baseline, she says.

But major new water projects, at any rate, are years away. And the immediate effects of this drought distract government leaders everywhere.

When the State Water Project announced February 25th that it would deliver only 10 percent of the usual amount to cities, the MWD had

already taken its share for the year. The MWD turned in desperation to the Colorado River, to groundwater and to asking its customers to cut use by 49 percent. San Francisco imposed 55 percent cutbacks — its strictest ever — and even Sacramento, embraced by two major rivers and without water meters, may soon ask residents to limit outdoor watering to twice a week.

Things are particularly difficult in communities that deliberately limited their water supplies. Marin County and the city of Santa Barbara both held back on water development as a way to restrict population growth. Now, they both must impose Draconian measures to curb water use. In Marin, households can use no more than 50 gallons per day per person, a third of what the typical Californian uses. In Santa Barbara, lawns long ago went brown, and the city now plans to build a plant to take the salt out of sea water.

In California's cities, the drought creates inconvenience. In the vast fields of the Sacramento and San Joaquin Valleys, the most productive in the country, it creates business dilemmas.

Generous aquifers eased growers through last year's cutbacks, but now many wells must be plunged deeper, at greater energy costs, and some in Monterey County are pulling up seawater. Farmers all over the state are planting the most valuable crops they can with whatever water they have.

"Cotton's going to take a big hit; rice is going to take a big hit," said Mike Henry, a California Farm Bureau Federation spokesman. "These guys are going to be planning for fruits and vegetables because they are the high-value crops."

Richard Howitt, an agricultural economist at the University of California, Davis, used a computer model that divides the state into six regions to estimate that farm losses this year will total $650 million. Regions with secure water supplies, such as the Imperial and Sacramento Valleys, will fare well, said Howitt, either by growing crops or selling water. About a million of California's 7.5 million irrigated acres will lie fallow this year, he predicted, and most farmers would survive but few would make profits.

Cattle ranchers are always hurt first in a drought because no rain falls to make grass grow. In 1977 livestock constituted $414 million of the state's $566 million agricultural losses. The California Cattlemen's Association estimates that 30 percent of the state's herds have already been sold. And with hay growers' stock of cheap, poor-quality hay gone, ranchers are paying up to $45 more per ton of cattle feed.

In Kern County, the country's third most productive farm county, the Kern County Water Agency estimates that of its 214,000 irrigated acres with no groundwater, some 83,000 acres are planted in permanent crops such as almonds, pistachios and grapes. If those trees and vines don't get water this year, the loss will top $8 billion over the next ten years in income and jobs, said Kern water resources manager Gary Bucher.

The Kern agency has about 200,000 acre feet of banked groundwater and is now hustling to fix old wells and drill new ones to get it into aqueducts.

"Next year dry is just incomprehensible," said Bucher.

Governor Pete Wilson, barely settled in his capital office, joined the high-stakes drought gamble in early February. With his emergency powers within easy reach, he announced a plan to stave off the drought.

A hastily organized "Drought Action Team" of state agency leaders, chaired by Department of Water Resources director David Kennedy, devised the plan. Like the budget Wilson unveiled in January, it asked for sacrifice from all Californians.

"We're going to have to apportion and share the pain on this," he said at a February 15 press conference, one day after the Central Valley Project announced its 75 percent cuts.

Wilson urged every community to get rationing plans in place and prepare to cut use by half if it did not rain soon. He stopped short of using his drought emergency powers to force such cutbacks.

"As a former mayor, I would certainly take no pleasure in usurping the prerogatives of local governments," said Wilson. "But I will not hesitate to assume emergency powers if such powers become necessary to protect Californians from the worst effects of the drought."

Wilson asked the Legislature to set aside $100 million for a drought fund and has created a state-run water bank to match water buyers and sellers. Some of the water gathered should stay in reserve in case the drought persisted, said Wilson.

He bolstered fire-fighting forces and urged the Department of Fish and Game to do everything "humanly possible" to help beleaguered wildlife, including transporting fish to better habitat in trucks.

And if it rains, announced Wilson, the state should re-evaluate its complete cut-off of water to agriculture.

The drought pulled Wilson into politically dangerous territory mined with anxious, powerful constituents such as agribusiness, which donated generously to his gubernatorial campaign. Making himself the leader makes him liable for blame in case of fiasco, such as saltwater contaminating the projects' delivery systems. But so far he seems to be making all the right moves.

"I was quite impressed with him, especially the way he fielded questions of a technical nature," said Don Maughan, chairman of the state Water Resources Control Board, who watched Wilson in action for the first time at the press conference.

The water board, four Governor Deukmejian appointees (there is one vacancy), oversees use of the state's water. They jumpstarted the state's slow response to the drought in late January by discussing rationing plans strict enough to alarm water agency directors, but they quickly acquiesced when Governor Wilson took charge and relegated them to team players.

"It's such an important matter I think it's going to take all of us to work it out," said Maughan later.

Whether Wilson continues to win praise for his leadership or must wield emergency powers to get water to the masses depends primarily upon the new state-run water bank.

No other response to the drought can get water to critical areas as quickly as selling water as a commodity. Although the Department of Water Resources has brokered transfers before, there is little financial incentive to sell water in years of normal precipitation and bureaucratic hurdles rarely make it worth the effort.

Any city with surplus or a grower willing to forgo planting can sell water. Prime candidates are Central Valley Project contractors who hold water rights so old that they still get, under law, 75 percent of their water while others have been cut to 25 percent. Many are Sacramento Valley rice farmers.

It takes about 7.75 acre feet of water per acre to grow rice (of the crops widely grown in California, only alfalfa uses more). It is also a surplus crop, subsidized by the government under a program that allows growers to fallow half of their acreage and receive almost full payment.

Rice farmers say that not planting will hurt the millers, truckers and salespeople who depend upon their harvests, and a simple lump sum for fallow acreage cannot be fairly distributed.

"Water marketing does not address third-party issues," said Bob Herkert, spokesman for the California Rice Industry Committee. "People are looking to rice for a very simplistic solution to this horrible problem."

Herkert said that whole rural communities would collapse without rice sales, and flooded rice fields are critical to migrating waterfowl now that most of the Central Valley's wetlands have been drained.

Rice growers are under special pressure these days since water diverted from rice planting could take care of more than 15 million people, but all of California agriculture is defensive.

For years politicians such as Congressman Miller and Assemblyman Phil Isenberg have argued that agriculture uses an inordinate amount of water for contributing only 7 percent to the state's gross product. California could solve its water problems, they say, if farmers used water more efficiently and stopped planting subsidized crops such as rice and cotton.

"A 25 percent savings from cities, business and industry in California would equal the same amount of water if agriculture saved less than three percent," says Isenberg, who suggests that the state pay farmers to take land out of production, especially where selenium in the soil leaches out to create poisonous drainage.

The drought does not seem to have driven a wedge between urban and rural California yet, despite the greater attention paid to agriculture's critics.

When polled by the *Los Angeles Times* in late January, 35 percent of some 2000 Californians said that they believed agriculture used water efficiently. Only 22 percent, on the other hand, said the same of residential users.

The poll showed, said Mike Henry of the California Farm Bureau Federation, that "contrary to some loud voices in the state, most people don't believe agriculture wastes water."

Nonetheless, Henry predicted an "explosion" of animosity as water for cities disappears, and only rain can change that. 🏛

A not-so-freeway future?

For whom the road tolls

By Debora Vrana

Reprinted from *California Journal*, August 1991

In 1991 California, it is the business of a fiscally strapped state and nearly broke counties to find innovative ways to pay for things such as roads. And what could be more modern than allowing private companies to build and pay for new transportation projects — such as toll roads — that can be operated by the state in 35 years?

A native may have trouble saying the words "California" and "toll road" in the same breath. But many Californians believe toll roads paid for by the private sector can answer two of the state's biggest problems: transit gridlock and fiscal shortfalls. With state transportation funds as scarce as an open stretch of Orange County freeway and the numbers of needed projects multiplying almost as fast as the state's growth rate, some beleaguered state transit officials envision a public-private trans-

Debora Vrana is a senior editor of California Public Finance, *a newsletter about public finance issues.*

portation system as utopia.

However, a historic $2.5-billion proposal for demonstration toll roads — one in the north and three in the south — has attracted enough scorn, opposition and downright hostility in the last six months to wreck the projects.

Critics angrily contend that the roads are the result of "secret deals" negotiated late last year between the state and developers. They say the roads could create a two-tiered transit system with the affluent motoring along well-kept tollways and the poor bumping along from pothole to pothole. Opponents, who include environmentalists and key legislators, say the toll roads will encourage unwanted growth, exacerbate air-quality problems and siphon local funds from needed areas. Legislation was recently introduced to cut off a key toll-road funding source in an attempt to kill the projects.

The controversy raging around the toll roads is not simply a battle over 116 miles of new asphalt. This conflict may demonstrate whether allowing

privatization of infrastructure will work. More important, the toll-road debate could help clarify California's transportation priorities and point to the need for a long-term state transportation plan.

"It's going to be a very bloody fight," said Mark Evanoff of Greenbelt Alliance, a San Francisco environmental group working to stop a Northern California toll road. "Whatever happens is going to set the destiny for future transportation development in California," he said.

The toll roads were part of former Governor George Deukmejian's $18.5-billion gas-tax package in 1989, but the idea really germinated at a place called The Reason Foundation, a libertarian-oriented think tank in Santa Monica. California transit officials were attracted to privately financed toll roads (not to be confused with three taxpayer-built toll roads now under construction in Orange County) after reading Libertarian Robert Poole's 1988 Reason Foundation transportation study. Poole proposed modern "Blade Runner"-like roads with toll booths that could read special toll microchips on cars, much like electronic grocery counters scan prices on canned foods. Auto occupants would then receive a monthly "toll road bill" not unlike a water bill. Poole's study also proposed a sliding toll price scale, including charging higher tolls at peak congestion hours.

Despite all the high-tech hoopla, the most radical aspect of the report was the use of private capital to pay for the roads. Privatization simply means transferring traditionally public projects to the private sector. It is the cornerstone of Reason Foundation philosophy and is attracting attention throughout the country at local and federal levels, especially in areas such as education. Poole's public-private transportation utopia was a vision for California officials anxious to find a way to pay for projects shelved for lack of money.

In 1989 only 19 legislators opposed legislation allowing the California Department of Transportation, CalTrans, to negotiate with private firms to build roads. The bill was introduced by Republican Assemblyman Bill Baker of Danville, who refused to be interviewed for this article. The bill required three things: at least one project in the south, one in the north and that a free road alternative be available to any proposed toll road. The bill allows the state to own the infrastructure and assume legal risks but lease the road and property to developers for 30 years. Developers were expected to fund the projects from the tolls.

Four contracts were approved under terms of the legislation:

• An 11.5-mile toll road extension of Highway 57 in Orange County that will use the Santa Ana River Channel. The $700 million road is to be build by the National Toll Road Company, a consortium that includes the Dallas-based Perot Group.

• A 10-mile toll road in San Diego near the Mexican border that is expected to cost $400 million and be built by California Transportation Ventures.

• A 10-mile toll road in the existing right-of-way on Highway 91 in Orange County to cost $88.3 million and be built by the California Private Transportation Corporation.

• An 85-mile toll road, known as the Mid-State Toll Road, to be built in Solano, Contra Costa and Alameda counties. Expected to cost $1.2 billion and to be built by the California Toll Road Company.

All was running smoothly for the toll roads until January 1991, when the contents of contracts were released. While the size and placement of the roads drew sparks, a fire storm of criticism erupted over the disclosure that developers planned to ask for state, local and even federal funds to help pay for the roads.

"A bunch of people came to us and said, 'We have a free lunch to offer you.' Now we find out the free lunch wasn't so free," said Democratic Assemblywoman Delaine Eastin of Fremont, who has vowed to support a bill designed to halt the toll roads. "These roads allow the general revenues of the state to build a highway for rich people."

Angry environmentalists, slow-growth advocates and legislators charge that public funds were never intended to even partially fund the roads and that they were deceived by CalTrans. Publications to the left of the political spectrum have had a field day with headlines such as "Highway Robbery" and "Monster Toll Road Threatens East Bay Green Belt." The *Los Angeles Times* ran an editorial titled "Toll roads can go off course — wholly private projects should not benefit from public funds."

"I feel we were deceived on AB 680," said Concord state Senator Dan Boatwright, a Democrat and a co-author of the Lockyer bill. "CalTrans sold out on these contracts. It far exceeds any authority they have. I'm never going to trust CalTrans again."

CalTrans officials say they are getting a bad rap from disgruntled legislators who do not understand the difficulty of negotiating contracts. Officials say the contracts are solid and point out that the 800-page documents were looked at by Price Waterhouse, an outside consultant.

"Fundamentally these are good agreements that we believe are balanced and yet still attractive to the private sector," said Carl Williams, CalTrans director. "These projects still have a good chance of being followed through on, although Lockyer's activities are making the projects appear more risky."

Williams is a strong supporter of privatization and believes that the federal government should allow states more flexibility.

"State governments should be allowed to put together any combination of funds for a facility," said Williams. "Let us use private capital in a designer concept."

Toll-road supporters charge that the legislation to prohibit public funds is a bad bill because it usurps local control. Many developers are concerned that the roads are mistakenly being perceived as "private roads" supplemented by public funds. They argue instead that the toll roads are not solely private roads, but public roads, "at all times ... owned by the state," and deserve public funds.

"These are public-private partnerships, not truly private projects," said Poole of the Reason Foundation. "Nowhere in AB 680 does it say that no public funds would be used. No one was under any illusions that these were just private projects."

But legislators contend that during committee discussion of AB 680 there were verbal reassurances from CalTrans that no public funds would be involved.

"They lied to us," said Lockyer. "I think they should keep the promise they made and keep public funds out. We all know that local governments have a susceptibility to certain lobbying interests."

Those in the local transportation trenches are gearing up for a bitter fight. Still uncertain about the future of Lockyer's bill (which some predict Governor Pete Wilson will veto even if the Legislature passes it), several local transit districts and governments have been approached about contributing to the planned roads.

"With the state of our county budget they might as well hold their breaths," said Solano County Supervisor Sam Caddle. "The toll road could be of some economic benefit but it does raise some deep concerns. When we were first approached by Parsons, we listened and were lukewarm to the idea. I guess they thought we'd be all enthused and write glowing resolutions."

While the Contra Costa Transportation Authority has voted not to authorize local funds for the Mid-State Toll Road, the Orange County Transportation Commission has approved $300,000 to help with environmental impact studies on toll roads in Southern California.

"This is a local-control issue," said Geoffrey Yarema, an attorney with Nossaman, Guthner, Knox and Elliott — a law firm working on the San Diego toll road. "Lockyer is telling Orange County and Santa Ana they can't have their projects no matter how much people want them. These toll roads did not come out of the air. The Santa Ana road has been discussed for more than 20 years. These are projects that the state would like to do but didn't have the money."

Big business does have the money. And one of the toll road critics' biggest beefs is that developers are allowed to make even more money on the toll roads.

According to the contracts, developers can make a 21.2 percent profit on the Mid-State Toll Road — an amount well above profit rates set for other public-private ventures, such as utilities. The profits on other toll roads range from 20.2 percent to 17 percent. Opponents of the toll roads say developers are guaranteed profits and that the roads should be subject to regulations by the Public Utilities Commission and that public hearings should have been held before profit rates were set. But developers contend that profits aren't guaranteed in the contracts and that the 21.2 percent figure is not a promise, but a cap.

"Even in our best case scenarios, we don't reach that rate of return," said Dennis Parker, manager of project development with Pasadena-based Parsons Municipal Services — a firm involved with the Mid-State Toll Road. "These projects are risky. All of sudden your project takes a dive and then you just sit. For a businessman that is deadly. Sitting still costs money."

But opponents dispute the developers' claims.

"They are lying like dogs," said Boatwright. "These people are trying to sell us burnt toast."

Developers continually reiterate how risky the projects are. In the contracts, CalTrans officials said they promised broad rights to developers in order to make up for the risks. The contracts include:

• Help from CalTrans if local governments attempt to build a road competing with the toll road projects. Williams and CalTrans would "use its best efforts to dissuade local governments" from building competing roads.

• Developers are granted the "air space" rights to the toll roads for 99 years. This allows developers to lease land along the roads to commercial companies. Critics say giving air space rights to developers will encourage growth and bring consumers to shop along the toll road. Developers dispute this scenario, saying that for every mall built along the road an off-ramp and toll booths would have to be built, which is too costly to be feasible.

"There's this misconception that H.R. Perot is going to laugh all the way to the bank and no one will benefit from these projects," said Poole. "That simply isn't true."

Some officials said the toll-road conflict is over more than public-funds-for-private-profit and charged that there is a "Wild West" mentality among California's public officials who have a gut opposition to paid roads. Some predict that toll roads, which are accepted on the East Coast and throughout the Midwest, will not work in California.

But historically, some of the roads that make up California's current freeway system were once toll roads. In 1863 California had more than 80 toll roads (mostly in the mining counties), in addition to 80 toll bridges and 111 ferries, according to an 1863 Sacramento newspaper. In subsequent years, the state bought many of these roads to supplement California's road system. Acquisitions included the Lake Tahoe Toll Road, the Muir Woods Toll Road and the Sonora-Mono Wagon Road, all of which were bought by the state, improved and made free roads. In late 1934 the state paid $25,000 for the 31-mile-long Death Valley Toll Road and eliminated the $2-per-car toll.

Today, the privately built and operated 17-mile drive in Monterey is the only toll road in California.

Highway building in California and the rest of the country has been stalled for many years. Since inauguration of the 1956 Federal Interstate Program, the United States has maintained a tradition of relying on public funds to build the network of roads connecting the country. But the federal highways program expires in September 1991, and many say that new alternatives must be considered. Some point to the success of privatization in Europe, where private firms have built more than 5000 miles of roads through Spain, Italy and France. California currently has $50 billion to $80 billion in highway needs alone in the next nine years.

At this point, many involved in the toll roads say it is unlikely that a way can be found to make all the projects work. Some sources predict the legislation and possible lawsuits expected to be filed against the Mid-State Toll Road will effectively kill the project. At this time it is unclear what will happen to the other three toll roads.

Some legislators are concerned in general about the privatization concept and say that there are some things — such as roads — that are a government responsibility. And some are concerned that with these toll roads CalTrans took on a bigger role than it should. Some legislators feel that this controversy points to the need for an integrated, long-term state transportation policy.

The state currently has a general transportation plan, according to Williams, but officials are watching a federal proposal to allow multi-layer plans that would be formulated at the urban level. The state would be in charge of services at the intra-urban level.

"I really do think that California needs a long-term state transportation plan," said Assemblywoman Eastin. "We need to stop thinking that we can get something for nothing. The toll-road plan was as if Harold Hill had arrived in the Legislature and promised us we'd have a fine band. Now we find out that we can't have 76 trombones and you can't get things for free."

Many believe that privatization of infrastructure is the wave of the future. Some developers say that business not only can finance and build roads better than local governments, it can assess needs and priorities more logically.

"We're talking about an important power that has traditionally belonged to local governments," said Parker of Parsons. "Business is perfectly capable of assessing, prioritizing and doing. The political process gets so bogged down and enmeshed that nothing gets done. Maybe it should just provide a forum for discussion."

The current toll-road controversy is a nightmare for many developers who feared such a scenario when the toll roads were being developed. But some developers said they plan to be in this for the long haul and that the projects may die and be resurrected many times before the conflict is over. Both developers and environmentalists said they were considering filing lawsuits against either the state or developers over the toll roads. To date, no such suits have been filed.

Reorganizing mental-health care — the counties take charge

By Kathleen Zimmerman McKenna

Reprinted from *California Journal*, July 1991

California lawmakers, after years of bleeding dry funding for community mental-health services, are stepping forward to stop the hemoraging by shifting control and money from the state to the counties. The plan, which hinges on successful enactment of a 1991-92 state budget, entails the biggest change ever in the relationship between California's 58 counties and the state government.

Assemblyman Bruce Bronzan, a Fresno Democrat and one of the chief negotiators who helped draft the proposal (embraced by Governor Pete Wilson in January), concedes mental-health services will still be grossly underfunded, but Bronzan says at least the current level of service will not continue to erode.

"It is not a panacea," said Bronzan. "It is not bridging the gap. It is not doing what should be done to mental health by any stretch of the imagination. But it

---

Kathleen Zimmerman McKenna is the Sacramento reporter for the Oakland Tribune.

is holding the line with a little bit of increase as compared to falling off the cliff, which is what they certainly are facing right now."

After years of suffering at the swing of the budget axe, newly elected Republican Governor Wilson arrived on the scene in January promising a more humane approach to funding of mental- and public-health programs for the medically indigent, even though, with a projected $14-billion shortfall, the state faced its worse deficit ever.

Taking a bold step, Wilson proposed a massive restructuring of 15 public- and mental-health programs totaling $2.1 billion that are run by counties but financed and overseen from Sacramento.

While helping out the state's budget woes by relieving it of $2.1 billion a year in expenditures, counties also are guaranteed proceeds from a half-cent sales tax increase and from the imposition of heftier vehicle license fees. Counties must provide some matching funds and will be given the right to seek voter approval for another half-cent increase on their own.

County officials breathed a sigh of relief at the prospect of complete control of programs and full funding to boot. Mental-health advocates saw an opportunity to radically reform the state's approach to treating the mentally ill. And Wilson basked in the bipartisan praise.

"This is the best hope the mental-health community has had in years," said Russell Gould, Wilson's secretary of health and welfare. "It provides stable funding and keeps them free of the vagaries of the budget process. They no longer have to fight education or other health programs for funding."

But what has emerged, after months of wrangling on the $745 million mental-health component of the realignment proposal, has not pleased everyone although the politicians finally signed off on the proposal. The final realignment bill package includes 300 pages on the transfer of mental-health programs — the thorniest component — with less than 150 pages for all the other public-health programs and revenue increases that will pay for them.

While taking care to praise Wilson's intentions, some mental-health advocates say they would rather no realignment take place if protections are not put in place to ensure that minimum standards of care for the mentally ill will be offered in all 58 counties.

"Nothing good is happening for the mentally ill and their families," complains Dan Weisburd, president of the California Alliance for the Mentally Ill. "We're in the midst of a stampede. The governor's intention is good ... But it would be impossible for me to say giving responsibility for the mentally ill to 58 counties is good. I don't think it is good. It will lead to chaotic and uneven services.

"... I'm really grateful we have a governor who's trying to protect funds for the mentally ill. But the funds are grossly inadequate and there is a great need for clear minimum standards."

Weisburd would rather have the state turn over administration of mental-health services to one strong central authority or allow for regional governance.

Even some supporters of realignment concede it will not answer the big-picture, mental-health-funding shortfall, but they argue that without it, the mentally ill will be much worse off.

"Realignment means the stabiliza-

tion of funds for the first time in years," said Bronzan.

"What many in the mental-health community are so enraged about ... is that we are going to settle on the current crummy status quo level of funding for mental health. And that's true. But the reality today is: Can we avoid catastrophe? And this is a way of avoiding catastrophe."

Up to a half-million Californians are believed to suffer from serious mental illnesses, but only 135,000 are currently receiving treatment. Strapped for money, many counties serve only the most severely and chronically ill, and officials concede the rest often end up in jails.

"It gives a little light at the end of the tunnel," said Francis Dowling, acting mental-health director for Los Angeles County, of realignment, "It gives us stability which we haven't had."

Los Angeles County treats 62,000 severely and chronically mentally ill residents each year, far below the more than 90,000 who used to receive treatment on an annual basis before budget cuts forced the county to limit care to the worst cases.

"There are a vast number of people who could use services, and we're not able to reach those people." said Dowling. "Look in our jail. Los Angeles County jail is the largest home to the mentally ill. On any given day, 3300 out of 23,000 can be classified as having mental illnesses. Had they been getting treatment, they might not have run afoul of the law."

Mental-health advocates want the state to require counties to provide food, shelter, medicine and treatment to the mentally ill.

"If there is not some kind of accountability, the county that does a better job will have clients drawn to it from all over," said Richard Van Horn, of the Los Angeles-based Mental Health Association. "... The mentally ill are ill — not dumb."

"They say, 'Trust us.' Why should we?" asked Weisburd. "There's a history of California shirking its responsibility to the mentally ill."

Bronzan said the state is hesitant to impose standards that could be construed as a mandate (beyond those already required by the federal government), giving the counties a way to come back to the state for additional money if funding proves inadequate.

A minimum array of services will

be required and counties will be evaluated on how those fared who sought treatment, rather than just looking at the numbers, Bronzan said.

"It's tricky to do all this and still avoid the unfunded mandate issue," he said. "You can't do everything in realignment. Realignment can't be everything to everybody. There's been so much desperation in this field for so long that when something like this comes along that does have the opportunity to do some things, it raises people's expectations and their anxiety and their frustration about how totally screwed up things have been for so long ..."

Weisburd is more than an advocate for the mentally ill, he is the frustrated father of a 30-year-old son who, 11 years ago, abandoned his bright future at Harvard University after realizing he was mentally ill when he began hearing voices in his head and imagined the football team, buck naked, was chasing him down the street. His son now lives in a board-and-care home, but after stays in 27 hospitals and talking to 32 psychiatrists, his mental health has not improved.

Weisburd said the state of most mental-health services is so poor that, "When you try and hospitalize someone, because the person is suicidal, you're asked, 'Well, how suicidal?'"

The deinstitutionalization, launched under former Governor Ronald Reagan that resulted when laws were passed to make it tougher to commit people to state hospitals, started the decline in mental-health services.

"We basically shut down that system and we gave counties absolutely nothing to care for those people," said Bronzan. "We just dumped them, the most severely mentally ill, with no money, no facility. Simultaneously, we started strangling their general community mental-health funds, giving them less and less while we were at the same time dumping on them the most severe mentally ill with absolutely no funding. That double whammy devastated the mental-health system."

San Diego County mental-health director Areta Crowell agrees realignment has to be a major improvement to the existing system.

"We shifted to a partnership with the state more than 20 years ago," said Crowell. "The problem was it wasn't equal and led to a lot of finger-pointing. With the regulations necessary to maintain Medicaid, there will be enhanced. We are very grateful to governor." 🏛

Runaway children face overwhelmed state programs

By Chris Ziegler and A.G. Block

Reprinted from *California Journal*, November 1991

They sleep anywhere they can find a space, often during the day when it's safer. They beg, steal, sell drugs and prostitute themselves for money for food. Most have been abused, and continue to be abused, by the adults around them.

An estimated 127,000 to 128,000 children live on the streets of California's cities, according to a 1985 UCLA study on homeless and runaway youth. The federal government estimates there are more than one million runaways nationwide. A large majority of the thousands of kids who run away from home each year return to their families after a few days, but those who do not are generally running from a life worse than that on the streets. An increasing number of homeless youth are "throwaways," kids who have been abandoned or kicked out of their homes by their families.

"One thing we have learned is that these are kids with very abusive histories," says Dennis Fisher, senior program specialist for the Child Victims Service branch of the Office of Criminal Justice Planning. "Most of these kids don't have a home to go back to."

Chris Ziegler was a California Journal *summer intern. A.G. Block is managing editor of the* Journal.

Officially considered status offenders if they are a runaway — homeless, truant or out of control of their parents — these youth fall between the cracks of government social services; they are not part of a homeless family, are not unemployed adults, disabled, veterans, or crime offenders. Runaways are also not eligible for child protective services.

California, "with its large population ... warm weather, numerous beaches and reputation for being a 'cool place,' has become a popular haven for homeless street youth," according to a position paper of the California Child, Youth and Family Coalition (CCYFC), which lobbies for children's rights.

"If you look under the Hollywood Boulevard overpass, there'll be 30 to 40 kids," Fisher says.

A 1981 United Way Planning Council study of Los Angeles County estimated there was 10,000 runaways in that county on any given day, according to a report on runaway and homeless youth by the Commission on California State Government Organization and Economy (Little Hoover Commission).

"There are real battles at bus stations between the pimps and the social service people ... to see who gets them," says Tony Cimarusti, assistant director of the California Youth Authority.

The state does not have a comprehensive policy to deal with status offenders, but rather a "hodgepodge" of state and local programs, says Catherine Sizemore-Barrankin, a lobbyist for the CCYFC, which advocates a more comprehensive policy.

Currently, there exists a loosely organized structure of runaway hotlines, after-school care, shelters, and non-secure receiving homes that provide food, shelter and counseling, as well as referral and health services to runaways. The basis of the state's services is a statewide hotline and the Homeless Youth Act of 1985, which created the Runaway Homeless Youth Projects to coordinate youth service agencies in San Francisco, Los Angeles, Santa Clara and San Diego counties. City, county and private programs also provide services, and are funded by a variety of sources.

Youth deemed to be status offenders by a juvenile court may no longer be held in juvenile hall or some other secure facility as they could until the mid-1970s, California Child, Youth and Family Coalition hotline director Marilyn Erickson says.

Now, if a youth is arrested for some petty offense, such as for loitering or stealing food, he or she is usually delivered to a shelter or receiving home after the charges are dropped. Unlike juvenile

The state does not have a comprehensive policy to deal with status offenders, but rather a "hodgepodge" of state and local programs.

hall, "the doors aren't locked from the inside," says Leonard Lloyd, manager of the Horizon Youth and Family Service in Livermore in Alameda County.

Kids can stay at shelters for seven to 90 days, depending on what the facility is equipped to handle, and receive food, counseling, medical assistance, a shower, and of course, a place to stay.

The CCYFC runaway hotline, created in 1984, provides crisis counseling and referrals, and handles several hundred calls per day, Erickson says. The number of calls has increased dramatically, from 1000 calls per month in 1989 to 2000 calls per month for 1991 so far, she says.

Each county decides how it will administer its services to runaways and homeless youth. The Horizon Youth and Family Service is one of a variety of programs that serve Alameda County, and provides assistance to approximately 250 runaways per year, 65 percent of them girls, Lloyd says.

A youth delivered by police to the Horizon Youth and Family Center receives immediate counseling, and his parents are notified and required to meet their child at the facility. The home situation is then evaluated, and family counseling is offered.

"You can't get anywhere working with just the kids," Lloyd says, adding that counseling just the child reinforces the parents' opinion that the problem lies solely with the child.

Lloyd also notes that many of the parents he encounters object at first to the idea of family counseling, or are displeased that the child was not taken to a secure facility, expecting the youth to be punished for running away. Some refuse to meet the youth at the center, or to take him home, he says, adding that when this happens, he reminds the parents that child abandonment is illegal.

Since so many runaways engage in prostitution or "survival sex" for drugs, food or shelter, the OCJP started the Child Sexual Exploitation Intervention program in 1987 as part of its ongoing effort to deal with sexual abuse, Fisher says.

The program, which has centers in San Francisco, Santa Clara, Los Angeles and San Diego, provides hotline services, drug and alcohol counseling, psychological counseling, shelter, and "independent living and survival skills to prepare the juvenile prostitute for a lifestyle free from contact with those who exploit them," according to the OCJP's 1991 report on the project.

OCJP hopes to expand the Child Sexual Exploitation Intervention program, but a bill proposed last session by Democratic Assemblyman John Vasconcellos of San Jose failed to receive funding. The OCJP also wants centers located in rural regions because most of the attention to the runaway problem has been focused on urban areas, Fisher says.

The state's Runaway and Homeless Youth Projects are funded through OCJP. "It's working really well. They're unique programs in the state," Fisher says.

California's policy toward status offenders, and toward children in general, has fluctuated over the past 150 years as society's attitudes have changed. Until about the mid-1970s a youth could be arrested and sent to juvenile hall for being a runaway. The segregation of youth from adults in correctional facilities was itself a reform done during the Progressive Era when juvenile court law was developed as separate from criminal law for adults.

Youth in juvenile lock-ups were categorized as "700s" depending on the offense until the early 1960s when a major revision in federal law divided kids into either "600s" (abused or neglected), "601s" (beyond control of supervising adult) or "602s" (delinquent).

Another federal change a few years later created the catagory of "300s," for abused children. Changing the numbers "was just to get us to think differently," Lloyd says.

The problem with the old policy, according to Lloyd, was that non-criminal offenders like runaways were housed with criminal youth. Over the years, probation officials found it increasingly difficult to get kids out of juvenile hall and into the parents' custody to await their court hearings. "They couldn't get them out," Lloyd says of the kids.

According to Lloyd, many parents of runaways saw the locking up of their child as a way of getting the state to punish their child for them, and so would refuse to have the youth released into their custody until the hearing.

Interestingly, parents of violent offenders often defended their children more than did the parents of runaways, so youthful criminals would wait for their court hearing at home, while runaways waited, sometimes up to three weeks, in juvenile hall, Lloyd says. "Even the kids would say, 'I don't get it,'" of why they had to remain incarcerated while other kids arrested for more serious crimes went home with their parents.

California Youth Authority officials and others who worked with status offenders also noticed that locking kids up in juvenile hall was ineffective in detering youth from running away.

To counter this problem of overcrowding youth facilities with non-criminal offenders, Sacramento County petitioned the state to place runaways and homeless children in non-secure receiving homes in 1970, with Alameda County closely following suit in 1971, Lloyd says. In 1976 the practice of incarcerating non-criminal offenders in juvenile hall in California ended. If California returns to incarcerating status offenders it would lose $5 million per year in federal monies.

After the incarceration policy ended, there was a period of several years while the state grappled with how to handle non-criminal status offenders. Until the youth projects started in the mid-1980s, "This category of kid didn't have services at all," according to Fisher.

State Senator Robert Presley, a Riverside Democrat and longtime opponent of the incarceration policy, could not explain the lag in legislation between the ending of incarceration and the beginning of providing non-secure shelter for status offenders. But of the current policy, he says, "I think we're moving in the right direction."

From 1976 until the Homeless Runaway Youth projects were created , the state moved slowly to devise a new policy for status offenders. The bill that ended the incarceration policy also mandated that the state fund community-based shelters, as it does now.

But "Prop 13 happened," says Gary Yates, associate director of the division of adolescent medicine at Children's Hospital in Los Angeles. Federal homeless programs and private agencies provided services to runaways, but growing budgetary problems during the late 1970s and early 1980s kept California from developing any kind of organized policy, besides continuing to lock up youths who committed violent crimes, says Yates.

By the early 1980s, probation departments, the agencies which were to administer school drop-out programs and other such juvenile crime-prevention projects, suffered budgetary cutbacks as much as 50 percent in a county.

Changing perception of runaways from that of juvenile delinquents to that of children often from abusive families also provided impetus for the state to support the shelter policy.

However, "there is still a lot of public sentiment that these kids are mini-criminals who should be locked up until they're 65," Fisher says.

The CCYFC has long been an advocate of alternative methods of dealing with runaways and lobbies for a more comprehensive policy. "We believe that the state of California should guarantee a shelter in every county," Erickson says, adding that there are only 39 shelters and 58 counties.

While the OCJP does not have a position on which policy is more effective or which it considers better policy, Fisher says, "The reality is that juvenile hall is jammed with really violent offenders."

Sizemore considers the current policy, "supportive, but wholly inadequate," and branded incarceration a "barbaric practice."

It is Sizemore's view that with the state's current fiscal woes, a comprehensive policy for status offenders, is "not going to happen anytime soon."

In the past few years there have been a number of bills to provide shelter and counseling for status offenders, including one that required the CYA to implement a model system of employment preparation and placement services for youth offenders. Another mandated that a youth may not be made a dependent of the juvenile court solely because of lack of emergency shelter for his family. In the early 1980s legislation was passed that authorized police to refer or deliver a minor taken into temporary custody to a public or private agency for shelter and counseling.

Republican Assemblyman Paul Woodruff of Redlands, another supporter of the shelter policy, believes drug and alcohol counseling and treatment programs should be added to the current policy.

Although the state has not sent status offenders to juvenile hall for 15 years, there are still some who advocate some form of incarceration. Assemblyman Curtis Tucker Jr., an Inglewood Democrat, has proposed a bill that would allow "a minor who has been adjudged a ward of the juvenile court by reason of various forms of non-criminal conduct may be confined in a suvervised facility or juvenile hall ... for no more than five days if the minor has willfully disobeyed an order of the juvenile court by leaving court-ordered placement on three separate occasions without adequate justification or permission," according to the bill, AB 119.

Tucker argues that his bill would handle those kids who "were headed down that slipperly slope."

However, "it costs a ton of money," McSweeney claims.

It costs the CYA $31,064 to house one youth for one year, CYA information officer Sarah Andrade says. Currently, the CYA has 8167 inmates, and 5965 youth on parole. Its 1990-91 budget was $387 million.

"It's going to take a lot of money to avert kids from a life of crime," argues Tucker. "It may be expensive, but we're talking about an even greater expense if you don't ... housing that person later."

McSweeney acknowleged that while Woodruff opposes Tucker's bill, "Everybody's trying to do the same thing," in dealing with the problem of runaways. 🏛